For Mary Anne

Abbreviations

EETS   Early English Text Society

ES   Extra Series

OS   Original Series

SS   Supplementary Series

OED   *Oxford English Dictionary*

References to Malory in the text and footnotes are to E. Vinaver, ed., *The Works of Sir Thomas Malory*, 3 vols, 3rd edn, rev. P.J.C. Field (Oxford: Clarendon Press, 1990). They are by page and line numbers. E.g., page 231, lines 14–23, is given as 231/14–23.

Acknowledgements

I am grateful to the University of Western Australia Press for permission to use in the Introduction and Chapter 3 material previously published as ' "The hoote blood ran freyshly uppon the erthe": A Combat Theme in Malory, and its Extensions' in Andrew Lynch and Philippa Maddern, ed., *Venus and Mars: Engendering Love and War in Medieval and Early Modern Europe* (Nedlands, WA: UWA Press, 1995) 88–105. Chapter 1 includes revised material from 'Good Name and Narrative in Malory', *Nottingham Medieval Studies* XXXIV, 1990, 141–51, and 'Why Misfortune Happens in Malory', *Parergon, Bulletin of the Australian and New Zealand Association for Medieval and Renaissance Studies*, New Series, no. 4, 1986, 65–72. Parts of Chapters 3 and 6 have been previously published as 'Gesture and Gender in Malory's *Le Morte Darthur*' in Friedrich Wolfzettel, ed., *Arthurian Romance and Gender* (Amsterdam: Rodopi, 1995) 285–95. I thank all the editors concerned for their kind permission to make use of this material.

Many people have at some time helped in the making of this book. I wish to acknowledge especially Bronte Adams, Philippa Beckerling, John Burrow, Mary Dove, Gillian Maddern, Philippa Maddern, James Simpson and Bob White. Karen Cherewatuk has been very generous in sharing unpublished work and work in progress. Thanks also to my academic and general staff colleagues in the Department of English, University of Western Australia, for their friendly support.

Thomas, Johanna and, lately, Peter Lynch have given me inspiration and encouragement along the way. The book is dedicated with deep gratitude to my wife, as the person to whom it owes most.

Introduction

In 1467, Lord Scales and the Bastard of Burgundy fought a challenge of arms at Smithfield, before King Edward IV. On the first day, the Bastard's horse was accidentally hurt in the face, reared back, and fell on its rider, concluding the combat. On the second day of foot-fighting, after some solid axe strokes had been exchanged, the King stopped proceedings, but each party retired well satisfied,

> and there they immediatly yafe yche to othir as courteis godely and frendely langage as coude be thoughte.[1]

The meeting had taken several years to arrange, and bore throughout a very high ratio of goodly language to deeds of arms. The later medieval English formal combat was as much a verbal as a physical and visual form, and the declarative virtue of its 'deeds' depended greatly on their discursive frame. In this instance, the King and the combatants 'ordain', 'show', 'give countenance' and 'behold' within a thoroughly textualised arena, dominated by literary models.

One possible modern response to its evident artificiality is to construe the Scales challenge as a literary fantasy out of touch with the mainstream 'reality' of English politics and warfare, at most an extravagant piece of Yorkist diplomacy and propaganda.[2] Another response would be to acknowledge the intense cross-influencing of literary and 'real life' events, and the overlapping discursive structures of the various 'realities' each generated.[3] Reading the Scales challenge this way, we are helped to reconsider the complex significance of combat in another text of the period,

---

1 See 'Tournament Between Lord Scales and the Bastard of Burgundy' in *Excerpta Historica, or, Illustrations of English History* (London: Samuel Bentley, 1831) 212. (I have silently expanded abbreviated forms.) L.D. Benson, *Malory's Morte Darthur* (Cambridge, Mass. and London: Harvard UP, 1976) 172–75, discusses this account also.

2 This is the view of Arthur B. Ferguson, *The Indian Summer of English Chivalry* (Durham, North Carolina: Duke UP, 1960) 18: 'It [the Smithfield tournament] was all very magnificent, very much by the book. It was prepared ... with all the courtly formality and frivolity that could be dredged from the romances of chivalry.'

3 See D.A.L. Morgan, 'The House of Policy: the Political Role of the Late Plantagenet Household, 1422–1485' in David Starkey, ed., *The English Court: from the Wars of the Roses to the Civil War* (London and New York: Longman, 1987) 34: '... the "feats of arms" of 1465–68 were integral to the formation of the Anglo-Burgundian alliance, and the king's personal declaration of his intent to resume a policy of outward war in France'.

Malory's *Le Morte Darthur*, completed three years later in 1469. Anthony Wydeville, Lord Scales, brother of Edward IV's wife Elizabeth Wydeville, has even been suggested as a likely provider of manuscripts for Malory, and as instigator of Caxton's imprint.[4] Caxton's first dated book printed in England was Wydeville's *Dictes or Sayengis of the Philosophers* in 1477. Wydeville was executed in 1483 by Richard III, two years before the *Morte* was published. He provides a good example of a great court nobleman-knight of this period, a man with whom an ambitious lesser gentleman like Sir John Paston would seek association both in person and through the medium of chivalric texts.[5]

In writing to the Bastard, Scales offered a romantic point of origin for his project. He had been talking to his sister the Queen, after mass, when he was surrounded by ladies of the court who bound on his thigh a gold collar, containing a flower of remembrance, and a note encouraging him to get on with the Burgundian challenge. The binding of the collar on his thigh contained, apparently, its own sexual import and challenge. Scales says, gallantly, 'whan I had it, it was nerre my hert than my knee'.[6]

If women provided the supposed spur to action, Scales soon converted the token of their interest into a close male union. He sent the flower to the Bastard, with a request to 'assemble by arms',

> principally to thentent that by the saide meane I may have the acquayn-taunce and frendshipe of you above alle oothir on erthe . . . and also trustyng that by you and youre alliaunce I may acquaynte me and have knowleche to the righte laudable and tryumphal hous of Burgoyne.

When the Bastard has touched the flower, Wydeville continues, he will 'bere it as my moost derest thing'.[7] The intimate gift of women is thus to be symbolically transformed into an object of exchange between noble men, as a token of their promised 'assembling' in combat.

---

[4] R.R. Griffith, 'Arthur's Author', *Ventures in Research*, Series 1 (Greenvale, NY, 1973) 7–43. R.R. Griffith, 'The Authorship Question Reconsidered: A Case for Thomas Malory of Papworth St Agnes, Cambridgeshire' in *Aspects of Malory*, ed. T. Takamiya and D.S. Brewer (Cambridge: D.S. Brewer, 1981) 159–77. P.J.C. Field, *The Life and Times of Sir Thomas Malory* (Cambridge: D.S. Brewer, 1993) 4, 144–45, offers some carefully qualified support for the idea. See also Karen Cherewatuk, 'Sir Thomas Malory's "Grete Booke" ' in D. Thomas Hanks, ed., *Malory and the New Historicism*, forthcoming.

[5] See Cherewatuk, 'Sir Thomas Malory's "Grete Booke" '. For discussion of possible links between Malory and contemporary chivalric ceremonies, see Richard Barber, 'Malory's *Le Morte Darthur* and Court Culture under Edward IV', *Arthurian Literature* XII, 1993, 133–55. Both Barber, esp. 146–55, and Cherewatuk, see above, and in a forthcoming article in *Arthurian Literature*, ' "Gentyl" Audiences and "Grete Bookes": Chivalric Manuals and the *Morte Darthur*', draw comparisons between the *Morte* and Sir John Paston's 'Great Book' as mixed genre chivalric anthologies.

[6] 'Tournament', 178.

[7] 'Tournament', 176, 185.

What else could Wydeville give as a reason for the challenge? He told the Bastard it was

> in augmentacion of knyghthod and recomendacioun of nobley; also for the vaillance thereof to my power to meynteyne & folowe; and for to voide sleuthfulnes of tyme lost, & to obey & please my feire lady.

King Edward's proclamation added that it was

> for the augmentacion of marcialle discipline and knyghtly honoure, necessary for the tuicion [protection] of the feith catholique ayenst heretikes and miscreantes, and to the defence of the ryght of kynges and princes and their estates publiques.[8]

As Mark Lambert has said of Malory's narrative, there is a multiple causality invoked here.[9] The formal challenge at arms apparently provides a time and place to display many things – nobility of birth and alliance, legitimate political and military power, sexual status, true love and religious piety. I draw attention to the Scales episode at length because it shows how readily all these major issues could be combined in Malory's period within the discourse of arms, and centred on a combat episode. And yet, although Malory's *Le Morte Darthur* is dominated by a similarly rich fight discourse, its critics have often tended to downplay the importance of the fights, or to treat them separately from what they see as the story's deeper interests and structures, just as some historians have dismissed the Yorkist tournaments as 'literary'. E.F. Jacob, writing in *The Oxford History of England*, may be taken to stand for a dominant twentieth-century attitude. He sounded a typical note of weariness with Malory's combat, selectively quoting Eugène Vinaver's influential view:

> It is not all fighting and as the stories went on, the drama of conflicting forces was worked out: the motive of the tale is primarily a conflict of two loyalties . . . the loyalty of man to man . . . on the other hand 'the devotion of the knight-lover to his lady'.[10]

In the following chapters, which take a very different approach, I use the term 'fighting' or 'combat' so as to avoid the assumptions normally connected with 'chivalry' and 'knighthood'. For I believe that it is in the thematics of combat themselves, more than in a wider pattern of moral conduct they may construct, that the significance of the fights, and hence of

---

8 'Tournament', 180, 208.
9 Mark Lambert, *Malory: Style and Vision in Le Morte Darthur* (New Haven and London: Yale UP, 1976) 158–76, esp. 160.
10 E.F. Jacob, *The Fifteenth Century: 1399–1485, The Oxford History of England VI* (Oxford: Clarendon Press, 1961) 657–58. The quotation from Vinaver is from *The Works of Sir Thomas Malory*, 1st edn (Oxford: Clarendon Press, 1947) vol. 1, xxv. See 3rd edn, 1990, xcvi.

the 'hoole book' (1260/16) which they dominate, can be best located. The language of Malory's combat episodes, consistent but polyvalent, far more than it imposing master pattern of divided loyalties and moral conflict, binds 'together' the participants and their actions in a volatile structure of imaginative relations.[11]

This book consists of a series of essays on major narrative preoccupations in Le Morte Darthur. They are of different kinds, touching virtually all areas of experience represented in the narrative, but each is related in some way to the central matter of combat. For the most part, instead of writing directly about narrative structure, style, or character, I have concentrated on a number of more material discursive strands, the kind of thing Roland Barthes once called 'existential thematics', a body of writing's 'organised network of obsessions'.[12] I do not treat such foci – blood, name, good and ill will, affective reactions – as 'organised' in the sense of consciously employed leitmotifs, nor do I argue for a total aesthetic pattern in Malory, nor for a mythic pattern in the narrative disposition of his episodes.[13] Still less do I see them as any direct reflection of fifteenth-century 'life'. Rather, I see these thematics, these habits of discourse, as omnipresent in the text because already part of its interpretative act, a product of the 'needs of meaning'[14] of Malory's cultural group, and therefore attesting some of its important habits of thought which may be reconstructed and revalued by a modern reader. Part of my effort is to construct a grammar for reading Le Morte Darthur out of some of its staple narrative terms, in the belief that the book is more self-articulate in its weight of unprocessed details than in the abstractions, such as 'chivalry' and 'love', sometimes employed (within and beyond the fiction) to manage them. The basic idea for this approach has come from the example of Jill Mann:

---

11 For the significance of 'together', see the important article by Jill Mann, 'Knightly Combat in Le Morte Darthur' in The New Pelican Guide to English Literature, vol. 1, part 1, ed. B. Ford (Harmondsworth: Penguin, 1982) 331–39.

12 The terms are cited in translation from Barthes in J. Culler, Roland Barthes (London: Fontana, 1983) 43. See Barthes, Michelet (Paris: Seuil, 1974) 5: 'Tel a été mon dessein: retrouver la structure d'une existence (je ne dis pas d'une vie), une thématique, si l'on veut, ou mieux encore, un réseau d'obsessions.'

13 'Thematics', therefore, differs from L.D. Benson's 'thematic structure'. See Malory's Morte Darthur, 73: 'By "thematic" I mean what is sometimes loosely called "mythic", the conformance of a narrative to some external, preexisting pattern.' My reference is instead to habitually privileged features of the narrative discourse, such as, in Barthes' reading of Michelet, 'blood' and 'liquefaction'.

14 See J. Culler, 'Story and Discourse in the Analysis of Narrative' in The Pursuit of Signs (London: Routledge, 1981) 178. See also below, Chapter 1, 3. A similar view is expressed by Benson, 73: 'thematic necessity rather than the requirements of the "plot" characteristically shapes the narrative structures'. See also Jill Mann, ' "Taking the Adventure": Malory and the Suite du Merlin' in Aspects of Malory, 71–91, esp. 78: 'not a logical sequence of cause and effect in the facts themselves, but in the perception of a kind of pattern in them on the part of the beholder'.

What modern Malory criticism needs to do – and has to some extent begun to do – is to work out a critical vocabulary and a way of reading that is appropriate for the structure and nature of his particular kind of narrative . . . the terms on which we should build our reading of Malory are those suggested by the work itself; the . . . narrowness and simplicity of his vocabulary directs our attention, by insistent repetition, to the key words and concepts of his narrative.[15]

Even within Malory's vocabulary, I have necessarily been selective, and have concentrated on terms which seemed able to connect important principles of Malory's ideology most directly, as I saw it, with the staple language of his many narrative 'days'. For instance, I have chosen to speak of the 'heart' more than 'love', of acts of 'seeing' or 'naming' more than 'worship', and of 'blood' and the various reciprocated actions of armed combat more than 'fellowship', 'knighthood' or 'adventure', though all those words, amongst others, have considerable textual prominence, as several excellent critical studies have shown.[16] Rather than follow further these ways of abstracting and co-ordinating Malory's incidents within broader terms, although it would be foolish to ignore them, my study seeks to trace the potential connections of some less explicitly over-determined narrative phenomena.

It could easily be objected to the emphasis of this method that at least some of Malory's ethical and moral statements, such as the institution of the High Order of Knighthood (120/11–27), Arthur's celebration of 'fellowship' (866–67) or the definition of true love (1119–20) are unavoidable landmarks in any reading of him. I agree, but would add that there is an advantage in delaying critical resort even to some of the text's own discourses of closure, because it lets one's reading take more account of the narrative silences, rough edges, gaps and co-existing contradictions which challenge or betray the preferred view. I have borne in mind Pierre Macherey's notion that 'literature challenges ideology by using it':

the work has an ideological content, but it endows this content with a specific form. Even if this form is itself ideological there is an internal displacement by virtue of the *redoubling*; this is not ideology contemplating itself, but the mirror-effect which exposes its insufficiency, revealing differences and discordances, or a significant incongruity.[17]

---

15 See Mann, 'Knightly Combat', 331–32.
16 See Lambert, *Malory*; Elizabeth Archibald, 'Malory's Idea of Fellowship', *Review of English Studies* XLIII, August 1992, 311–28; Beverly Kennedy, *Knighthood in Le Morte Darthur* (Cambridge: D.S. Brewer, 1985; 2nd edn, 1992); Jill Mann, ' "Taking the Adventure" '; Beverly Kennedy, 'Notions of Adventure in Malory's *Morte Darthur*', *Arthurian Interpretations* 3 (2), 1989, 38–59.
17 Pierre Macherey, *A Theory of Literary Production*, trans. Geoffrey Wall (London: Routledge and Kegan Paul, 1978) 132–33.

By virtue of such 'internal displacement' of ideology by itself, I argue, there are many effects in Malorian narrative with a more developed existence in practice than in his theory, and more textual outcomes are evident than he had a will or means to acknowledge. What such a long and complex story 'proves', as Malory might have said, can be read in different ways from those he sometimes prefers, without forfeiting proper attention either to the text or to its historical moment.

As I frequently observe in later chapters, even Malory's most heartfelt generalisations refer primarily to their local context. We should not make a few speeches, whether by Malory's heroes or himself, into unbending rules for interpreting the whole narrative. Malory is basically a descriptive, rather than prescriptive, author, and his famous axioms are generated in the enthusiasm of the moment. I am tempted to compare him as translator, very respectfully, with a live sports broadcaster, who from time to time gathers the events he describes into one of a set of thematising formulae. The formulae are adopted according to preconceptions of genre, but they must be applied *ad hoc* to incidents dependent on the chances of play, which in themselves may not be very suitable for exemplary purposes.[18] Malory's stories are selected and partly re-shaped, of course, and bent in the telling towards certain interpretative needs, but they still come first, ahead of the moralising commentaries they occasionally receive, and not necessarily well-fitted to them.

I place the description of armed combat, undeniably Malory's most common subject matter, centrally in my reading of his work. Until relatively recently, not very many critics have adopted this attitude. The marked reaction against arms for arms' sake in the nineteenth-century revival of Arthur, abetted by Tennyson's huge influence, gave Malory criticism a bent towards the judgement of morality in the conduct of individual characters which it has never lost since.[19] In popularising Malory, a stream of critics, editors and abridgers complained of repetition and moral mindlessness in the fight material, and either cut or marginalised it to produce a *Morte Darthur* devoted instead to issues such as Lancelot's and Guenevere's infidelity, Arthur's culpable weaknesses and the tragic decline of the Round Table.[20] W.E. Mead's scholarly selected edition typifies the critical attitude

---

[18] See Eugène Vinaver, ed., *The Works of Sir Thomas Malory*, 3rd edn, rev. P.J.C. Field, 3 vols (Oxford: Clarendon Press, 1990) xxvi–xxxiv: Vinaver points out (xxxiii) that Malory had to 'supplement' his French sources with 'remarks of his own on the art and meaning of chivalry'.

[19] See Elizabeth Brewer and Beverly Taylor, *The Return of King Arthur* (Cambridge: D.S. Brewer; Totowa, New Jersey: Barnes and Noble, 1983) 134: 'The possibility of analysing and dramatising the Arthurian stories was one of the great discoveries of the nineteenth-century writers on these themes. They detected a lack in the medieval version of the stories, and were quick to supply what was felt to be a deficiency in characterisation.'

[20] For examples of nineteenth-century critical hostility to Malorian arms, see Marilyn Jackson

reached by the turn of this century. Mead claimed that his selections 'contain some of the choicest portions of the *Morte Darthur*, and are really representative of its character'.[21] He excluded everything between the Balin story and the Holy Grail, so leaving out, as was common, Arthur's Continental wars, and all the major stories of knight errantry: Lancelot, Gareth and Tristram. Mead's justification was typical: 'The episodes are too frequent and too long, and, though interesting, they have too little to do with the main current of the narrative.' 'The story here and there drags a little. A reader must have a well-developed appetite for unimportant detail who can take in the entire description of a medieval battle without wincing.'[22] To such an extent had the major portion of Caxton's text been rendered 'unimportant' and 'unrepresentative' of its 'main' story, with effects on the critical reception of Malory that have lasted a long time, in a way oddly counter to the view of modern historians that the chivalric 'conception of secular virtue ... was narrowly martial'.[23]

In more recent years, Malory critics such as Larry D. Benson and Beverly Kennedy[24] have treated the issue of fighting very carefully, mainly through constructing narrative patterns and typologies of knighthood by studying the sequence or comparative morality of combat episodes, drawing attention, respectively, to the models provided by other romances and manuals of chivalry. In distinction, this book looks in the repeated language of Malory's fights themselves for features below the level of aesthetic pattern or conscious code, for what one might think of as the more primitive building-blocks of Malory's imaginative structures, or the raw outcropping of his ideological predilections. But to stress the importance in Malory of certain material discourses of, say, the body or the emotions, as I do, is by no means to exclude the other approaches which these critics have taken, and to which my reading is often indebted. Indeed, Benson and Kennedy, amongst others, have gone into the broader aesthetic and ethical issues so fully that I have felt more justified in treating the combat episodes in a different way, just as I have tried not to duplicate too often the definitive work of Field[25] and Lambert on Malorian style. In my analyses, I have

Parins, ed., *Malory: The Critical Heritage* (London and New York: Routledge, 1988) 89–90, 120–33, 133–52, 240–51, 379–82. For abridgements and selected editions which severely cut the fighting material, see J.T. Knowles, *The Story of King Arthur and His Knights of the Round Table* (London: Griffith and Farrar, 1862); Ernest Rhys, *Malory's History of King Arthur and the Quest of the Holy Grail* (London: Walter Scott, 1886); W.E. Mead, *Selections from Sir Thomas Malory's Le Morte Darthur* (Boston: Ginn and Co., 1897); Andrew Lang, *Tales of King Arthur and the Round Table* (London: Longman, Green and Co., 1905).

21 Mead, *Selections*, iv.
22 Mead, *Selections*, liv.
23 Maurice Keen, *Chivalry* (New Haven and London: Yale UP, 1984) 177.
24 See notes 1, 16, above.
25 P.J.C. Field, *Romance and Chronicle* (London: Barrie and Nelson, 1971).

outlined an idea of 'goodness' in Malory more strictly related to military prowess than others are, one relatively inattentive to patterns of conduct, individual motivation or moral ends. In short, I have treated the narrative of combat as I have seen it, a web of discourses in which progress towards chivalric perfection, or moral teleology, are only single strands.

One practical consequence of my approach is that several of the following chapters tend to refer fairly widely to evidence drawn from over the whole *Morte*. Vinaver's edition of the Winchester manuscript, my chosen text, is not treated book by book, and my more detailed analyses usually concentrate on the basic unit of narration, the episode. While this method pays less attention to the structure of individual tales, or to their formal inter-relation, than some readers might wish, I have used it to articulate more extensively, and in reasonable depth, the features treated. It is just because these discourses are so prevalent and multifarious that discussion of their effect cannot be confined neatly to individual tales, although they may be especially visible in some and less so in others. When my reading does touch on the broader issue of structure in Malory, it is through showing the various expressions and outcomes of some consistent thematic factors when they are subjected to the pressures of multiple narrative contexts. For example, in discussion of Malory's combats, I relate major preoccupations found throughout the text – vision, blood and gesture – to military, religious, genealogical, sexual and medical discourses of Malory's period. I see the *Morte* as bound together by the sheer consistency of its discursive habits, more than by patterns of episodic sequence, or strict respect for chivalric conduct, and I hope therefore that a reading of the kind offered here can still respond to 'the hoole book', without needing to re-visit directly the old discussions about its structure.

The long *Book of Sir Tristram*, more than a third of Malory's total work, and frequently neglected by critics, receives at least proportionate attention in this study, and I hope it is more accessible than usual to the approaches taken here. The great difficulty of getting one's mind around the *Tristram*'s narrative mass has naturally led critics to prefer shorter tales more easily contained within summarising strategies. I have followed three critical trails into the *Tristram*: one, outlined above, is through studying the thematics of combat; the second considers the narrative and ideological functions of dilation, repetition and delay in the presentation of events; the third concentrates especially on the developing role of particular personages, mainly Dynadan and Palamides, and on their involvement with the supreme knight Tristram, embedded in a study of the envy and good will generated within knightly power relations. Rather than consider the knights principally as autonomous agents whose conduct is offered for moral analysis, I have treated their actions, and the 'characters' these construct, as produced in the service of an ideology committed to defending the attachment of 'right' to military success. In the interaction of Tristram and his satellites can also be observed how the text shapes and polices its response to the basic problem of inequalities of power. Eventually, however, I have credited the situation created by these inequalities with a potential for psychological narrative, especially in the case of Palamides.

There are two further chapters, framing the central section on combat, which approach the question of identity and consciousness in Malory, both group and individual, from rather differing perspectives. I first consider the importance of a 'name' externally conferred, and how an apparent need to rank the reputation of major figures in the narrative may override the declarative power of its incidents, good or ill, challenging the concept of adventure as either 'proof' or 'chance'. The work of Mark Lambert on Malory's publicly-oriented 'shame-culture' has been an inspiration here, but in the final chapter I pay attention also to the textual representation of emotion and the 'inner life'. In considering these, along with some aspects of speech and gesture in the narrative, I outline an important role for personal feeling – the 'herte' – in the Malorian ethos, in an attempt to take the discussion of mentality and agency in the *Morte* beyond the modern inner/outer dichotomy. Through close analysis of several narrative incidents, the gendering of Malory's discourse of gesture and consciousness is also examined. I argue that the role of Malory's women can often be interestingly understood through their implication in the language of knightly combat.

I have treated the text as one produced in and for a fifteenth-century English cultural milieu, and read by me in the late twentieth century. This means that I have not restricted the study of 'Malory' to the differences he made from his originals. In adapting his sources, Malory effectively permitted the co-existence of many narrative effects which are problematical but fascinating when taken together. It is hard, for example, to reconcile Lancelot's complete bonding with Bors at the conclusion of the Grail Quest, and the equation of their adventures at that time (1036–37) with the moral difference between them observable in earlier incidents (e.g., 894–95; 933–35; 954–56) and specifically noted by the hermit expounding Ector's dream (946–47). Malory no doubt wanted 'to make Lancelot appear at the end of the Grail adventures as their chief protagonist', as Vinaver remarked, and added this scene to fit the purpose (1584). But in so doing he created, in effect, a new thing, a hybrid which neither the values of the French *Queste* nor the apparent tendencies of the adaptation can adequately describe. We see something similarly complex at the start of Malory's next book, where Lancelot returns to sexual passion with Guenevere (as in the French source), while still yearning for 'the hyghe servyse' (1046/13) of the Grail (a new touch). In my reading, I have not sought to privilege a supposedly characteristic Malorian difference from the source, but to register the presence of the varied impulses which, whilst perhaps stemming from the tension between source and adaptation, find an equal home in *Le Morte Darthur*.

The fifteenth-century text in which they fruitfully co-exist is the object of study I call 'Malory' here.

In offering a kind of historically aware literary criticism, attempting to construct and scrutinise a mind-set which might have permitted *Le Morte Darthur* to come into being, I do not pretend to operate from a position somehow beyond ideology, or to have found a special way of reading which transcends the processes that have formed modern Malory interpretation. Any acquaintance with the long history of the *Morte*'s reception must dispel that illusion.[26] Rather, in the attempt to understand the necessarily hybrid creation I call 'Malory', I have tried to stress the multiple, overlapping, contested potential in a text which reads differently depending on the differing critical assumptions and interpretative strategies (often eclectic, always problematical), brought to bear upon it. For this reason, I have sometimes returned to the one liminal episode or issue – the death of Lot, the fate of Balin, the conduct of Palamides, the healing of Urré – in several different places in this book, with varying analyses. It also follows that although I speak, for convenience, of a 'Malorian' attitude, one which the work of many scholars has helped to realise for me,[27] the responsibility for the 'Malory' so created rests on my own late twentieth-century reading, not on an ideal Sir Thomas or an ideal historical era whose mind would or could have agreed with mine. Although the chosen method necessarily leads to generalisations about the norms of Malory's writing, I have tried to make evident how such views were arrived at (and therefore how differing views can be obtained), and to let statements of the norm come under fair question from the unruly wealth of narrative detail. Malory, like other great writers, can provoke very mixed feelings. If my readings appear to contain self-contradictions, that is at least preferable to representing his text as ideally consistent – 'The experience woot wel it is noght so.'

Finally, an explanation. In articulating differing ways of reading the *Morte*, I have sometimes cited the opposing views of others as signposts in the argument, without trying to give a full account of how their readings parallel or contrast mine. If this has meant that the names of some scholars to whose researches I owe much appear mainly at moments of disagreement, it is certainly out of no desire to pick factitious quarrels with their work. In any case, I am interested in extending the tensile multiplicity of meaning in Malory, not in trying to knock others' opinions out of court. *Le Morte Darthur* is a very big book, with room and delight for many readers.

---

[26] For surveys of Malory reception and adaptation, see Parins, ed., *Malory: The Critical Heritage*; Brewer and Taylor, *The Return of King Arthur*.

[27] See the works by Vinaver, Field, Lambert, Benson, Mann, Kennedy, Barber and Cherewatuk already cited above. See also especially Stephen Knight, *Arthurian Literature and Society* (London: Macmillan, 1983); Felicity Riddy, *Sir Thomas Malory* (Leiden: E.J. Brill, 1987).

1

'Suche a man I myghte be':
Good Name, Identity and Narrative

Name and Identity

Proper names are a staple of narrative interpretation. As Thomas Docherty remarks,

> In the mainstream Realist tradition, a proper name is ... perhaps the one identifying mark which remains unproblematical for the course of the entire novel, for it remains unchanged, unlike other 'characteristics' or 'qualities'.[1]

A name, says Docherty,

> create[s] a gap in our understanding which requires plenitude, a gap therefore which prompts us to read on and 'fill' with meaningful signifi- cance the empty space in the name as it occurs in the fictional world.[2]

Docherty distinguishes broadly between two attitudes to names in fic- tion: firstly, the 'essentialist' or 'ceremonial' kind,

> consonant with a plot-oriented fiction, a fiction in which the mechanics of the intrigue subsume the characters into the effecting of a design (often called the 'world' of the novelist, and always the 'plot') whose hermetic nature precludes the illusion of a character having any existence outside of its boundaries.[3]

The opposing method of nomination is described as 'existentialist' or 'historical'. The character assumes

> the authority to exist subjectively and make history. Will the character accept an anterior authority which gives it a name, as in a patriarchal

---

[1] Thomas P. Docherty, *Reading (Absent) Character* (Oxford: Clarendon Press, 1983) 45.
[2] Ibid., 47.
[3] Ibid., 49.

heritage, or will the character revolt against this in the subjectivist impulse
to be the authority behind his or her own existence and name?[4]

We see here two models for the operation of names in narrative. Names
may be places for the readers' aggregation of narrative events into subject-
'characters', or names may be instead objects of an authoritative naming
plot. This latter function, as Docherty observes, is seen most clearly in
allegory, in such names as Obstinate or Pliable.[5] But to what extent plot
claims authority over character, or vice versa, in the reading of a text such
as *Le Morte Darthur*, is a harder question to answer. After all, Malory's names
are not Obstinate and Pliable, but Lancelot, Guenevere and Tristram. The
body of Malory criticism reflects the difficulty of the problem.

The issue of name as character lay beneath the long controversy over
unity in Malory. The Lumiansky school defended its vision of a coherent,
organic narrative by appealing to the continuity of naming between separate episodes. Discontinuous qualities associated with such names were
seen as changes in character behaviour, themselves forming the plot of
tragic decay, worked out within a complex chronology.[6] In contrast,
Vinaver's emphasis on the formal divisions and other discontinuous elements of the Winchester Manuscript granted less power of subjectivity to
repetitions of name, and hence, by implication at least, more to the local
demands of romance plot, with its patterned themes. This tendency, taken
to its extreme, would see *Le Morte Darthur* as a succession of unrelated
narrative events about personages with the same names, but without
consistent or developing 'character'.

Later critics have shifted the grounds of Malory debate, but without
resolving the conflict between name as subject and name as object. Whilst
influential analyses like Larry D. Benson's have stressed the function of
thematic or 'vertical' structure in Malory, and hence the role of named
personages as demonstrative objects within the plot, Benson, like other
critics, has not denied the status of 'character' to the major names, finding
at crucial moments in the text a tension between comic thematising and a
tragic historical effect.[7] Something of the same tension is betrayed in the
work of Beverly Kennedy. Her attempt to locate a consistent typological
hierarchy of knighthood in Malory paradoxically relies on the assumption
that the types are also autonomous characters, whose motives and actions
extend implicitly beyond the text, as well as explicitly within it. Accord-

---

4   Ibid., 51–52.
5   Ibid., 49.
6   See, e.g., Wilfred L. Guerin, '*The Tale of the Death of Arthur*: Catastrophe and Resolution'
    in *Malory's Originality*, ed. R.M. Lumiansky (Baltimore: Johns Hopkins Press, 1964) 269:
    'The fall of this society comes as the climactic and artistic conclusion of a unified epic-ro-
    mance, a tragedy which results, however, from the sins and errors of the characters as
    individuals over a lengthy period of time.'
7   L.D. Benson, *Malory's Morte Darthur*, Chapters 4 and 12.

ingly, she detects a narrative criticism of Tristram for his devotion to hunting, on the grounds that it impairs Tristram's service to his temporal lord, causing his absence at a crucial moment for Cornwall.[8] Behind such a suggestion we see a strong belief in the primacy of the demands of psychology over those of the story in the formation of 'character'.[9] It is a little like blaming Dr Watson for neglecting his patients. The problem arises because the repeated name 'Tristram' has been overloaded with subjectivity by the critic, who has credited the metaphorical 'world' of Malory with the complexity and inter-relatedness of an actual world. The opposing view is that the text simply requires Tristram's absence at this moment, and explains it by reference to his favourite pastime, with no thought of blame attached.

The subject/object problem Kennedy's approach reveals is a real one and perhaps irresolvable, especially since Malory's text has such a wide gap between story and discourse, between bald narrative event and full narrative treatment. Jonathan Culler warns us of the double logic of narrative:

> at certain problematic moments story events seem to be produced by the requirements of the narrative discourse, its needs of meaning, rather than vice-versa, as we normally assume.[10]

In Malory's case, the solution of this problem is made more difficult by a tricky mixture of potential genres: quasi-history, in which the basis of narrative is its notional actuality as the record of autonomous beings, and romance, in which events attached to names are manipulated into the expression of a ritual, a providential pattern. I do not suggest, of course, that these are the only available generic models, merely that they can represent the poles of a reader's response to named individuals in Malory. And I suggest that Malory readers can gain some assistance in mediating between these models by first looking neither at notions of subjective character, nor at thematic patterning, but at the culturally specific practice of naming which underlies both.

One can say, I think, that proper names are very prominent in Malory's 'existential thematics'.[11] In the Winchester manuscript, all personal names, some place and feast names, and the word *Sankgreal* are written in red and in a special script. To accomplish this the scribes were required to change pens every time they came to a proper name. N.R. Ker states that the distinguishing of proper names was evidently a 'matter of great consequence' to them.[12] The red names stand out very boldly from the page; they

---

8   Kennedy, *Knighthood*, 2nd edn, 173.
9   See Tzvetan Todorov, *The Poetics of Prose*, trans. R. Howard (Oxford: Blackwell, 1977) 67, for the distinction between psychological and apsychological character, typified respectively by Raskolnikov and Sinbad.
10 Culler, *The Pursuit of Signs* (London: Routledge, 1981) 178.
11 See Introduction, xiv.
12 See the introduction to *The Winchester Malory, A Facsimile* (EETS SS 4 London: Oxford UP,

might be thought of either as a key index to the text, or as its major concern, what the rest of the writing is *for*. Lists of names are prominent, as in the Healing of Sir Urré episode with its careful reprise of past events, and there are many others associated with battles, tournaments and court occasions. We can get a rough idea of the frequency of naming from looking at the incidence of words like 'sir', 'king', 'queen' and 'lord', which are usually or often accompanied by personal names. Taken together, these amount to more than one word in twenty of the text.[13]

We know also, from Robert Wilson's researches, that *Le Morte Darthur* has a tendency to cut anonymous characters from its sources, and to give names to those whose actions are kept in.[14] Thereby, Elizabeth Pochoda says, Malory creates 'a familiar society of people who recur in successive tales'.[15] More simply, I would add, this habit ensured that a name became in Malory's text an index of power and prestige, something seen as a good in itself. The unnamed tend markedly to be the other ranks of this militaristic fiction: squires, dwarves, churls, and a predictably large number of anonymous ladies, damsels and gentlewomen.

If we look within Malory's story, we find its personages themselves preoccupied with the issue. Eighty per cent of the occurrences of the word 'name' are in speech, though speech is less than half of the text as a whole.[16] This is because the knights so frequently require each others' names, and reveal or guard their own with great care.[17] The story makes much of its moments of identification, when names are disclosed.[18]

I take the interests of the named and the namers to be identical here, for the text itself also guards and discloses names to the reader very carefully. A striking example is in Book III, *Sir Launcelot*. When Tarquin is first seen, by the reader and by Lionel, who does not know him, he is unnamed (254). Tarquin's name is not disclosed to the reader until the capture of Sir Ector (255), and not to Lancelot until some while later (264). The reader and Lancelot do not learn until the succeeding mortal battle that Tarquin's vendetta against Round Table knights is motivated by his obsession with Lancelot's killing of his brother, Carados of the Dolorous Tower (266), in a

1976). For another discussion see Dhira B. Mahoney, 'Narrative Treatment of Name in Malory's *Morte D'Arthur*', *ELH* 47, 1980, 647–55, esp. 654–55.

13 See T. Kato, *A Concordance to the Works of Sir Thomas Malory* (Tokyo: University of Tokyo Press, 1974).

14 'Malory's Naming of Minor Characters', *Journal of English and Germanic Philology* XLII, 1943, 364–85.

15 Elizabeth Pochoda, *Arthurian Propaganda: Le Morte Darthur as an Historical Ideal of Life* (Chapel Hill: University of North Carolina Press, 1971) 10. See also Mahoney, 'Narrative Treatment of Name', 646–55, esp. 648ff.

16 See Kato, *Concordance*, 'name'.

17 See Jeanne Drewes, 'The Sense of Hidden Identity in Malory's *Mort Darthur*' in D. Thomas Hanks Jr, ed., *Sir Thomas Malory: Views and Reviews* (New York: AMS Press, 1992) 17–41.

18 See, e.g., the stunning revelation of Tristram's identity to Palamides, 696–97.

parallel episode involving Gawain, mentioned later in Book VIII (1162, 1198). And it is not until we learn that, that Tarquin discovers his opponent is Lancelot himself. Malory reserves Lancelot's elaborate naming of himself to Tarquin for the occasion when he must prove himself as great an upholder of the Round Table as Tarquin is an enemy. The length and formality of his response to a request for his name, in part Malory's own addition to the French, indicates its major significance in the action:

> '. . . all shal be delyverde [says Tarquin], so thou wolte telle me thy name, so be hit that thou be nat sir Launcelot.'
> 'Now se I well,' seyde sir Launcelot, 'that suche a man I myght be, I myght have pease; and suche a man I myghte be that there sholde be mortall warre betwyxte us. And now, sir knyght, at thy requeste I woll that thou wete and know that I am sir Launcelot du Lake, kynge Bannys son of Benwyke, and verry knyght of the Table Rounde. And now I defyghe the, and do thy beste!' (266–67)

At a moment like this, it might well seem that the named figure, in fulfilling his function as an exemplary object of the plot, also asserted his own name as a subject, 'suche a man I myghte be', and that further adventures might make him another man.[19] What happens instead, I wish to argue, is that the knight's 'name' becomes primarily the property of others, his *reputation*. In making his choice for 'mortall warre', Lancelot is already respecting his previous reputation, one which in this context the mere utterance of his name can activate. And the fight with Tarquin, like nearly all his further adventures, seems to *add* to his 'name', without fundamentally changing an understanding of the identity it signifies. At the end of Book III, Lancelot has 'the grettyste name of ony knyght of the worlde' (287). This 'name' or reputation he keeps on throughout the text. It will accompany him permanently, as long as his name is known. Outrageous actions that he performs while in disguise (564ff), including callous killings (564/11–29, 570/34–5), do no damage at all to his public name when once he makes it known again (570–72). Lancelot repeatedly insults Arthur and even Guenevere (566/2–5) in order to provoke fights, and as a means of disguising himself (571/17–18). Vinaver's explanation for this episode 'quite out of keeping with . . . [Lancelot's] character' (1484/n.571/9–18) is that Malory's love of supplying names caused him to identify the anonymous manslayer from the French original as Lancelot, with unhappy results. One might equally argue another case: Malory wanted to add extra adventures to Lancelot's account, as he had done before in *Arthur and Lucius*

---

[19] See Felicity Riddy, *Sir Thomas Malory*, 56: 'There is a profound sense here of a potential other self he carries with him: of choices that might have been made . . . of the person that might have been.' I agree, but would point out that the sense is retrospective, of a potential realised, but not thereafter fully available to the narrative to alter.

(220/15–17 and n.). Unmindful of Vinaver's sort of 'character', and not very disturbed by these incidents, which are common enough in the Tristram book, he thought their attachment to Lancelot's name sufficient to make them fully acceptable.[20] Even the humiliations of the Grail Quest can cause no permanent loss of Lancelot's reputation, at least once he repents.[21] Although a damsel tells Lancelot his status as 'best knyght of the worlde' has gone (863/10–864/4), it is restored as soon as Galahad, and with him the unusually stringent moral outlook of the *Sankgreal* story, leave the scene. By the reckoning of this very passage, Galahad is the only knight who is ever better. When Lancelot says ' "I know well I was never none of the beste" ' he is flatly told ' "Yes . . . that were ye, and ar yet, of ony synfull man of the worlde." ' (863/29–31). Even then, Guenevere attributes most of Galahad's worth to his father: ' "he muste nedys be a noble man, for so hys fadir ys that hym begate" ' (862/5–6). One cannot be at all sure that her view is presented as unreliable. Lancelot's amazing resilience shows how a 'name', once gained, strongly resists alteration in the eyes of others, and how others may know better than the bearer what a name is truly worth. One can either see Malory as inconsistent in characterisation here, or, preferably, as consistent in his own way in maintaining his hero's reputation.[22]

There are degrees of difference in the syndrome I am outlining. In the free-wheeling, loosely motivated *Tristram*, as I have briefly indicated, Lancelot's identity is very much a public and externally negotiated matter, and especially a product of his military prowess. In the *Sankgreal*, there is much more attention paid to moral self-awareness. Lancelot's enlightenment comes from outside, through shame, but is intimately registered within: 'tho wordis wente to hys [Lancelot's] herte, tylle that he knew wherefore he was called so' (895/32–33).[23] The healing of Sir Urré, concluding a series of tales beginning under the shadow of the Grail Quest's values, but re-asserting Lancelot's earthly yearnings, is poised between these extremes. It offers an instance of a potential split in Malorian identity between a knight's self-consciousness and the objective proof of his worship in the eyes of others.[24] Urré's healing 'proves' that Lancelot is 'the beste knyght of the worlde' (1145/19–20); but Lancelot's reluctance to act, his humble yet priest-like

---

[20] For a further discussion, see Riddy, *Sir Thomas Malory*, 108–09. See also Jeanne Drewes, 'The Sense of Hidden Identity', 23; Mahoney, 'Narrative Treatment of Name', 648.

[21] See 894/32–895/2: ' . . . many men seyde hym shame, but he toke repentaunce aftir that'.

[22] For a related view of Lancelot in Book VII, see Robert L. Kelly, 'Wounds, Healing and Knighthood in Malory's *Tale of Launcelot and Guenevere*', in *Studies in Malory*, ed. J.W. Spisak (Kalamazoo: Medieval Institute Publications, 1985) 173–97, esp. 197: 'Having decided that Lancelot was to be "the hede of al Crysten knightes", Malory felt the need to show him in possession of the virtues of knighthood even when his actions reveal that he is not.' See also my analysis of the 'Poisoned Apple' story, Chapter 6, 150ff.

[23] See Riddy, 120–21, for Lancelot's growing self-condemnation.

[24] I argue below, Chapter 2, 44ff, that the values and discourse of combat chiefly determine the overall significance of this scene.

prayer 'secretely unto hymselff' (1152/19–20) and his weeping (1152/35–36) perhaps allow an equal importance to moral self-searching, even to feelings of guilt. Is Lancelot's identity chiefly vested in its ties to external forces, rather in the spirit of early French epic, as R. Howard Bloch sees it?

> Within an immanent universe the world accessible to the senses is, as Marc Bloch observed, a 'mask behind which the truly important events take place.' . . . In a universe which places little value upon individuality or interiority, the assumed targets of divine judgement – inherent innocence or guilt – can never be known directly. They become apparent only through the secondary effects, recompense or penalty, which they engender.[25]

Or, as in Foucault's view of a later development in identity, is Lancelot 'authenticated by the . . . truthful confession he . . . [is] able or obliged to pronounce concerning himself'?[26] Do his prayer and weeping attest his wrongfulness?

Perhaps these two views need not be seen as completely contradictory. At any rate, there seems to be an attempt to combine them in this episode. Lancelot's reluctance and his humble prayer stress that he is not acting out of presumption (1151/17–32), clearing the way for God to prove him the best *against his will*, precisely countering suggestions of pride in his motivation. Lancelot has already confessed in the *Sankgreal* that

> 'never dud I batayle all only for Goddis sake, but for to wynne worship and to cause me the bettir to be beloved, and litill or nought I thanked never God of hit.' (897/19–22)

In the Sir Urré episode, Malory's text, very much his own conception, shows that it anticipates such a charge, that it has learned to be conscious of interior motivation. Lord Scales had been careful to guard against similar interpretations in his challenge to the Bastard of Burgundy:

> And that no man thenk that I doo it or undirtake the thynges abovesaide by any arrogance, presumpsion, envye or any outrage to be callid worthly: for uppon Gode and myne honour I doo it not but fortoo obeye my faire lady, and to have coyntance of you, and principally of a gode knyght, the whiche ye be my choice.[27]

---

[25] R. Howard Bloch, *Medieval French Literature and Law* (Berkeley: University of California Press, 1977) 22.

[26] Michel Foucault, *The History of Sexuality: An Introduction*, trans. Robert Hurley (Harmondsworth: Penguin, 1981) 58.

[27] 'Tournament', 187–88. It is interesting that Wydeville follows Malory's prescription here (1119): 'But firste reserve the honoure to God, and secundely thy quarell muste com of thy lady.'

Malory also covers this ground very effectively: Lancelot's humble and copious weeping can be seen as a proof that he is not arrogant and does now thank God in a heartfelt way. Yet he still asks God to save his 'symple worshyp and honesté [credit]' (1152/20–22). The text has broadened its idea of what that worship includes, but the public perception of his goodness is still paramount.

The common behaviour of Malory's text when knights' names are hidden reveals a clear privileging of the external view of identity. When Tristram disguises his name as 'Tramtrist' (384) the text also begins to call him that, reflecting its concern with how he is known, rather than with the abstract notion of 'Tristram' as pure identity. But as more and more people suspect or discover that he is not 'Tramtrist', the text reverts by degrees to 'Tristram'.[28] Lancelot's madness, the state of not knowing himself, persists as long as he is not known as Lancelot by others: 'And so he ran two yere, and never man had grace to know hym' (806). He is helped by two knights who have an inkling that he may be Lancelot, 'But in his wytte they cowde nat brynge hym ageyn, nother to know hymselff' (819). He is cured, brought to know himself, only after Elayne 'felle in remembraunce of hym and knew hym veryly for sir Launcelot' (823). Gareth incognito remains 'Beaw-maynes' until he tells his name to Lancelot (299). He is then called 'Gareth' for the first time, but the text reverts to 'Beawmaynes' when he leaves Lancelot's company for that of Lyonet (300), who knows him only as the kitchen knave. He tells Persaunte his true name, because 'I wolde fayne be of good fame and of knyghthode' (316–17), but commands him to secrecy, and so does not become 'Gareth' permanently to the text until a dwarf makes his real name known (329). Unlike Chrétien's Perceval, Gareth does not have to find his name through adventures. He knows it, but the real meaning of his name is as it is known by others.[29]

---

28 E. Vinaver, *Le Roman de Tristan et Iseut dans l'oeuvre de Thomas Malory* (Paris: Champion, 1925) 38ff, speaking of Caxton's edition, attributed the text's apparent hesitation between 'Tramtrist' and 'Tristram' to authorial confusion: after writing 'Tramtrist' where his French source still had 'Tristram', Malory was supposedly distracted by the French manuscript. I think it likely that *Le Morte Darthur* was moved to anticipate its French source because it naturally thought of Tristram in terms of the new name he was known by in this section of the story. The Winchester Manuscript only seems to become confused over this issue after a squire who knows Tristram's real identity appears. Even then, it makes a fairly clear effort to call Tristram one name or the other depending on the changing narrative focalisation. See 386: 'Than there cam the same squyre that was sente frome the kynges doughter of Fraunce unto sir Tramtryste, and when he had aspyed sir Trystrames he felle flatte to his feete. And that aspyed La Beale Isode, what curtesy the squyre made to Tramtryste. And therwithall suddeynly sir Trystrames ran unto the squyre – his name was called Ebes le Renownys – and prayde hym hartely in no wyse to telle his name.' For another discussion of this passage, see Mahoney, 'Narrative Treatment of Name', 649.

29 See Mahoney, ibid., 649–51, for a fuller discussion of Gareth's naming, and 655: 'Thus, it is clear that Malory sees his characters in terms of the roles they are filling at the time, and as narrator uses the titles that are proper and appropriate.' See also Lambert, *Malory*, 179: 'The important thing is not one's own knowledge of what one has done (the inner

Malory's fondness for names has points of contact both with his own English context and the earlier French milieu from which his originals emerged. Georges Duby's researches have shown the growth of chivalric narratives from genealogy.[30] Names, originally taken from a place, became the 'cement' binding a loose group of kinsfolk and associates into a powerful abstraction – a 'house', 'name' or 'race'. After the early twelfth century, Duby claims, family history existed not only to prove ownership of property and other rights, but to praise a string of individuals. Being of name and being a knight were vitally connected from the beginnings of chivalric romance. The self-awareness of the French aristocracy centred on knighthood from as early as the tenth century, when *miles* begins to replace *nobilis* as a descriptor in documents, until by the thirteenth century a knight has higher prestige than an unknighted noble.[31] Knighthood, though clearly not the same concept from time to time or from place to place, has the common feature of binding together different levels of upper society. This is still seen quite clearly in Malory: Mador de la Porte says to Arthur: 'thoughe ye be oure kynge, in that degré ye ar but a knyght as we ar, and ye ar sworne unto knyghthode als welle as we be' (1050), whilst Sir Lavayne, son of an obscure 'olde barown' of Guildford (1066), becomes companion of Lancelot, who seems to be king over most of modern France (1204–05), and is richly rewarded for it.

Historians have also shown us the high, but different, value placed on name in both its senses in Malory's England. Du Boulay writes: 'What counted was how you were called and how you behaved. Even names mattered. It was much better to have a name derived from a place than from a trade or a nickname.'[32] He also stresses the psychological and practical need to be of 'worship', of good name and fame, in a society where class-consciousness had grown as a result of the actual blurring of class-divisions in the late fourteenth and fifteenth centuries.[33] David Starkey reminds us that the nobility of England, unlike in France, was a 'tiny status group (numbering only fifty to a hundred) at the head of the much larger class of gentlemen'[34] which formed about one per cent of the population as a whole. The nobility were few, admired and imitated. But entry into the group of gentlemen was 'casual in the extreme'. 'Gentility was a question

---

life is not very significant in Malory), but public recognition of one's actions.' But see Chapter 6, 137ff.

[30] G. Duby, *The Chivalrous Society*, trans. C. Postan (London: Arnold, 1977), Chapter 10.

[31] Ibid., 157.

[32] F.R.H. Du Boulay, *An Age of Ambition* (London: Nelson, 1970) 73.

[33] Ibid., Chapter 4. See also Riddy, *Sir Thomas Malory*, Chapter 3, on uncertainty about class amongst the English gentry of Malory's times.

[34] David Starkey, 'The Age of the Household' in *The Later Middle Ages*, ed. S. Medcalf (London: Methuen, 1981) 227.

of lifestyle, and hence of the wealth that supported it.'[35] It depended upon being *known* for a gentleman.

Malory's text asserts both the levelling-up effect of knighthood/gentility and his century's fascination with great lords and their households. Its big names are great aristocrats, or royalty, and also wealthy men, with a few exceptional 'poor knights' like Balin, but they are mainly brought into the story as *knights*. Though they are nobles by birth, emphasis falls on the proof of this in knighthood, a status which has to be given by others, and which, as Kennedy has shown, forms a strong bond between conferrer and receiver, between Lancelot and Gareth for instance, or between Arthur and Lancelot.[36] Gareth chooses to build his identity on knighthood from Lancelot before he claims nobility from kinship to Arthur. Sir Torre, whose mother is a cowherd's wife, is admitted to the Round Table before King Bagdemagus, because Arthur has 'sene hym proved' (131). When Tristram comes to court, Arthur says ' "Wellcom . . . for one of the beste knyghtes and the jentyllyst of the worlde and the man of moste worship." ' (571). Knighthood is mentioned before nobility, whether of birth or spirit, and 'worship', it seems, comprehends both, in a way that must have been congenial to sections of Malory's audience. Balin's knightly sentence – ' "manhode and worship ys hyd within a mannes person" ' (63) – moved one early reader of the Winchester Manuscript to copy a version of it into the margin.

Malory's narrative appeals to its readers as 'men of worship' and as 'gentle' knights, on two occasions within the Tristram book:

> all jantyllmen that beryth olde armys ought of ryght to honoure sir Trystrams for the goodly tearmys that jantylmen have and use and shall do unto the Day of Dome, that thereby in a maner all men of worshyp may discever a jantylman frome a yoman and a yoman frome a vylayne. For he that jantyll is woll drawe hym to jantyll tacchis and to folow the noble customys of jantylmen. (375)

> Here men may undirstonde that bene men of worshyp that man was never fourmed that all tymes myght attayne. (484)

Here we see worship as a group activity; whether it is the knightly peer group of the narrative, or the worshipful readers, who confer it, the response is similar. Identity is the amount of worship that qualified judges attach to a name on the basis of the 'proof' supplied by behaviour. Usually, some weighty personage in the text – Arthur, Lancelot, Merlin – is used to pronounce 'worship'. (Most of the important evaluative words – 'noble', 'prowess', the 'worship' group, and 'false' – are considerably more prevalent in dialogue than in other narrative.) And such assessments of events

---

[35] Ibid.
[36] See Kennedy, *Knighthood*, 130–36.

are often written down - an inscription, on a tomb (when things go badly), in a letter, the 'grete bookes' of the Sankgreal stored at Salisbury (1036), the ubiquitous 'French book' that the text calls 'auctorysed' (1260) and the text itself, 'the hoole book of kyng Arthur and of his noble knyghtes of the Rounde Table' (1260). Malory's book can be described as a circumstantial promulgation of the 'name' of Arthur and his knights. Caxton, printing it at the request of 'many noble and dyvers gentylmen' (cxliii), promises an increase of worship to the names of its readers: 'Doo after the good and leve the evyl, and it shal brynge you to good fame and renommee' (cxlvi). (He makes little distinction between good fame and moral, even spiritual virtue.[37]) So a community, a wider fellowship of the worshipful, is formed from the names of the text and its readers. The reader, by participating in the naming process, is not encouraged to individualise the named personages as subject-others, but rather is encouraged to subsume the names into his or her own subjectivity. Even a being of 'passyng' worship, the best of knights or ladies, is, ideally, not estranged, but made more similar to, and drawn closer to, others by his or her preeminence. He 'bears them up' (1052) as Bors says of Lancelot, and 'maintains' them, as he says of Guenevere (1054).[38]

In Malory, 'name' remains much the same throughout the 'whole book' where circumstantial evidence, the stuff of novelistic character and of providential patterning alike, does not. A reader, following either the 'historical' or the 'thematic' model, fails to explain the high incidence of narrative amnesia, by which events that do not add to 'name', sometimes including the very circumstances of its winning, are permitted to sink without trace. The reader is discouraged from drawing any inferences unfavourable to the 'name' of worshipful characters, and where the narrative fears that historical change may cause this unawares, it is quck to step in, as in the case of Baldwin, the hermit:

> For in thos dayes hit was nat the gyse as ys nowadayes; for there were none ermytis in tho dayes but that they had bene men of worship and of prouesse, and tho ermytes hylde grete householdis and refreysshed people that were in distresse. (1076)

Malory evidently fears that Baldwin, as a hermit, may be taken for one of Langland's 'Grete lobies and longe that lothe were to swynke'[39] and moves to save the dignity of his story, and of a chief associate of his hero

---

37 See Caxton, cxlvi, 'But al is wryton for our doctryne, and for to beware that we falle not to vyce ne synne, but t'exersyse and folowe vertu, by whyche we may come and atteyne to good fame and renommé in thys lyf, and after thys shorte and transytorye lyf to come unto everlastyng blysse in heven.'

38 For the pressures exerted on this ideal by envy and ill will, see Chapters 4 and 5, below.

39 William Langland, *Piers Plowman: The B Version*, ed. G. Kane and E.T. Donaldson (London: Athlone Press, 1975) Prologue, line 55.

Lancelot. The reader sees here, I suggest, a model for the text's treatment of changes in its own history. Its primary 'need of meaning', in Culler's phrase, is to represent these changes without permitting them to reflect adversely on 'name', a narrative trait that can cause both the character-hunting and the pattern-making reader considerable problems.

Sir Bors' career provides a good example of how good name is impervious to narrative change. Is the all but perfect knight of the Sankgreal the same person who is drawn into Lancelot's dangerous ambience in Book VII, wishes to kill King Arthur in Book VIII, as if totally caught up in a blood-feud, and then dies on a Good Friday as a knight for Christ's sake? It sounds like a history or a pattern of moral crisis and regeneration. And yet, at any stage of the proceedings, the 'name' of Bors would be the same – 'worship-ful' – and there is no 'proof' allowed to the narrative events that might suggest otherwise. Bors is 'Bors', the same to himself as to others. In moments of crisis, a Malory character consults his 'worship' itself, as if from an external viewpoint. Gareth says after the Great Tournament ' "he [Lancelot] made me knyght, and . . . methought hit was my worshyp to helpe hym" ' (1114). Arthur agrees ' "ever hit ys . . . a worshypfull knyghtes dede" ' to do so (1114). In this all-important respect, the major figures of the narrative never change, only their fortunes and their contexts.

It may seem strange to make such a claim, since criticism has made so much of Lancelot's instability and Arthur's weakness,[40] either as causes of the ending in a 'horizontal' chain, or else as thematic figures in the 'vertical' pattern of the text. And I will admit that critics such as Benson and Kennedy have made a good case for narrative 'adventure' as the expression of Providence's reaction to knightly identity. Yet one can also see that such patterns are very selectively formed. Arthur acts like the tyrant Herod on one occasion, drowning all the children born on May Day (55–56), and yet remains the 'most noblest Crysten Kyng'. Lancelot says he is 'shamed . . . for evir' by his failure to guard Pedyvere's wife when she is under his safe-conduct (285), but that turns out to be a great exaggeration. Very few events in Malory have permanent consequences, though many predictions of the kind are made. 'Name' is not formed by an inexorable discursive response to narrative events, but on the basis of a desire to preserve the ranked community of worship. To put it another way, name becomes a primary 'need of meaning' for the story, making it very difficult for further narrative events to tell us anything *new* about its personages. The narrative acts like them, ignoring or pardoning aberrations, as, for instance, Tristram repeatedly ignores and pardons Palamides:

'No forse', seyde sir Trystram unto sir Palomydes, 'I woll take youre

---

[40] For a recent example, see Ginger Thornton, 'The Weakening of the King: Arthur's Disintegration in *The Book of Sir Tristram de Lyones*' in Hanks, *Sir Thomas Malory*, 3–16.

exscuse, but well I wote ye spared me but a lytyll. But no forse! All ys pardoned as on my party.' (756/15–17)

The attitude and language of Tristram's reaction are legal, his purely personal knowledge of events set aside. On a later occasion, this is done explicitly for the sake of 'name'.

Than sir Trystram remembyrde hymselff that sir Palomydes was unarmed, and of so noble a name that sir Palomydes had, and also the noble name that hymselff had. Than he made a restraynte of his angir. (780)

The text similarly 'makes a restraint' of its reaction to troubling narrative event, in deference to name. Arthur may look weak in refusing to hear of Lancelot's infidelity with Guenevere, but his behaviour is actually at one with the narrative practice in this. It is Aggravain and Mordred, bringing private and personal obsevation of events into collision with Lancelot and Guenevere's 'name', who are its transgressors, models for the worshipful reader to avoid.

A concomitant of this collective, public and legalistic ethos is that the text seems under-equipped to deal with notions of individuality, privacy and change, when the story might seem to 'prove' something incompatible with, or more complex than, reputation. Malory's vocabulary for personal difference is rather small, perhaps because difference in 'worship' is a matter of degree rather than register of quality; the small number of villains, like Mark, are simply conceived of as the opposites in worship of the heroes. There are very few characters acknowledged to be problematical, Palamides being the only major figure. Malory's Mordred, for instance, is entirely without the moral torment of Mordred in the alliterative *Morte Arthure*. The most important word in Malory for the nature of individual identity, as we know it from later narratives, is perhaps 'condicion/s'. Yet it has to serve both for crucial moral alignments, such as Bors' worthiness or Gawain's 'vengeable' tendencies, and for relative trivialities: Gawain's love of fruit, Galahalt's dislike of fish, Lancelot's habit of talking in his sleep.[41] The usage in all cases shows belief in the essential habitualness of behaviour, the belief that people don't change, even when, as in Gawain's case, their behaviour seems very inconsistent.[42]

This overall lack of characterising power in changing narrative 'history' may reflect other features of fifteenth-century life, in particular the dependence of nearly all participants in great affairs on the fortunes of their protectors, their 'good lords'. Even a great nobleman like Bors gains 'worship' by following the fortunes of his even greater kinsman. He does not

---

[41] See Kato, *Concordance*, for Malory's uses of 'condicion' and related forms of the word.
[42] See Bonnie Wheeler, 'Romance and Parataxis and Malory: The Case of Sir Gawain's Reputation', *Arthurian Literature* XII, 109–32.

make all his own developmental choices, unlike the autonomous individuals that have been associated with the rise of the bourgeois novel. The bonds
formed between people in the past are usually seen to dictate their courses
of action in the present. Lancelot is told by his kinsmen and friends 'with
one voice' (1172) that 'hit ys more youre worshyp that ye rescow the quene
from thys perell, insomuch that she hath it for your sake' (1172). And as
Nick Davis points out, the man of most worship, Lancelot, is the man with
the best memory.[43] Worship, it seems, always requires an attempt to maintain the status quo, whatever new adventures have occurred, and the
readers' granting of worship to those who do so requires that *they* also put
'name' above narrative 'proof' of anything else. To think the taking of
Guenevere with Lancelot more probative than her noble name is to align
ourselves, as readers, with those who by 'evyll counceile' (1172) make a
sudden judgement based on 'othir the menour other the takynge wyth the
dede' (1174) and are 'over hasty' (1174) to condemn. We are expected,
instead, to try to *save* her, as Lancelot and Malory both do. Mark Lambert's
comments on Malorian 'shame-culture' provide a classic analysis of the
narrative attitude to this question.[44]

It seems that two things follow from the idea of name in Malory advanced here. Firstly, name does not mean Docherty's 'existentialist'
subject- *character*, as we understand the word from the classic realist novel.
It is far too static for that, too unchanged by other changes within the
narrative. On the other hand, neither does a name function purely as the
object of a thematic pattern 'proving' the identity of the named figure. To a
large extent, the special discursive status of name as worshipful reputation
deforms the patterns and devalues what they tell us. The will to save name,
freer and more opportunistic in its operations than a pattern tied to narrative event, can deal with all opposition from the story piecemeal.

For us to credit the patterns, we are required to think that the identities
of the text's personages are expressed in the adventures they undergo. Such
a notion is aesthetically attractive; it allows us to see connection and
progression in episodic structures; it provides a greater articulation of
identity through plot than the text has abstract terms to manage; it can be
seen to agree with historical ideas of providential outcomes in human
actions, such as underpinned the idea of trial by combat, for example, and
much medieval historiography. Yet at crucial moments in the narrative, it
is hard to see the text placing much faith in the 'proof' supplied by narrative
adventure. For instance, if it did, it would surely accept the killing of Gareth
as an adventure responsive to Lancelot's sin. The event would prove

---

[43] Nick Davis, 'Narrative Composition and the Spatial Memory' in *Narrative: From Malory
to Motion Pictures*, ed. J. Hawthorn (Stratford-upon-Avon Studies, 2nd Series, London:
Arnold, 1985) 25–40.
[44] Lambert, *Malory*, 176–94.

Lancelot a traitor. And yet the only personage who takes that view is Gawain, whose 'vengableness', a frequent theme of the text, can be invoked to explain and devalue his reaction (1189–90), and who eventually retracts every bit of his charges before he dies. (We note, incidentally, that this 'vengableness' always retains its potential to affect Gawain's 'name' though it is only intermittently part of his actions: Gawain has never been less vengeance-seeking than in the episodes preceding the death of Gareth, specifically exonerating Lancelot from blame for killing his sons (1175–76).[45]) The text, in fact, strongly supports Lancelot's view that the killing of Gareth is an 'unhap', a terrible accident, which cannot be attached to Lancelot's name, just as Lyonet tries to deprive Gareth of the credit for a victory by calling it accidental (302).

In short, the thematic pattern is seen to be at the mercy of the narrative's desire to save name. If anyone's difficult situation is 'proved' by the great 'unhap' of the final book, it is poor Gareth's. His presence at Guenevere's burning is in deference to his uncle Arthur, for he is 'yonge and full unable to say . . . nay' (1176). But the fact that he is unarmed, and hence unrecognised, is in deference to Lancelot, who made him knight. The worshipful reader shares Gareth's plight in this new turn of events, responding, as he does, to *two* great names, but unable to cope with their sudden hostility towards each other. The high regard for name places both Gareth and Malory's implied reader under great pressure, through its incapacity to respond to change in the story. In this respect, perhaps, the narrative conservatism of *Le Morte Darthur* reproduces the tension of a cultural moment in which a dominant element of discourse was outpaced by events.

Adventure, Misfortune and Reputation: The Case of Balin

Thematic narrative structures, by giving little importance to psychological motivation, direct our sense of individual characters' agency into general categories ('worship', 'prowess') in which the knight's adventures mainly prove his degree of attainment, his relative perfection or imperfection. For instance, Lancelot's motivation, at the start of the *Noble Tale*, is merely that 'he thought hymself to preve in straunge adventures'. At the end of the tale he has 'the grettyste name of ony knyght of the worlde, and moste he was

---

45 Wheeler, 'Romance and Parataxis', denies my view, *Nottingham Medieval Studies* 34, 1990, 148, and 11ff above, that 'name is impervious to events'. See Wheeler, 132: 'Sir Gawain has a name, but it is contingent, subject to constant change. The paratactic mode amplifies cracks in the shattered mirror of Sir Gawain's discordant selves.' My point is simply that at moments of narrative necessity the appeal to 'name', in this case a bad one, overrides the more complex view we might derive from considering the full range of a knight's actions. This is just what happens in 1189–90 when Malory ignores Gawain's recent unvengeful forgiveness of the deaths of his sons, but invokes through Lancelot his murder of Lamerok.

honoured of hyghe and lowe' (287/24–25). The adventures create the 'name'. This theory of significant structure in Malory, admirably expounded by Benson,[46] has met some opposition. Jill Mann, in a powerful article on 'Balin', denies that Balin's adventures reveal his identity, because of the major role *chance* plays in them. Balin's tragic actions 'do not manifest his self, they merely manifest his destiny'.[47] Mann is not confident of our ability to detect more than an intermittent 'aesthetic'[48] pattern in this story, involving stylistic features such as repetition, irony and balance, bafflingly isolated from familiar cause-and-effect. For Mann, 'adventure' is *chance*, and the final shape of events

> does not result from the effort of an organizing author, – or even of an organizing God – but in the chance completion of a single pattern among the countless others which remain unfulfilled.[49]

This analysis is extended by her to cover the last two books of the *Morte Darthur* as well: 'this final cataclysmic adventure equally impossible to link with any will or intention, human or divine'.[50] In my own approach to the 'Tale of Balin', which follows, I argue that Balin's 'name', his poor reputation and social reception, may be read as cause, rather than effect, of his unhappy career. To adopt Mann's term, I see the 'will' behind his mischances as the narrative's own, in its need to rank Balin's adventures below those of greater knights to come.

Whatever the verdict in Balin's case, a look at its close context – *The Tale of King Arthur* – shows Malory happy to acknowledge a great variety of causes for events. Causes are personal and emotional – Uther falls sick 'for pure angre and for grete love' (8/8); providential – Arthur is king 'for God wille have it soo' (14/20); personal and political – 'Thys was the causis of the northir hoste, that they were rered for the despite and rebuke that the six kyngis had at Carlyon' (25/20–22). Often they are mixed – Arthur is chosen king 'by adventure and by grace' (97/2); Pellinore says ' "God may well fordo desteny" ' (120/10), but Merlin cannot avoid his ' "evil adventure" ' (125/19–22). Arthur says of Morgan's temporary petrifaction ' "here may ye se the vengeaunce of God! And now am I sory this *mysaventure* is befalle" ' (151/24–25).

Multiple causes co-exist peacefully in the minds of the author and his characters throughout the text of *Le Morte Darthur*.[51] When Lancelot is trapped in Guenevere's bedroom, he cries:

---

46   Benson, *Malory's Morte Darthur*, 81–82.
47   Mann, ' "Taking the Adventure" ', 84.
48   Ibid., 78.
49   Ibid., 87–89.
50   Ibid., 91.
51   Lambert, *Malory*, 166, demonstrates Malory's penchant for multiple causes: 'The ruin [of the Round Table] is the fault of Aggravain, and of Gawain, and of Guinevere, and of

'God deffende me frome such a shame! But, Jesu Cryste, be Thou my shylde and myne armoure!'
    And therewith Sir Launcelot wrapped hys mantel aboute hys arme well and surely. (1167/4–7)

So Lancelot, caught by the 'unhappy' Mordred and Aggravain, acknowledges that all is in God's hands. He reveals his personal motivation ('shame'). He trusts in the particular providence of Christ, for whose 'plesure' he has 'applyed hym dayly to do' (1045/24–26), and he proceeds to make a provisional earthly shield out of his mantle. His reactions indicate an easy acceptance of the co-existence of chance, malicious enemies, God's activities, and his own power to act, just as Arthur has seen God's vengeance in a 'mysaventure' (151/18–23) which Morgan, for her part, regards as a proof of her own power:

'tell hym I feare hym nat whyle I can make me and myne in lyknesse of stonys, and lette hym wete I can do much more whan I se my tyme.'
                                                                                            (152/25–28)

We do not, then, normally find Malory or his characters baffled by inexplicable adventure seen as 'chance'. (Even in 'Balin' the characters themselves are able to *accept* the apparently illogical and disproportionate consequences of the hero's actions, whilst they pity and lament them.) We find, instead, that Malory and his characters like, if possible, to draw connections between people's actions and the fates they have or should have: 'quene Gwenyver . . . whyle she lyved she was a trew lover, and therefor she had a good ende' (1120/11–13). Implicitly, the good end is God's work as well as Guenevere's, just as Lancelot's reception into heaven is definitely *his* reward from God. Such endings are more (or less) than aesthetically congruent; still less are they a tribute to the power of chance. They represent a narrative's commandeering of the notion of providential intervention in history, in order to aggrandise certain figures in the text. This apparent dependence of 'destiny' on the need to save the name of the protagonist shows out strongly when the knightly hero is uncannily preserved in his adventures from the operations of mischance. In what Benson calls the 'proof of perfect knighthood' adventure – *The Noble Tale of Sir Launcelot* – Lancelot is conventionally imbued with the ability to act correctly even when the significance and likely consequence of his choices are obscured. At the Chapel Perilous he has this exemplary exchange with a damsel:

Launcelot; it is also an unhap, a misfortuning. Malorian tragedy is multicentric: we understand all the parts, but not the whole.'

'Sir Launcelot, leve that swerde behynde the, other thou wolt dye for hit.'

'I leve hit not', seyde sir Launcelot, 'for no thretyng.'

'No,' seyde she, 'and thou dyddyste leve that swerde quene Gwenyvere sholde thou never se.'

'Than were I a foole and I wolde leve this swerde.'

'Now, jantyll knyghte,' seyde the damesel, 'I requyre the to kysse me but onys.'

'Nay,' seyde sir Launcelot, 'that God me forbede.'

'Well, sir,' seyde she, 'and thou haddyst kyssed me thy lyff dayes had be done. And now, alas,' she seyde, 'I have loste all my laboure, for I ordeyned this chapell for thy sake and for sir Gawayne.' (280/35–281/10)

How does Lancelot know to answer this damsel correctly, just as in another adventure he feels free to say to another importunate female ' "As for to kysse you . . . I may do that and lese no worshyp" ' (1136/20–27)? The answer is that such good adventures are conventionally reserved for knights 'proved' worthiest by the narrative. The story's wish to demonstrate Lancelot's consummate knightly identity necessitates that the action he takes is right in both cases.

A good part of the 'worship' that comes from an adventure accomplished lies in the retrospective understanding of how grave the unforeseen consequences of failure would have been, as in the episode above, and how unknowably fitting the correct course of action was. So, when Lancelot delivers a castleful of distressed ladies, he finds that the castle is Arthur's (Malory's alteration) (272). When he leaps out the window to assist one unknown knight against three, the knight is disclosed as Kay (273–74). These are good 'adventures', apparent matters of chance, but still credited to their achiever's name. Generally speaking, therefore, however strong the sense of sudden, unforeseen 'adventure' as a disruptive force in Malory, we are also aware of it as *necessary* to the action, a recurring source of opportunity. The hero's special gift of ruling his environment will restore or even improve on the status quo. The *Noble Tale* is a classic instance of this kind of romance, where all 'chances' exist ultimately to serve Lancelot, increasing the unique distinction of his name. In that sense, they are not 'chances' at all.

By contrast, the course of events in Malory's 'Balin' bears no direct narrative relation to its protagonist. Not only is the hero's path constantly crossed by those of others, as in most romances, but the *story* itself is never fully his own, the events never purely fitted for his self-declaration. Although 'Balin' is well presented as a separate short tale, it is connected to many other stories extending long before and after. Quite unlike the *Noble Tale*, or the *Gareth*, there is no single point of origin, nor can everything be tidily accounted for at the end. The ideal disponibility of actants and events in romance seems superseded here by the messy contingencies of history. In no other story of Malory's is there at once so much surprise and so much prophecy, as if the narrative laboured to repair its crumbling sense of providentiality. Everyone comes on stage already with a history, enemies, friends, serious consequences to face from the past, and a projected future. Balin has already killed Arthur's cousin and the 'Lady of the Lake''s brother before the story starts. The 'Lady of the Lake', Arthur's ally, has killed Balin's mother. Arthur has already antagonised King Lot for ever, and incurred God's displeasure, by sleeping with Morgawse. King Pellam, 'the moste worshipfullist man on lyve in tho dayes' (85/28–29), still supports his fiendish brother Garlon, the invisible knight. In this way, despite the 'marvellous' nature of many of the events, existence is far more contingent and situational in this romance than in most of Malory's. Instead of domi-nating the course of action, Balin appears trapped within it.

One sees this theme of entrapment strongly realised in the text, especially in the unavoidable 'evil customs' of the castle where both brothers die. Balan laments to Balin

> 'I had never grace to departe fro hem syn that I cam hyther, for here it happed me to slee a knyght that kept this iland, and syn myght I never departe, and no more shold ye, broder, and ye myght have slayne me as ye have and escaped yourself with the lyf.' (90/19–23)

A moral reading of the story may consider this an emblem of the self-perpetuating nature of revenge and feuding, in which Balin has become enmeshed through his violence.[52] Alternatively, Balin can be seen as the victim of an inscrutable destiny or chance.[53] I would like to suggest that Balin's unusual lack of power to control his environment may be read also as a product of the narrative closure constantly enforced in this tale by the stronger claims of the wider story-cycle (Malory's) in which it is inserted. The effect of intertextual over-determination inherited from Balin's French source is maintained in Malory, at least in the sense that the 'Tale of Balin' is only a small part of his 'hoole book' and its protagonist is a minor figure in comparison to many others - Arthur, Merlin, Lancelot, Tristram, Gawain, Galahad - that the story mentions. Although Malory's 'Balin' is in some ways less carefully intertextual than the French original, as Vinaver points out (1275–79), it still retains a strong effect of being embedded in a much larger story, and is augmented also with that of Arthur's defeat of Lot. Balin is, from the start, mainly alone and at cross-purposes with the series of events in which he figures, and his identity is asserted *against* the course of the action, rather than 'proved' by it. The normal romance system of punishment and reward is disabled in his case. Balin demonstrates the prowess and the 'truth' of a supreme nobleman knight. He is ' "a passynge good man of hys hondys and of hys dedis, and withoute velony other

---

[52] See Kennedy, *Knighthood*, 227ff.
[53] See Mann, ' "Taking the Adventure" ', 87.

trechory and withoute treson" ' (61/34–62/2). As Merlin says, ' "there lyvith nat a bettir of proues, nother of worthynesse" ' (75/10–11), but Balin is still doomed. What does this mean?

The opening episode, in the rather confused version of it by Malory, sets the ambiguous pattern for the whole tale. We cannot tell at all from the narration that the sword-bearer is 'the falsist damesell that lyveth' as Merlin later says (67/22–32). The sword-test looks comfortably familiar, like a version of the sword-drawing which has proved Arthur's right to the kingdom (13–16), and a forerunner of the sword-drawing which will prove Galahad the destined achiever of the Holy Grail, predicted later in this tale (91–92). Balin sees the adventure as a good one, which can assert his inner value, like his true nature, over his current lowly situation caused by fortune. Asserting that 'manhode and worship ys hyd within a mannes person' (63), he relies on the adventure to 'prove' it. At first events seem to do so. The magic sword, which identifies Balin as both a great fighter and a loyal nobleman, singles him out as the perfect person to defeat King Ryons of North Wales, in Arthur's current political crisis. The normal happy ending of reward seems already in sight. Things are seen to go wrong when Balin refuses to give back the sword, and so receives its curse. The damsel, again not seeming very false, warns Balin of exactly what will happen, that with the sword he will kill his best friend, and that the sword will be his own destruction. He still refuses to return it; if we require a motive, it is perhaps through stubbornness, or perhaps because he 'takes the adventure' as a divinely-ordained path for himself, whose consequences he must accept.[54]

We could see Balin as morally rash here, subject to a recklessness that easily leads to unacceptable violence.[55] He has already been imprisoned for the manslaughter of a cousin of Arthur's. He is just about to take a personal vengeance on the 'Lady of the Lake', Arthur's chief benefactor, the giver of Excalibur. In this, and later in King Pellam's hall, when he kills the invisible knight (83–84), he seems to act without proper discretion as to place or time: ' "telle hem in Northhumbirlonde how my moste foo ys dede" ' (66/26–27). One can generalise the point and see Balin as representative of an older blood-feuding ethos, of revenge, as opposed to a higher loyalty to king and fellow-knights, which will be necessary to the not yet established 'Order of Knighthood', devoted to rule by law, centred on Arthur, and especially exemplied by Lancelot.[56] The story might also be thought to encourage this view in referring directly to several future civil and family conflicts. There is mention of the clash between Tristram and his uncle King Mark of

---

54 Ibid., passim.
55 Tennyson's 'Balin and Balan', the last-written (1872–74) of his *Idylls of the King*, is an influential 'reading' of this kind.
56 See Kennedy, *Knighthood*, 98–102.

Cornwall over Isoude (72), also of the very bitter blood-feud between the families of King Lot and King Pellinore (77, 81/16–18), and of the crucial quarrel between Gawain and Lancelot (91/21–25), chief cause of Arthur's war against Lancelot. There is also prophecy of the final war between Arthur and his incestuously-begotten son Mordred (79/3–8). The curse on the sword looks highly symbolic of a certain kind of civil violence, and violence within the one family, which must have been very meaningful to Malory, an old campaigner of the Wars of the Roses.

In the original symbolism of the French story, which Malory has altered, the sword of Galahad was to be the first of Balin's two swords, which would be employed only against spiritual enemies. In medieval political theory, the idea of the 'two swords', taken from Luke's Gospel (22, 38), had often been used to describe the division of spiritual and secular authority.[57] But in Malory's version, famously, the neat division of the French is confounded. The same sword will be used for both purposes: battle between Round Table knights and the spiritual chivalry of Galahad.[58] Beverly Kennedy considers Malory's alteration shows that 'Balin's heroic code of ethics and his fatalist world-view must be transcended if Arthurian society is to avoid self-destruction'.[59] But this may be an overstatement of the Morte's symbolic neatness. It is not certain that Balin's keeping of the second sword is connected with his manslayings in a way that declares failings in his knighthood. After all, Balin fairly soon recovers from Arthur's displeasure by doing him such good service against King Ryons and King Lot. Arthur seems prepared to admit that Balin might have had a good reason to kill the 'Lady of the Lake'; it was the shame of having her killed under his safe-conduct that the king could not bear: ' "For what cause soever ye had . . . ye sholde have forborne in my presence . . . for such anothir despite had I nevir in my courte" ' (66/15–19). In support of Jill Mann's view, that the curse on the sword does not reflect on Balin's moral character or exercise of choice,[60] Merlin and Arthur (68, 75, 78, 92), and the sword-damsel herself (64/15–19) repeatedly pity Balin, rather than blame him, and insist on the uprightness of his conduct. Merlin reads it all as a plot by a jealous and deceitful woman seeking revenge on good knights (67–68). In terms either of Benson's 'horizontal' cause and effect, or of psychological motivation, Balin cannot be blamed. Nevertheless, his story is represented as a wrongful one in the sense that it is a failure or travesty of the normal chivalric pattern.

---

[57] See Walter Ullmann, A History of Political Thought: The Middle Ages (Harmondsworth: Penguin, 1965) 110–11.

[58] See Vinaver, 1322/n.91, 23;

[59] Kennedy, Knighthood, 9. See ibid., 221–23, which sees both Balin's and Arthur's 'first swords' (i.e., the one Balin received in knighthood, and the Sword from the Stone) as good, but their second swords (Balin's from the Sword-maiden, and Excalibur from the Lady of the Lake) as bad.

[60] Mann, ' "Taking the Adventure" ', 87–89.

Balin's breach of protocol in beheading an enemy before Arthur en-
throned stamps his story as one of imperfection, but not because it indicates
an ordinary moral flaw. The sign of imperfection is conventional: instead
of being able to begin his 'straunge adventures' properly (as Lancelot does),
with the riding-out he had already commenced – the first stage of the basic
tripartite pattern – riding-out/accomplishment/return – Balin is *sent* from
court in disgrace. The courteous departure he intended, with Arthur's
traditional regret for his going, and request to return, foreshadowing reward (64/24–65/6), is converted into ignominious flight. Balin remains
caught on the wrong foot throughout the adventure, and is never reinte-
grated fully into Arthurian society. This is despite his repeated good intentions (66, 69, 70) and Arthur's (75, 78). When at last Balin is restored to
Arthur (79–80) – the conventional ending Malory uses for the *Noble Tale of
Launcelot*, the *Gareth* and the *Tristram* – he must immediately go off to find
the sorrowful knight, and becomes caught up in a new chain of events from
which there is no return.

In short, the reader receives two sets of signs from the tale. One, based
on our awareness of the probative pattern gone wrong, tells us that Balin's
story has an indefinable wrongness. When a false damsel says to *him*,
' "Now, jantyll and curtayse knyght, geff me the swerde agayne" ' (64/4–5),
Balin, like Lancelot at the Chapel Perilous, refuses – but *he* is in error. The
second, based on the proof of the sword-drawing, and the direct statements
of Malory, Merlin and others, tells us that he is 'a passynge good knyght . . .
and moste of worship withoute treson, trechory or felony'. The record of
Balin's adventures combines both significances. His misfortunes, culminating in the 'unhappy' custom of the castle, the 'unhappy' knight who makes
him change his shield, and the fatal stroke with the 'unhappy' sword,
express a conventional wrongness, but the only explicit prompting Malory
gives us is to pity such a good knight. The broken 'vertical' pattern assures
us of the rightness of Balin's end; the 'horizontal' features of the story
present it as pitiably undeserved. This combination of impressions is what
gives the adventure its unusual power.

Another failed narrative pattern is made evident through frequent textual reference: Balin is fated, it seems, to take part in a history which he does
not understand, the Holy Grail. The Grail and sacred lance are waiting for
Galahad, who will heal the Maimed King and recover the Waste Land from
the suffering which Balin causes. Balin's subordinate role in this process
must be already determined, since Merlin (not to speak of God) can predict
it (72/25–32, 78/12–14). Merlin's view is that Balin strikes the Dolorous
Stroke because of the death of the lady Colombe who killed herself after
Balin killed her lover, Lanceor (72/19–32). The moral arbitrariness of the
connection reflects strongly on the subordinate position of Balin in the story.
Were Merlin's words to refer to the killing of 'The Lady of the Lake' in
Arthur's court, as has been claimed, the major issue might be Balin's moral

culpability,[61] but the reference must be, where it stands, directly to Colombe; the story requires only Balin's action, not his motive. Balin's slaying of Lanceor in fair fight is in itself 'knightly', and would be quite unexceptionable in nearly all other contexts of the *Morte*. The boastful Lanceor has demanded a combat, despite Balin's express discouragement (69/1–6). Balin has not tried to kill him, and fails even to realise at first that he is dead (69/12–16). He tries also to stop the lady killing herself, but fails (69/24–70/2). Why does Merlin select this one incident to connect with the Dolorous Stroke, and why is Balin made culpable in such a huge way because of something that happened against his will and his best efforts to stop it? (In the French version he is held culpable because he violates the Holy Grail chamber and touches the lance.[62]) In Malory the connection is not explained; there is not even 'poetic justice'. Balin is not understood here as an independent moral agent, but rather by his significance in an intertextual process which wants to compare and contrast his story with other knights', to their advantage. The demands of relative 'name' fashion his identity, one externally over-determined, not an interior self 'proven' by deeds whose reception is just and equitable, nor even 'providentially' neat. In this way, Balin's adventures simulate the career of a 'poure knight', as he is, required to serve the self-realisation of those more powerful; his otherwise arbitrary 'unhappiness' exposes as fantasy the notion that romance closure signifies a just or providential reward for deeds done.

Wherever Balin goes, we find that he is a precursor of some more important and successful knight who is to come. Very often, the events he partakes in have already been preordained, so that he seems to be living backwards, fulfilling the narrative plan (which in this way oddly resembles a psychological 'script' for him) yet always a step behind the action, unaware of its cryptic interconnectedness, or unable to believe it, until too late (73/1–3, 89/1–4). He is always wandering into someone else's story, to be made a figure in his pageant. Significantly, when Balin kills Lanceor, Merlin identifies the field as the site of a later battle between Lancelot and Tristram, which will totally eclipse this combat in both prestige and good fortune:

> 'Here shall be', seyde Merlion, 'in this same place the grettist bateyle betwyxte two knyghtes that ever was or ever shall be, and the trewyst lovers; *and yette none of hem shall slee other.*'
> And there Merlion wrote hir namys uppon the tombe with lettirs of golde, that shall feyght in that place: which namys was Launcelot du Lake and Trystrams. (72/5–11)

When Balin buries Perin de Mount Beliard in a tomb, he finds a prophecy

---

61 Kennedy, *Knighthood*, 226.
62 See Vinaver, 1309/n.72.25–27.

of Gawain, Lot and Pellinor (81/15–18). Balin's damsel, who bleeds to save the sick lady, is to be outdone by Sir Perceval's sister in the Holy Grail story (81/19–82/14).[63] When Balin takes up a lance to defend himself against Pellam, it turns out to be the lance that killed Christ, the very implement which Galahad will later use to heal Pellam (84/27–85/30). Balin's sword is reserved for the later use of Lancelot and Galahad (91/15–26). Merlin rigs up a wonderful bed at the scene of Balin's death, which only Lancelot can destroy, and a bridge which only Galahad can cross (91/11–14; 91/27–31). And, of course, the sword-drawing with which the tale begins is to be outdone by Galahad's adventure, copiously predicted at its end.

In all this, Balin is very much the image of a *'poor* knight', rather than a bad one. Try as he may, his efforts can never achieve the recognition or the reward of other names more favoured, and he cannot manage to fashion events into a prestigious declarative pattern chiefly about himself. On him consequences are visited, especially for deaths, that others more wealthy and socially powerful can normally evade. Balin's main difference from a Lancelot or a Tristram is not one of conduct. It is that he cannot control the public reception of his deeds. From the very start, his success in drawing the sword is emphatically discounted by fellow-knights: 'Than had the kynge and all the barownes grete mervayle that Balyne had done that aventure; many knyghtes had grete despite at hym' (63/32–34). 'Than the moste party of the knyghtes of the Rounde Table seyde that Balyne dud nat this adventure all only by myght but by wycchecrauffte' (65/6–9). Similarly, his killing of the 'Lady of the Lake' is not condemned as a moral failing, but in terms of its poor reception: ' "Alas! . . . ye ar gretly to blame *for to displease kynge Arthure"* ' (66/30–31), a theme harped on in this tale (70/14–24). (We may remember that Arthur himself has displeased God by sleeping with Morgawse, and received a punishment to be worked out through Mordred (44), yet will remain throughout the *Morte* 'the most noblest Crysten kynge', hardly a moral cripple.)

We find, in short, that the force which fore-ordains Balin's doom, whether we call it providence or chance, bears an uncanny relation to his inability to gain widespread social acceptance of his actions. The crucial point is whether Balin is right when he says that it is the inner worth of a man, made visible in his deeds of arms, that counts in his assessment, not his wealth and social image (as displayed in clothing) and his reputation:

> 'A, fayre damesell,' seyde Balyn, 'worthynes and good tacchis and also good dedis is nat only in araymente, but manhode and worship ys hyd within a mannes person; and many a worshipfull knyght ys nat knowyn unto all peple. And therefore worship and hardynesse ys nat in araymente.'

63 See Chapter 3, 70ff, for more analysis of this episode.

'Be God', seyde the damesell, 'ye sey soth. Therefore ye shall assay to
do what ye may.' (63/23–30)

The sword-maiden's agreement with Balin's view might be the falsest trick
she plays. For in actuality 'The Tale of Balin' maintains a strong distinction
of rank and power in the way it consistently treats the role of Balin in
relation to greater men's careers. It is clearly not enough for success to be
brave and without treachery, if England is filled with utterances and inscrip-
tions subordinating you to other men, and putting your actions in a bad
light. These include the majority accusation of witchcraft (65); the 'Lady of
the Lake' 's accusation of manslaughter (65); the bad opinion of Arthur,
Balan and the squire (66, 70); the words of the dwarf (71), warning Balin
that the kin of Sir Lanceor will be after him; the inscription on the tomb of
Lanceor and Colombe (71–72);[64] Merlin's prophecy of the Dolorous Stroke
(72); the blame of the people of the Waste Land, warning of vengeance (86);
the accusation of Sir Garnish (87). Then, to avoid an accusation that he has
killed Garnish, his lady, and her other lover, Balin rides away (88), but only
towards the island where he is to die, with Merlin's definitive inscription
on his tomb: ' "here lyeth Balyn le Saveage that was the Knyght with the
Two Swerdes *and he that smote the dolorous stroke*" ' (91). Balin tries hard to
reveal the quality that is 'hid' within him, but after some initial success in
changing Arthur's opinion, each further step only seems to conceal it more
and more. For this knight of limited name, 'nat knowyn unto all peple'
(63/26), the weight of adverse external evaluations proves too much, and
he dies accordingly, not 'known' until too late, in fatal misrecognition
(88/35–39, 89/11, 90/5–14). He is pitied, but he is not to be spared. Indeed,
the pity of others seems to accompany a general acceptance of the fact that
Balin will be expended sooner or later.

   Balin's unhappy fate is not probative pattern, symbolic punishment, or
chance. It is part of the least dispensable function of his tale, its preservation
of the hierarchy of 'names'; the story is told so as to keep from Balin's actions
the prestige and declarative power that belong to Lancelot, Galahad, Tristram and others. His 'adventures' turn out to be carefully ranked according
to his lesser importance in the scale of heroes, and so, accordingly, are the
ways of interpreting them. Those of the great are allowed to be 'proofs',
providential dispositions which supposedly represent heaven's answer to
their greatness. Balin's are a 'poor knight''s hard luck story, their 'unhappiness' stemming ultimately from his lack of money, influence and social
standing, specifically as these are determined by clothing, confident appearance and social favour:

---

[64] This does at least specify that Lanceor jousted at his own request.

> But for he was poore and poorly arayde, he put hymselff nat far in prees
> . . . for hys poure araymente she thought he sholde nat be of no worship
> withoute vylony or trechory. (63/5–18)

(In this context, it may be significant that the honorific 'sir' is usually omitted from Balin's name, even in formal addresses to him.) Despite all his efforts, and his touching faith in the proof of 'adventure', Balin finds that 'worship' is externally derived, determined by appearances and reputation rather than by anything hidden 'within' a man. The Paston family received very similar counsel about their son John, at Edward IV's court:

> there shal no thyng hurte hym but youre streytnesse of mony to hym, for
> withoute he haue mony in hyse purse so as he may resonably spende
> amonges hem, ellys they wyll not sette by hem.[65]

Clement Paston also wrote to John Paston I lamenting that young John 'is not yet verily aqweyntyd in the Kyngys howse, nore wyth the officerys of the Kyngys howse . . . fore he is not bold y-now to put forthe hym-selfe', and stressing the need for more money, 'fore the costys is gretter in the Kyngys howse quen he rydythe that ye wend it hadde be'.[66] Young John's letters home reveal the same, the equal need for money and high acquaintance if one is to succeed at court.[67]

Elsewhere in the *Morte*, Malory tends to prefer the story of 'levelling-up', in which previously obscure young men, like Torre or Lavayne, win a name for themelves. As the *Noble Tale* puts it,

> som there were that were but knyghtes encresed in armys and worshyp
> that passed all other of her felowys in prouesse and noble dedys, and that
> was well proved on many. (253/4–7)

Malory may have been thinking of Edward IV's high promotion of fighting men like Sir John Astley.[68] And yet, revealingly, he immediately adds 'But in especiall hit was prevyd on sir Launcelot de Lake' (253/8), forgetting in his enthusiasm that Lancelot is not 'only a knight', but a French king, and

---

[65] John Russe to John Paston I, 23 August 1461, no. 643 in *The Paston Letters*, ed. N. Davis (Oxford: Clarendon Press, 1976) vol. II, p. 247. Also, Thomas Playter to John Paston I, June 1461, no. 631, telling him that he is on the list to be knighted, warns him to get the appropriate gear ready 'for the gladnesse and plesour of al your welwyllers and to the pyne and dyscomfort of all your jlle-wyllers'. See also Philippa Maddern, 'Honour among the Pastons: Gender and Integrity in Fifteenth-century English Provincial Society', *Journal of Medieval History* 14, 1988, 357–71, esp. 361–62.

[66] *Paston Letters*, vol. I, no. 116, pp. 199–200.

[67] E.g., *Paston Letters*, vol. I, no. 231, p. 391; no. 232, pp. 392–93; no. 243, p. 406, all asking for money; no. 240, p. 401, advising his brother on a livery for attending the Duke of Norfolk; no. 318, p. 524, boasting of his acquaintance with Lord Hastings and members of the King's household.

[68] See Barber, 'Malory's *Le Morte Darthur* and Court Culture', 138ff.

'the grettist jantillman of the worlde' (865/12). To *his* story, there are virtually no limits. 'The Tale of Balin', by contrast, realises in its protagonist's marvellous adventures his 'bandes', the boundaries that a 'knyght alone' can not break down:[69]

> And within thre dayes he cam by a crosse; and theron were letters of gold wryten that said: 'it is not for no knyght alone to ryde toward this castel.'
> Thenne sawe he an old hore gentylman comyng toward hym that sayd,
>   'Balyn le Saveage, thow passyst thy bandes to come this waye, therfor torne ageyne and it will availle the.' (88/3–8)

The episodes of 'Balin' concerning King Lot have been considered a mere excrescence to the main narrative,[70] but actually parallel Balin's story quite closely in their combination of respect for the loser (Lot) with the political recognition that he has to go if he will not be subordinated. Like Balin, Lot is admired and pitied, as I demonstrate in the next chapter, but still he must be defeated, because he stands in the way of Arthur, and this is Arthur's story, not his.[71] Lot is not to blame; he has a very good reason to dislike Arthur; like Balin, he is a supreme knight. But he is, ultimately, a dispensable figure in the context of the broader story:

> And well Merlion knew that one of the kynges sholde be dede that day; and lothe was Merlion that ony of them bothe sholde be slayne, but of the tweyne he had levir kyng Lotte of Orkeney had be slayne than Arthure.
>   (76/16–20)

Put simply, the demands of the following books, in which Arthur, Lancelot, Tristram and Galahad will in turn be permitted adventures which 'prove' their greatness, require the misfortunes of lesser figures here. Balin's fate, Lot's defeat, are not ultimately matters to be left to chance.

---

69 For discussion of a rather different phenomenon, the periodic guise of major Round Table figures, and even Arthur, as 'poor knights', see Chapter 4, 86.
70 See E. Vinaver, *King Arthur and his Knights: Selected Tales of Sir Thomas Malory* (London: Oxford UP, 1956) Introduction, xx.
71 See Chapter 2, 39–41.

2

'Vertuous dedes' / 'Tedious havoc':
The Vision of Combat

> . . . honest King Arthur, will never displease a soldier.
> (Sir Philip Sidney, A Defence of Poetry)[1]

A Book of Arms

Le Morte Darthur consists mainly of descriptions of martial combat, a subject of supreme interest both to its author and its implied audience – 'all jantyllmen that beryth olde armys' (375/23–24). Along with Shakespeare's Henry V, Malory's text remains the most influential English story of fighting. The 'noble actes of chyvalrye, the jentyl and vertuous dedes' of which Caxton's Preface speaks (cxlv/32–33) are deeds of arms. Most of Malory is to do with men of the knightly caste fighting each other – in wars, tournaments, jousts, knight errantry, quests and private quarrels. These 'acts' are in no way secondary to any other narrative interest, nor even necessarily subordinated to any broader themes of conduct and political fortunes. Rather, combat narrative is both a means and an end in Malory. It provides the dominant expressive medium for nearly all the interests of the story, and its major rationale: to be, as Caxton saw it, a memorial of British arms.

There is little purely theoretical about Malory's understanding of knights as fighters, and, as his re-emphasis of the French Holy Grail stories indicates, he proved incapable of thinking of fighting as possibly wrong in itself. Where the French book had set up a moral distinction between a sword of killing, for Lancelot, and a sword of healing, for Galahad, Malory 'makes the two swords into one which is to be handled either by Lancelot or by Galahad' (91/8–26 and n.).[2] Those with less respect than Malory and his heroes for fighting (not to say killing) are the malcontents and ingrates of Arthur's realm:

for than was the comyn voyce amonge them that with kynge Arthur was never othir lyff but warre and stryff, and with sir Mordrede was grete joy

---

1 Philip Sidney, A Defence of Poetry, ed. J.A. Van Dorsten (London: Oxford UP, 1966) 56.
2 See Chapter 1, 21.

and blysse. Thus was kynge Arthur depraved, and evyll seyde off; and many there were that kynge Arthur had brought up of nought, and gyffyn them londis, that myght nat than say hym a good worde.

(1228/35–1229/5)

Conversely, the recollection of deeds of arms, properly accredited to the men who achieved them, and recorded in detail, is the basis of the text's idea of 'goodness' – of what is worthy, and therefore worthy to be remembered. Although it is possible to construct a teleology of combat in Malory, there is no absolute need. His fights are not necessarily *for* anything, other than the pleasure of witnessing to the great deeds themselves. As T.H. White half-playfully insisted, Malory and Wisden have something in common,[3] and though Malory did not construct an actual scoring table, as later tournament writers sometimes did,[4] his impulse to quantify, detail and conclude each passage of arms often produces something similar in effect:

So whan sir Launcelot was horsed he ded many mervaylouse dedis of armys, and so ded sir Trystram, and sir Palomydes in lyke wyse. Than sir Launcelot smote adowne wyth a speare sir Dynadan, and the kynge off Scotlonde, and the kynge of North Walys, and the kynge of Northumbirlonde, and the kynge of Lystenoyse. So than sir Launcelot and his felowys smote downe well-nye a fourty knyghtes. (740/20–26)

The mode is sequential and quantitative, concerned to record the names of the principal combatants, the 'score' (40–nil) and the winners.

Chaucer had wonderfully captured the excitement with which a tournament crowd discussed the prospects of the contestants and the action itself:[5]

The paleys ful of peple up and doun,
Heere thre, ther ten, holdynge hir questioun,
Dyvynynge of thise Theban knyghtes two.

In Malory this nameless crowd voice is often heard – 'the cry huge and grete' (739/10), the 'cry of herowdys and all maner of comyn people' (734/30–31) – but greater personages are more articulate and more specific. They gather regularly to discuss the day, comparing and ranking others in terms of their prowess, so that the description of actual combat and the evaluative discussions about it slip without resistance into each other. Malory's reinscribing

---

[3] T.H. White, *The Once And Future King* (London: Fontana Books, 1958) Book III, Chapter 2.

[4] See Sidney Anglo, 'Archives of the English Tournament – Score Cheques and Lists', *Journal of the Society of Archivists* vol. 11, no. 4, 1961, 153–62. See esp. 155: 'It was the business of the attendant heralds to record the scores of the contestants, and they performed this task according to conventions for which the only modern parallel would seem to be the scoring method in cricket.'

[5] *The Riverside Chaucer*, ed. L.D. Benson (Oxford: Oxford UP, 1988), *Knight's Tale*, 2513–22, 2719–41.

of 'the book' to which he often refers is represented as continuous with this conversational preoccupation of the aristocracy and knightly classes; it is a rewriting of adventures as 'told' by knights.[6] Quality counts, but the evaluation of knighthood is mainly built on the quantity of deeds performed, so that certain recurring figures dominate the incidents of the book just as they do the knowledgeable conversation of their peers within the fictional narrative. The nature and function of these (supposedly) spoken and written discourses is ideally identical, so that they can be seamlessly merged, whether it is the book's personages who are 'talkynge' or the book itself that 'seyth', as in this example:

> And all this was talkynge off in all the howsis of the kynges, and all kynges and lordis and knyghtis seyde, of clyere knyghthode and of pure strengthe and of bounté and of curtesy sir Launcelot and sir Trystram bare the pryce of all knyghtes that ever were in kyng Arthurs dayes, and there were no knyghtes in kynge Arthurs dayes that ded halff so many dedis of armys as they two ded. As the booke seyth, no ten knyghtes ded nat halff the dedis that they ded, and there was never knyght in there dayes that requyred sir Launcelot othir ellys sir Trystram of ony queste, so hit were nat to there shame, but they parformed there desyre. (742/23–33)

It seems likely that Malory conceived of his book as an extension and guide to this kind of professional discussion. Reading and speaking of great deeds could be seen as a sure step on the way to achieving them, as we observe from Caxton's Preface to *The Book of the Ordre of Chyvalrye*,[7] and could even be a form of keeping company with chivalric heroes, and participating in their prestige.[8] As a narrative of martial 'virtue', *Le Morte Darthur* must have held something of the same relation to knightly conversation and practice as did a book of hours in relation to prayer and religious devotion.[9] It was

---

6   See, e.g., 1036/11–22. Maurice Keen, *Chivalry* (New Haven: Yale UP, 1984) 138, referring to the Kings of Arms' and heralds' written reports, shows how by Froissart's time 'the heralds' old function, of crying out the names of the valiant at tournaments, has . . . developed into something much more professional'.

7   *The Book of the Ordre of Chyvalry*, ed. A.T.P. Byles (EETS OS 168, London: Oxford UP, 1926) 121–25.

8   For further discussion see Karen Cherewatuk, ' "Gentyl Audiences" and "Grete Bookes" '; Richard Barber, 'Malory's *Le Morte Darthur* and Court Culture under Edward IV', 133–55, esp. 152: 'His [Malory's] wide range of reference is best explained in an oral context, such as that of the squires of the household "talking of chronicles of kings and other policies" after supper'. Felicity Riddy, *Sir Thomas Malory*, 44, notes also that the *Morte* exhibits a 'blurring of the boundaries between writing and reading'.

9   For an analogy, see *Knyghthode and Bataile*, ed. R. Dyboski and Z. Arend (EETS OS 201, London: Oxford UP, 1935) Proemium 33–88. The author imagines his work, a translation of Vegetius' *De re militari*, reaching the notice of Henry VI through the verbal recommendation of 'my lord Beaumont': ' "For my seruyse/ Heer wil I rede (he seith) as o psaultier . . . I fynde it is right good and pertynente/ Vnto the kyng . . . /I halde it wel doon, hym therwith presente." '

an imaginative structure to be used as a resource for personal betterment in their lives, as well as a pastime, by its readers.

Quite early in his story Malory gives an indication of how a fight should be described, stressing the equation ('worde by worde') of oral and written accounts, as if the story were not fabricated from writerly imagination or literary formulae, but simply written up as the record of the day's activities in the field. Merlin tells his master Bloise

> how Arthure and the two kynges had spedde at the grete batayle, and how hyt was endyd, and tolde the namys of every kynge and knyght of worship that was there. And so Bloyse wrote the batayle worde by worde as Merlion tolde hym, how hit began and by whom, and in lyke wyse how hit was ended and who had the worst. And all the batayles that were done in Arthurs dayes, Merlion dud hys mayster Bloyse wryte them. Also he dud wryte all the batayles that every worthy knyght ded of Arthurs courte. (37/29–38/2)

This idea of the narrative, supposedly passing verbatim from eye-witness oral report to authoritative written record, works on the assumption that all right-thinking men will share one view and one language for describing and evaluating combats. As Lambert says, there is 'an impression of careful, accurate record-keeping'.[10] There seems to be no doubt made of Bloise's account, even though one could easily see him as a propagandist, a court historian directly manipulated by Arthur's chief of council. Instead, the circumstance is related to increase respect for the authenticity and the value of the present story. The formulaic nature of the description functions as a guarantee of authority; the story follows an approved course, and simulates a general judgement shared by the knightly peer group in response to known events. The formula invokes collective speech rather than the singularity of individual writer and book-readers. In this way, though the narrating of the content of combat might seem to display conflict and division within the chivalric ranks, both its manner of description and the implied circumstances of communication, reception and re-communication stress instead a solidarity of outlook, and coerce the would-be 'jantyll' reader-hearer to conform his or her judgement to the chivalric norm. To be worshipful, one must see things the same way, speak with the same voice as the 'kynges and lordis and knyghtis' who are so convinced of Lancelot's and Tristram's preeminence, and of how it can be known. There is a strong illusion of a judging presence and 'voice', established by, rather than in spite of, the heavy reliance on written formulae.

Caxton directed *Le Morte Darthur* to 'alle noble prynces, lordes and ladyes, gentylmen or gentylwymmen, that desyre *to rede or here redde* of the noble and joyous hystorye of the grete conquerour and excellent kyng, kyng

10 Lambert, *Malory*, 49.

Arthur' (cxlvi/19–22). He seems to have envisaged the written account's being turned again into the speech from which it came, and received back into the stream of aristocratic and gentry conversation. This 'hystorye' had, according to his Preface, long been perceived by 'many noble and dyvers jentylemen' as worthy to be 'remembred emonge us Englysshemen'.[11] Walter Ong has observed of the medieval period that writing served largely to recycle knowledge back into the oral world, as in medieval university disputations, the reading of literary and other texts to groups, and the habit of reading aloud even to oneself.[12] Within this context, Malory's *Morte* assumes the status, then, not of an invented fable (or its translation), nor even of a book of *exempla*, what Caxton called 'ensaumples and doctryne', but of a 'hystorye' made available for oral purposes already in existence and already sanctioned.[13] Its value and meaning seem thoroughly appropriated from the outset to the interests of a broad social group, the 'jantylls'. This assumed homogeneity of reception can be read as part of the appeal of the book, no doubt comforting for those of Caxton's audience who aspired to share the values of gentility with people actually well above them on the social scale. The precise meaning of 'gentle' is so broad and so ill-defined, under fifteenth-century English conditions, that the text's insistence on community of values can be seen as necessary to create a strong sense of a united audience, and to disguise their differences from each other.[14] In short, though the *Morte* may look like a story of conflict, it much more strongly upholds a myth of solidarity amongst the 'jantyll' group.

Even within a discourse specific to a social group, Malory's ideal of a perfectly informed and universally acceptable fighting narrative is a patent fantasy, if one thinks of the babble of conflicting accounts succeeding a real late-medieval battle, such as Bosworth Field,[15] or the predictable bias of onlookers describing a real formal combat, like that between Lord Scales and the Bastard of Burgundy.[16] But the *Morte* is 'true to life' in the sense that it naturalises a particular ideologically-derived view – the winning of

---

[11] Some indications of 'orality' in Malory's reception of his exemplars can be seen in his occasional preservation of the *sound* of the French text, where the sense would require another phrase. See Vinaver's notes to 942/16–17, 944/4, and further comments on p. 1538. One can also note Malory's preservation of alliteration and metre, and possible addition of new alliterative lines, in adapting *Arthur and Lucius* from the alliterative *Morte Arthure*. See, e.g., 209/16–24, 241/19, and Vinaver's notes. See also P.J.C. Field, *Romance and Chronicle*, 75ff.

[12] Walter J. Ong, *Orality and Literacy* (London and New York: Methuen, 1982) 119.

[13] For Malory's likeness to chronicle 'history', see Riddy, Chapter 2.

[14] See Riddy, p. 11: '[Caxton] . . . seems to assume the old socially-cohesive readership united by a shared chivalric culture, but the book must in fact have sold to a much more diverse readership than this.'

[15] See Michael Bennett, *The Battle of Bosworth* (Gloucester: Alan Sutton, 1985).

[16] See 'Tournament', in *Excerpta Historica*, 212ff, for the *Memoirs* of Olivier de la Marche, which give a much more favourable account of the Bastard's arms than the English herald's report does.

knightly worship – as the predominant meaning of the story. Within these terms, the Malorian narrative apparently wishes to be entirely explicit, to suggest virtually no opacity or indeterminacy in its events, and to produce a meaning to which all (all who matter) will assent so readily that the possibility of other meanings is suppressed. For the modern reader, *Le Morte Darthur* has, in consequence, a strange double-life: the text so perfectly embodies the ideology it was born to serve that one has relatively little difficulty in hearing its 'voice', and containing all interpretations within the discourse of chivalric 'worship'. Such an approach may seem 'historical', any other approach inappropriate, and easily disprovable. Certainly, it is hard to see that the text shows any conscious leaning towards other kinds of interpretation, especially those that are critical of normal chivalric values. There seems no point in modern readers inferring an authorial attack on Tristram's conduct, for instance,[17] or insisting that Malory means to display the hollowness of chivalry,[18] if the text tells us specifically (through Lancelot) that ' "all that sir Trystram doth is thorow clene knyghthod" ' (760) and, in general, that 'worshyp in armys may never be foyled' (1119/27–28). On the other hand, our consciousness that this is in fact extremely stylised *writing*, that it dwells on certain possibilities of closure and neglects others, alerts us to the self-censorship, mainly naturalised and unconscious, necessary to such a degree of interpretative containment. In these circumstances, to suggest a plurality of potential meanings in Malory may be, I contend, a necessary strategy of historical criticism, because it permits greater awareness and scrutiny of the text's ideological affinities, not merely an endorsement of their dominant interpretative effects. It is in that spirit, to learn more about Malory as a *text*, rather than as an ideologically-contained pseudo-'world', that I shall sometimes challenge below the normal view of his combat stories.

In Merlin's instructions to Bloise, we see the stress on the literal recall of events (the text as record of what has already occurred), and the ambitious claim to be totally inclusive.[19] The 'namys of every kynge and knyght of worship' and 'all the batayles' of Arthur's time are to be related, the latter not only in terms of their beginning, conduct and conclusion as fights, but also with consideration of each worthy knight's individual involvement

---

[17] See the discussion in Riddy, p. 86, citing Donald G. Schueler, 'The Tristram Section of Malory's *Morte Darthur*', *Studies in Philology* 65, 1968, 51–66, and Maureen Fries, 'Malory's Tristram as Counter-Hero to the *Morte Darthur*', *Neuphilologische Mitteilungen* 76, 1975, 605–13. See also William Matthews, *The Tragedy of Arthur: A Study of the Alliterative Morte Arthure* (Berkeley and Los Angeles: University of California Press, 1960) discussed by Vinaver, 1369–71. Beverly Kennedy, *Knighthood*, 150ff, sees Tristram as a prudent vassal and 'worshipful knight', of a lower type than Lancelot's.
[18] For readings of this kind, see n. 17, above; also Charles Moorman, *A Knyght There Was: The Evolution of the Knight in Literature* (Lexington: University of Kentucky Press, 1967) 99, 126; Pochoda, *Arthurian Propaganda*, 104.
[19] See also 347/18–19.

and, it seems, all their other individual combats. The book is represented as a perfectly adequate and capacious repository for deeds. In Malory there are no *topoi* of inexpressibility employed about fighting,[20] relatively few brevity *topoi*, and very few gaps noted, unless the original material is mentioned as unavailable (1154/1).[21] The general implication is that the tales are otherwise complete. Bors and Lancelot are able to relate after dinner to Arthur's 'grete clerkes' all the adventures of the Sankgreal which they have seen, and '*all* thys was made in grete bookes and put up in almeryes at Salysbury', which in turn are the basis for the true French 'cronycle' Malory's version is drawn from (1036/11–22).[22] Like other medieval war stories, such as the history of Troy, this one seeks its authority from the voices of participants, but goes even further in making almost no discrimination between eye-witness account and the subsequent narrative of clerks. It is not until very late in the piece that Malory represents himself as uncertain on a point of importance, and even then he has a good source: 'thys tale sir Bedwere, a knyght of the Table Rounde, made hit to be wrytten' (1242/21–22). Ideally, in Malory, writing and clerical learning are something which an orally-oriented society commands for its own purposes, much as Dynadan pens the abusive 'lay' to be sung in Mark's hall, or 'kyng Arthure lat ravyshe [fetch] prystes and clarkes in the moste devoutiste wyse to brynge in sir Urré into Carlyle' (1153/1–2). There is no question that it is the voice of the powerful[23] – 'kynges and lordis and knyghtis' – that we hear, a voice with its own interests at stake, which seeks to prevent adverse scrutiny of its values, and with which readings of the text which question those values must necessarily clash, as the history of Malory reception from Ascham onwards records.

Prowess and Goodness: A Critical Relation

Caxton seems to have had no trouble in viewing deeds of arms as 'virtuous'. But many subsequent readers have found it hard to relate the fights to the rest of Malory's text, and to understand what their 'virtue' consisted in. The sixteenth-century writer Roger Ascham was disgusted at the lack of proper

---

[20] Some examples of this *topos* are: 493/2–6, the joy of Tristram and Isoude; 662/19–22, a knightly reunion; 868/3–5, a knightly parting; 1017/6–13, Lancelot's vision of Christ's 'grete mervayles of secretnesse'.

[21] An exception is 845/31, where the 'third book' of Tristram is expressly omitted.

[22] At 947/31–33, a hermit says that Lancelot will tell only 'a party such thyngis as he hath founde' in the Grail quest. The statement probably refers to the ineffability of Lancelot's heavenly vision (1016–17).

[23] See Barber, 'Malory's *Le Morte Darthur* and Court Culture', 137, pointing out the small, elite nature of Edward IV's court. I am not suggesting that Malory's knights are always in complete agreement, or truly a 'fellowship', only that they share very much the same values and frame of reference. For analysis of some contrastive strategies in knightly conversation, see Catherine La Farge, 'Conversation in Malory's *Morte Darthur*', *Medium Aevum* LVI 2, 1987, 225–37.

motivation for fighting in Malory and the resulting deficiency of his fight description as a medium for moral example. He complained that 'those be counted the noblest Knightes, that do kill most men without any quarell'.[24] Such an attitude is almost inevitable once the *Morte* is read without sympathy for its military values. The remark already had precedents in earlier English writing, such as the fourteenth-century poem *Cleanness*, commenting on the violent age of giants mentioned in Genesis 6,4: 'He watz famed for fre that feght loued best,/ And ay the bigest in bale the best watz halden'.[25] Ascham was right, I think, to notice the limited sense of 'beginnings' in many Malory combats, and he could well have had the books of knight errantry most in mind, where frequent and apparently gratuitous deaths occur.[26] To think differently from Ascham, one must be more willing to accept fighting as the unmotivated narrative currency of 'worship'. Otherwise, Gareth, for instance, who fights fourteen knights on the outward leg of his first quest (killing six of them), will seem a sociopath, quite unlike the 'true' knight Lancelot later celebrates:' "he ys jantill, curteyse and ryght bownteuous, meke and mylde, and in hym ys no maner of male engynne, but playne, faythfull an trew" ' (1089/1–3). Bridging such a moral valuation and the bare facts of a knight's violent career has remained a potential problem for the Malory reader since Ascham's time.

Philip Sidney, in aristocratic vein, was more sympathetic to the martial narrative, but correspondingly patronising about Malory as thinker:

> For poetry is the companion of camps, I dare undertake, Orlando Furioso, or honest King Arthur, will never displease a soldier; but the quiddity of *ens* and *prima materia* will hardly agree with a corslet.[27]

'Honest' is here 'a vague epithet of appreciation or praise, especially as used in a patronising way to an inferior'.[28] Malory can be 'the companion of camps' because his supposed simplicity is considered suitable for 'active men'.[29] The text's credit ('honestas') is bound up with a soldierly straightforwardness that has no intellectual pretensions, and specifically lacks philosophical depth or subtlety. For Sidney, *Le Morte Darthur* is like *Chevy Chase*, a stirring call to deeds of arms whose moral direction and purpose must be sought elsewhere.

---

[24] Roger Ascham, *The Schoolmaster*, ed. L.V. Ryan (Folger Documents of Tudor and Stuart Civilization, Ithaca, NY: Cornell UP, 1967) 68–69.

[25] *The Poems of the Pearl Manuscript*, rev. edn M. Andrew and R. Waldron (Exeter: University of Exeter Press, 1987) 275–76, spelling slightly modernised.

[26] See, e.g., Lancelot's behaviour in 564/11–29 and 570/34–35, discussed above, Chapter 1, 5–6.

[27] Sidney: *A Defence*, 56. 'King Arthur' is a reference to Wynkyn de Worde's edition of Malory, 1498.

[28] *OED*, 'honest' 1.c.

[29] Sidney, *A Defence*, 57.

John Milton does not figure in the Malory *Critical Heritage*, but may well have had the *Morte* in mind when he declared himself unwilling

> ... to dissect
> With long and tedious havoc fabled knights
> In battles feigned.[30]

This seems to echo two words from Caxton's Preface – 'that alle suche bookes as been maad of hym [Arthur] ben but *fayned* and *fables*' (cxliv/12–13). By pointedly doubting the *Morte*'s historicity, Milton destroys its chief value from Caxton's point of view, as a record of deeds done, and therefore as a memorial to British arms. Caxton had given his readers 'leisure' to regard Malory's fine detail as history or fiction, but insisted on its essential truth. Milton is more uncompromising: the fight stories are untrue ('feigned'), and worthless as fables, in any case, being long and boring digressions from important moral issues such as his own true story foregrounds. Without the sanction of history, the fights must seem facile and otiose, spun out of the writer's mind without care or purpose. At best they are morally irrelevant, at worst obnoxious lying.

Samuel Johnson, though he had a private love of chivalric stories, publicly stressed their obligation to provide a moral example:

> In narratives, where historical veracity has no place, I cannot discover why there should not be exhibited the most perfect idea of virtue; of virtue not angelical, nor above probability, for what we cannot credit we shall never imitate, but the highest and purest that humanity can reach.[31]

By these standards, Malory must fail, since for most of his knights, excluding Galahad and Perceval, 'virtue' in Johnson's sense is not the motivation. The 'adventurous' fight stories in Malory, and particularly the long books of knight errantry, combining and recombining their participants in variations of the combat formulae, are not only improbable in their copious demonstration of one kind of knightly 'virtue' – arms –, but deficient in providing examples of the other kind. Tristram, Lamerok, Lancelot and Palamides are clearly sinners.

It was to counter the problems raised by these attitudes, I believe, that nineteenth-century critics, of whom the majority were troubled or bored by the fights, still desired an approach which could treat them as models of good conduct. Robert Southey likened Malory's knights to bare-knuckle prize-fighters,[32] but his wish for something more was clear. He wrote,

---

30 *Paradise Lost* IX, 29–31, in *Milton, Poetical Works*, ed. D. Bush (London: Oxford UP, 1966).
31 *The Yale Edition of the Works of Samuel Johnson*, ed. W.J. Bate and A.B. Strauss (New Haven: Yale UP, 1969), The Rambler, no. 4, 21.
32 *The Byrth, Lyf and Actes of Kyng Arthur*, 2 vols (London: Longman, 1817) xxxi.

wistfully, 'the morals of the chivalrous romances were . . . always taken at the highest standard of the age . . . but the ferocious spirit of the times frequently appears'.[33]

An unsigned writer in the *Dublin University Magazine* for 1860 solved the problem only by distorting Malory to supply a sense of punishments for misconduct where little or nothing of the sort exists:

> we find in these romances of Arthur that no crime goes unpunished. For all his courtesy, his high-bred courage and deeds of arms, Tristram of Lyones dies miserably, stabbed in the back by his most despised enemy; Lamoracke de Galis is murdered by the sons of his unlawful love . . . Lancelot, even – but we must not forestal the main incidents of the romance.[34]

It is a severe misreading of Malory to justify the means by the end in this way. The killings of Lamerok and Tristram are appalling precisely because they are not by 'knightly means', in fair combat, but back-stabbing murders 'in a pryvy place' (699/22). Contrasting this misplaced ability to see in Malory 'the leaven of revealed ethics'[35] is the view expressed in 1858 by W. Lucas Collins, that the fighting is merely juvenile fun:

> The plot and the machinery are of the simplest kind, most intelligible to the schoolboy mind, and appealing strongly to his sympathies, fresh from foot-ball. Everybody runs full tilt at everybody he meets is the general stage direction. Whether the anatagonist be friend or foe by right, is quite a secondary consideration.[36]

Collins rightly sees the prevalence and narrative self-sufficiency of the fights, but wrongly concludes that this makes them purely trivial. Spread between these poles of opinion, the spiritual and the sporting, nineteenth- and earlier twentieth-century critics from Southey onwards failed to find a discourse which convincingly related the details of combat to the moral function they required of the *Morte*. It was left to Eugène Vinaver, in the best introduction to this issue, to limit the search for moral example. His view is that Caxton's Preface 'mistakes, – perhaps deliberately – Malory's practical intention for a moral one', and that the knight-errantry of Malory's main sources was 'less of a school of courtly service than a peculiar mode of living, characterized by a constant search for new adventures'.

---

[33] Ibid., xxix.
[34] *Dublin University Magazine* no. 55, April 1860, 497–512, quoted in *Malory: The Critical Heritage*, 134ff.
[35] Ibid., 151.
[36] *Malory, The Critical Heritage*, 122.

And so his work has neither the light-heartedness of romance nor the doctrinal poise of a moral treatise; its dominating feature is a kind of earnestness one usually associates with early epic. (xxxiv)[37]

More recent critics have generally considered issues of character, structural patterning and thematic development in the fights, rather than their direct narrative content. The view of the text as offering patterns of moral conduct has re-emerged and morally condemnatory readings have remained popular, as noted above.[38] But Felicity Riddy, pointing to the *Morte's* wide generic variation, has shown that stylistic features, mainly of parataxis, can make some of Malory's 'romance' narratives particularly resistant to moral analysis:

> The effect of the style is to diminish the reader's sense of physical reality and to reproduce a feeling of discontinuity in things we normally assume to be continuous. There is a relation here between the style and the structure of the tale; 'so' links episodes with an intricate flexibility, at times allowing us to make logical, temporal or spatial connections and at times leaving relationships in doubt.[39]

Such flexibility of linking has implications for the romance narrative of arms, since the thematics and consequences of a fight can be invoked or played down if necessary. Riddy notes that in a 'chronicle' section such as *Arthur and Lucius* the killing of the giant of St Michael's Mount is rendered by an object-centred prose about a world which is 'out there'.[40] But Lancelot's killing of a churl in the *Noble Tale* is told in a different way that

> ensures that we do not respond to it as manslaughter. There is no pain, nor is there any blood . . . at crucial moments the fiction does not reach out to some confirming reality but remains closed, opaque and of itself.[41]

The differing narrations here might represent an issue of class also: a giant, however uncouth, is an opponent on whom a knight can win honour, whilst an ordinary churl is not. However we read the difference, Riddy's analysis reminds us that there can never be one code, one generic pattern or one thematic register to describe the narrative function of Malorian arms. Nevertheless, the *Morte's* stories of fighting, 'Malory's favourite topic' (xxxiii), are so vast and densely detailed that some primary organisation of their component values must be attempted here. Not all the values can be

---

[37] See Vinaver, xxvii–xxxiv, for the full discussion.
[38] See 33, above.
[39] Riddy, *Sir Thomas Malory*, 52, and see 31–59 for the broader discussion of generic variance. For the non-committal effects of parataxis, see also Bonnie Wheeler, 'Romance and Parataxis and Malory', 109–32, esp. 112.
[40] Riddy, *Sir Thomas Malory*, 52–53.
[41] Ibid., 53.

apparent in every fight. Nor is the honour of fights always exactly 'like', for there is a comparative element. But the basic methods of fight description can be broadly stated, with their significant variations, and their important links with features of Malory's ideology. More important than the structure of these episodes, or even their conscious themes, is 'what goes without saying', the discursive reflex of the text's ideological assumptions.

The Essential Value Placed on Fighting

In Malory, to be of worship is to be named, and therefore to be named is (usually) to be worshipful; there is some prestige in being mentioned as a participant, even as a loser. Chronically unsuccessful figures like Sir Barraunte, 'The King with the Hundred Knights', never seem to lose face on the tournament circuit. Because the names of the unworthy are largely excluded from the story, the record tends to suppress failure, giving the impression that chivalric society is made up of the successful, some more so than others, certainly, but all bonded in their enjoyment of a common good. Participation in the narrative is worship enough for all but a few. One can compare the contemporary formula of tournament prize-giving: 'John hath wele justid, Richard hath justid bettir and Thomas hath justid best of all.' As Sidney Anglo comments,

> in the proclamation, everybody 'did well' or 'did very well' . . . There was, apparently, an ancient chivalric convention which forebade the heralds . . . from informing the assembled ladies just how miserably their knights had performed.[42]

Malory seems to extend this generous view even into mortal war. So when the valiant and worshipful names must be thoroughly defeated, even for the soundest political reasons, the ethos of collectivity is placed under some pressure, since *both* sides are doing 'as good men ought to do'. The text therefore often betrays some anxiety about a good knight's defeat, through expressions of pity, exclamations and appeals to proverbial wisdom.[43] The successful war against Lot and the eleven kings, though necessary for Arthur to claim his right inheritance, produces several moments of this kind. When Arthur is 'passynge wrothe' (34/31) with his enemies, Ban and Bors give him important advice:

> 'blame hem nat, for they do as good men ought to do. For be my fayth,' seyde kynge Ban, 'they ar the beste fyghtynge men and knyghtes of moste prouesse that ever y saw other herde off speke. And tho eleven kyngis ar

---

[42] Sidney Anglo, 'Archives of the English Tournament', 158–59 and notes.
[43] For a discussion of the use of proverbs about combat, see Chapter 4, 89.

men of grete worship; and if they were longyng to you, there were no
kynge undir hevyn that had suche eleven kyngis nother off suche worship.'

'I may nat love hem,' seyde kynge Arthure, 'for they wolde destroy me.'

'That know we well,' seyde kyng Ban and kynge Bors, 'for they ar your
mortall enemyes, and that hathe bene preved beforehonde. And thys day
they have done theire parte, and that ys grete pité of their wylfulnes.'

(34/32–35/8)

The obligation to do one's 'part' involves the acceptance that each side
('party'), once established, has a right to exist and offers the chance to win
worship. The political necessity that sets Arthur against Lot is at least
momentarily less important to the narrative of combat than the valour of
the combatants. (Even when one 'party' is deeply tainted by treason, as
Mordred's is in the last battle, Malory can write approvingly that Mordred
'ded hys devoure that day and put hymselffe in grete perell' (1236/4–5).[44])
In fighting, Lot's political stubbornness becomes heroised as bravery.
Arthur's kingly and necessary anger at his opponents' resistance is matched
by his professional appreciation of their valour:

Than they [the eleven kings and their army] amended their harneyse and
ryghted their sheldis, and toke newe speris and sette hem on theire
thyghes, and stoode stylle as hit had be a plumpe of woode.
    Whan kynge Arthure and kynge Ban and Bors behelde them and all hir
knyghtes, they preysed them much for their noble chere of chevalry, for
the hardyeste fyghters that ever they herde other sawe. (35/31–36/2)

Once battle is joined, Lot and his fellows become the chief object of
narrative vision. The eleven kings' army is said to be 'ever in the visage of
Arthure', never turning back, constantly present to his appraising view.
Merlin intervenes to warn Arthur that his military advantage is only
through God and Fortune (36/26–37/4). Otherwise he and Lot are one: 'ye
have macched thys day with the beste fyghters of the worlde' (37/3). In the
last campaign against Lot, Merlin's crafty intervention is again required
(75/26–28, 76/6–20), and the battle description mainly concerns Lot's prowess and the pity of his death:

'As for me,' seyde kynge Lott, 'I wolde that every knyght wolde do hys
parte as I wolde do myne.'
    Than they avaunced baners and smote togydirs and brused hir sperys.

---

[44] In a similar case, the otherwise hostile Polydore Vergil wrote that Richard III 'was killed
fighting manfully in the thickest press of his enemies'. See the modernised translation of
Polydore Vergil's *Anglia Historia*, ed. H. Ellis (London: Camden Society, 1844) 221, quoted
in A.R. Myers, ed., *English Historical Documents: 1327–1485* (London: Eyre and Spottis-
woode, 1969) 346. Thanks to Sonia Middlemiss for this reference.

And Arthurs knyghtes with the helpe of the Knyght with Two Swerdys and his brothir Balan put kynge Lotte and hys oste to the warre. But allwayes kynge Lotte hylde hym ever in the fore-fronte and dud mervey-lous dedis of armys; for all his oste was borne up by hys hondys, for he abode all knyghtes. Alas, he myght nat endure, the whych was grete pité! So worthy a knyght as he was one, that he sholde be overmacched, that of late tyme before he had bene a knyght of kynge Arthurs, and wedded the syster of hym. And for because that kynge Arthur lay by hys wyff and gate on her sir Mordred, therefore kynge Lott helde ever agaynste Arthure. (76/26–77/7)

To the very end, Malory's text is uneasy about Lot's death, giving him a tomb made 'passynge rychely' and 'by hymselff' (77/33), yet including him amongst the twelve gilt brass and copper figures of the conquered in the propagandist memorial Merlin designs for Arthur (78/1–8). The political necessity to defeat Lot, the military point of this war, is substantially disguised throughout by the urge to portray him as Arthur's fellow in combat, his 'match', and a credit to the knighthood they share. Arthur's growing appraisal of Lot's valour is as important to the narrative as his defeat of him, for by this means the continuity of the British tradition of martial bravery is stressed. The victor carries on the spirit of the van-quished, asserting his worthy succession more than the fact of his politi-cal enmity. The fighting is made to seem as important for its own sake as for its outcome.

Fights as Discrete Narrative Occasions

Merlin's stipulation that a fight description should include 'how it began' and 'how it was ended' might seem to deny the narrative tendencies I note below to downplay the political motivation of fighting and to draw atten-tion away from causes and consequences beyond the fights themselves. There *are* some important indications of motive, as seen above in the account of Lot's opposition to Arthur, stemming from the adultery with Morgawse. But commonly a 'beginning' means no more than a first blow or an entrance to the field or a new stage in battle: 'And there began a grete medelé of brekyng of speres' (31/23–24); 'than there began a new batayle whych was sore and harde' (34/20–22); 'bycause sir Palomydes beganne fyrste' (741/1); 'And ever kynge Bagdemagus ded beste, for he fyrste began and ever he was lengyste that helde on' (659/12–13). An 'ending' is the conclusion of the fight, at which one side or combatant is left to occupy the field alone (e.g., 69/7–8, 626/5–7), while the other has 'the worse', unless, especially common when great knights encounter, there is an honourable draw. In between, the narrative of a good fight stresses *duration* more than *progress.* In Malory's day, tournament prizes could be awarded simply for 'staying in the field longest and still helmed'.[45]

With this limited notion of beginnings and endings, the fight narrative has a tendency to turn in upon itself as a discrete rhetorical unit, avoiding or neglecting other contingencies in terms of plot and individual motive. This seems more natural in the more inconsequential encounters of tournaments and knight errantry, but is a factor even in the cases of Lot and Mordred, as we have seen, where there are very extensive plot ramifications. In the last battle, when only four participants are left alive, it is still shown that Arthur has 'won the fylde', as Lucan says (1237/1), and although that seems a grisly irony to us, it may well not have been so for Malory's audience. Though his long-predicted destiny with Mordred remains to claim Arthur, a combat still has its own start and finish, a standard enclosed shape, even when the causes are important, or the political backwash, as in the feud between Lot's kin and Pellinore's, is endless. In this way, fight narrative often more resembles the 'apostrophic' celebration of the moment characteristic of lyric than the historical narrative's longer view over time,[46] and sometimes even generates the tone and cadence of lyric complaint: 'Alas, he myght nat endure, the whyche was grete pité!'[47]

Although Malory's work considerably abbreviates his French originals, its use of the brevity topos in relation to fights is infrequent, and carefully employed to effect gradations of worship. The exploits of Palamides, Dynadan, Lavayne and Urré may be condensed 'for to shortyn this tale' (1153/17), but hardly those of Lancelot or Tristram.[48] To speak generally, and as if the book were one continuing narrative, fighting description 'becomes' rather less detailed after the Tristram book, and is more closely implicated with other plot issues, especially in Books VII and VIII, but there remains a willingness to regard fights as places for independent narrative expansion. If Malory had not 'loste the very mater of Shevalere de Charyot' (1154/12–13) we might have heard a great deal more of Lancelot's forty battles in the year missing from the story. And even when Malory is ostensibly talking about what we would regard as something else, such as in the famous passage on love in *Launcelot and Guinevere*, he naturally

---

45 See Tiptoft's Ordinances, cited in Christopher Gravatt, *Knights at Tournament* (London: Osprey, 1988) 25. See also 741/1–6: 'bycause sir Palomydes beganne fyrste, and never he wente nor rode oute of the fylde to repose hym, but ever he was doynge on horsebak othir on foote, and lengyst durynge, kynge Arthure and all the kynges gaff sir Palomydes the honoure and the gre as for that day'.

46 See David Lindley, *Lyric* (London: Methuen, 1985) 3; Culler, *The Pursuit of Signs*, 149.

47 See also laments for the death of Lamerok (698–99) and Gareth (1189/20–21; 1199/25–28).

48 There is only one use of the brevity topos in connection with Tristram's fighting (507/13); some of Lancelot's prowess at the Castle of Maidens is given in summary form, 'to make short tale in conclusion' (533/27ff), but the narrative is otherwise rich in details of his fighting there.

introduces the topic and discourse of arms, the deeds in which the valorous ('vertuouse')[49] power of the knightly 'herte' is displayed:

> Therefore, lyke as May moneth flowryth and floryshyth in every mannes gardyne, so in lyke wyse lat every man of worshyp florysh hys herte in thys worlde: firste unto God, and nexte unto the joy of them that he promysed hys feythe unto; for there was never worshypfull man nor worshypfull woman but they loved one bettir than anothir; *and worshyp in armys may never be foyled*. But firste reserve the honoure to God, and secundely *thy quarell* muste com of thy lady. And such love I call vertuouse love. (1119)

The Fundamental Importance of Prowess

Malory contains relatively few examples of knights fighting against other than knights. Though he may have invented Sir Severause, who 'had never corayge nor grete luste to do batayle ayenste no man but if hit were ayenste gyauntis and ayenste dragons and wylde bestis' (1148/29–32, and n.), he tells us nothing more about him. His uses of the word 'chivalry' seem to mean, basically, either 'knights' or 'cavalry'; 'prowess as a knight' or 'reputation as a knight'.[50] Malory does display also, though intermittently and partially, concepts of true justice, of right and wrong quarrels and of proper conduct in fighting.[51] Karen Cherewatuk has recently suggested that the *Morte* is influenced by and represents the separate categories of material in contemporary chivalric anthologies, from instruction in kingship, love and religion to the 'practical treatise of chivalric combat', with accordingly varying emphases.[52] Felicity Riddy speaks of the *Morte* as pulling in the direction of four main interests – 'history, good manners, right living and the next world'.[53] Both critics are surely right to stress the varied, overlapping and sometimes contradictory concerns of the narrative. It must be recognised, all the same, that the depiction of military prowess is the factor which all these narrative tendencies hold in common, and which is essential to their realisation in the story. A 'good knight' is first and foremost 'a passyng good man of his hondis' (158/35). Moreover, the text's enthusiasm

---

[49] See *OED*, 'virtuous', I, 1, 'Distinguished by manly qualities; full of manly courage; valiant, valorous', quoting Caxton (1474): 'stronge and vertuous in bataylle'. Malory's idea of knightly goodness seems to merge this sense with 5, 'Producing, or capable of producing, (great) effect; powerful, potent, strong' and 6, 'Endowed with or possessed of inherent or natural virtue or power . . .; potent or powerful in effect, influence or operation on this account'.

[50] See Kato, *Concordance*.

[51] See Vinaver, xxix–xxxiv, and Kennedy, *Knighthood*, 28–55.

[52] Karen Cherewatuk, ' "Gentyl Audiences" and "Grete Bookes" '.

[53] Riddy, *Sir Thomas Malory*, 30.

for the courage, strength and skill needed to fight well can rarely be confined within purely technical bounds. The attitude taken towards a 'good knight' is that he is a good man as well for that very reason, unless otherwise indicated. There is not usually much differentiation of the kind of goodness involved:[54]

> 'I knowe hym well,' seyde sir Uwayne, 'he is a passynge good knyght as ony on lyve, for I sawe hym onys preved at a justys where many knyghtes were gadird, and that tyme there myght no man withstonde hym.'
>
> (159/8–11)

Although Malory assents to the principle that no one should be blamed for the outcome of a fair fight, this certainly does not mean that such fighting is morally justified in the modern sense. It means that it is in general seen as 'knightly', not dishonourable, without a further need to probe its significance in other terms, including moral ones. When blamed for a killing, Gareth can reply simply ' "I slew hym knyghtly" ' (305/20).[55] Denying any personal motivation, through an implicit appeal to the known risks of combat, the slayer makes moral analysis of the act irrelevant. His proof of greater prowess becomes a sufficient justification. These are not primarily stories told to teach men to fight fairly, with that as their main point. That task was left to ordinances and manuals of chivalry. In narratives such as Malory's, the requirement to fight fairly occurs precisely because the 'proof' of sheer prowess is so important: 'worship' must be attached to the superior fighter beyond any suspicion of foul play or improper advantage. To approach the deeds of knights from this business end removes many of the problems we encounter when the text is treated principally as a moral fable of a 'goodness' separate from military strength. Prowess is a great good in itself; in Malory's mind, rather different from Langland's, it is simply to 'do well'.

Since to be named in the text is to be 'of name' (renown), there is always much more praise than blame in Malory. Mark and Meleagant are perhaps the only instances of frequently named knights who are worthless in fighting. Fighting descriptions have the primary purpose of praising the combatants. Knights are supposed to fight, so their participation in combat is a sign of a social duty properly performed. And even in contexts where other knightly qualities are celebrated, fighting remains the ruling discourse. In this connection, the healing of Sir Urré (1145–54) provides an interesting case study. It is sometimes cited as a summarising climax of

---

[54] See Chapter 6, 138–39.
[55] See also 321/7–8: Gareth resolves to 'wynne worshyp worshypfully othir dye knyghtly in the felde'.

Malorian pageantry,[56] or as a scene of religious interiority,[57] an issue I examine elsewhere. Yet more than anything else this episode demonstrates the all-importance of combat. The roll-call of names, whilst it shows Malory's love of 'fellowship', also functions as a grand memorial to the military careers of Lancelot, Gareth, Tristram, Lamerok and others, recalling earlier episodes, and listing the knights they have 'won'. Urré's background is established only through fighting, as 'an adventurys knyght, and in all placis where he myght here of ony adventures dedis and of worshyp there wold he be'. When Urré recovers from his seven-year illness, Arthur immediately asks ' "Than woll ye juste and do ony armys?" ' His potential in the fighting role has determined the description of Urré's person – 'a full lykly man', 'passyngly well made and bygly'. His renewed health – 'never so lusty' – his finding of a 'good and gracious lorde' who provides him with 'all that longe[s] unto justis', and his prescient 'harte' that inclines him to Lancelot, his healer, and, as it were, his re-maker as knight, all demand an issue in fighting. Even though Malory abbreviates the description of the ensuing tournament 'for to shortyn this tale', the formula 'he overthrew and pulled down a thirty knyghtes' is sufficient at this time to secure the impression of Urré's bodily and social resurrection, through which he is called to the Round Table and given 'a barony of londis'. As Lambert says, Urré 'does not exist except in relation to chivalric activities'.[58]

Through Lancelot, Urré is connected with Lavayne, the brother of Elayne of Ascolat, and Lavayne marries Urré's sister. Although Elayne's sad story, and that of Urré, have in their different ways admitted that chivalry has its 'envy' (1146/9) and its victims, including Elayne's wounded older brother (1067/14–17), fighting prowess is still made the medium for the reconstitution of the two stricken families, and their continuance of the culture of arms. Lancelot, Lavayne and Urré form a fellowship, and, we are told, 'ever sought uppon their dedis' (1153/29). Though the whole Urré story is not specifically of fighting, its structure and discourse remain centred on knightly prowess, and the other virtues involved – courtesy, humility and faith in God – are really adjuncts to the prime value placed on arms. It is greatness as a knight which in Malory's eyes (and presumably God's) makes Lancelot worthy to perform the healing miracle, and the tale seems precisely designed to allow Lancelot his particular version of the healings performed by Galahad in the previous book. The whole episode shows us that the

[56] See Stephen Knight, *Arthurian Literature and Society*, 134–35. L.D. Benson, *Malory's Morte Darthur*, 227ff, gives a handy summary of some critical attitudes to Lancelot's weeping in this scene. See also Lambert, *Malory*, 65: 'Lancelot weeps because of the contrast between this success and his earlier failure [in the Grail quest]; but for the reader these are the *lacrimae rerum*, tears for the fall of the Arthurian world.'

[57] See above Chapter 1, 6–8. See also, e.g., C.S. Lewis, 'The English Prose *Morte*' in J.A.W. Bennett, ed., *Essays on Malory* (Oxford: Clarendon Press, 1963) 20.

[58] Lambert, *Malory*, 58.

importance of prowess is by no means confined to the description of actual fights; it provides a more comprehensive discursive field for the 'hoole book' of Arthur than any other of its matters.

Fights as Places

In either the dramatic or the novelistic sense, there is very little physical 'setting' in Malory, and very little interest in landscape.[59] The brief descriptions of terrain are scarcely present for themselves, but act as markers between one episode and the next. Knights ride through these empty spaces (mainly forests) only in order to be present at their next combat. Fords and bridges are chiefly locations for *pas d'armes*, and 'a lytyll leved wood' is mentioned only as the place where armed men can be lodged or hidden.[60] The 'environment' in Malory is almost entirely supplied by other people and their dwellings, with occasional help from the next world. In particular, no incident is ever far (in narrative proximity) from society and speech. As a rule, relatively brief moments of solitude in the wilderness are soon overtaken by more social occasions, chief amongst which are 'encounters' with other knights.

Fights provide, therefore, the major *places* in Malory. As has been remarked by Riddy,[61] the *Morte* has a spatial as much as a temporal relation of events, and readers are usually more aware of their place within the book than in a fixed geographical or temporal scheme.[62] The sense of narrative development over time is scanty and frequently disrupted. Time is the time we take to read from place to place. History is the (selective) memory of the preceding story and its prophecies. Location is the knight's place on the page, the 'field' on which the Winchester manuscript's red-letter names stand, and these sites of narrative expansion are most frequently the places of combat. (Rather as in some late-medieval English painting, the spatial field is used to separate incidents on a loose temporal continuum, and to display different episodes relating to the same personage.[63]) Alternations between solitude and society, exterior and interior, nature and culture, are mainly employed to occasion new fights. Fighting articulates geography,

---

59 Vinaver, 1369, notes that Malory cut descriptions of scenery in adapting the alliterative *Morte Arthure*. See also Lambert, *Malory*, 75, 78ff.

60 See 262/14, 485/37, 1069/28, 1070/18. For a view which characterises the forest less functionally, see Sally Firmin, 'Deep and Wide: Malory's Marvelous Forest' in D. Thomas Hanks, ed., *Sir Thomas Malory: Views and Reviews*, 26–39.

61 Riddy, *Sir Thomas Malory*, 139.

62 D.S. Brewer, *Malory: The Morte Darthur: Parts Seven and Eight* (York Medieval Texts, London: Arnold, 1968) 9–10 points out the increased specificity of time and location in the last two books. Felicity Riddy, *Sir Thomas Malory*, 46ff, sees *Arthur and Lucius* as 'physical, solid and detailed'.

63 See, e.g., the fifteenth-century painting of the life of St Eustace in Canterbury Cathedral.

giving a meaning to place and chronology. Merlin prophesies famous combats,[64] and knights errant appoint each other 'days' and places to meet in arms.[65] Combat provides the map and the calendar of most stories in Malory. The great feasts of the Christian Church are celebrated by tournaments and the beginning of quests. Even the special value given to Pentecost in the *Morte*, as celebrated in the tales of *King Arthur*, *Gareth* and the *Sankgreal*, may well be related to its climatic suitability for beginning deeds of arms. As Trevisa wrote:

> Aboute pentecost is tyme of cheualrie and ek of orpidnesse [valour] and thanne yonge knyghtis beth igurde with the swurde of cheualrie . . . Also thanne is tyme of hardinesse and of booldnesse, for that tyme by strong impressioun of hete of the sonne colera is tend [excited] and by tendinge therof aboute the herte wrathe and hardinesse is excitid in bestis; and therfore that tyme is most couenable [suitable] to meue werre and bataile ageynes enemyes.[66]

After combat, solitude is briefly necessary as the condition of winning, to possess the 'field' alone for a while, dominating both the battlefield of the fiction and the spatial field of the book page. But the return to society must finally occur for the bestowal of appraisal and reward, the true conclusion of a major episode or sequence. Malory chose to end both his *Noble Tale of Launcelot* and his *Gareth* in this way, with a recapitulation at court of the hero's progress. As I have indicated above,[67] even the morally pointed failure of either Galahad or the Grail to return to Camelot did not deter Malory from giving his version a much more positive ending at court. His conclusions enact within the text a model for Malory's reader, with their summarising and evaluative responses from worthy judges.

An account of an episode-sequence in *Gareth* will illustrate some of the processes I have been outlining. Gareth is in search of a bed for the night:

> And than fell there a thundir and a rayne, as hevyn and erthe sholde go togydir. And sir Gareth was nat a lytyll wery, for of all that day he had but lytyll reste, nother his horse nor he. So thus sir Gareth rode longe in that foreste untyll nyght cam; and ever hit lyghtned and thundirde as hit had bene wylde. At the laste by fortune he cam to a castell, and there he herde the waytis uppon the wallys. Than sir Gareth rode unto the barby-can of the castell, and prayed the porter fayre to lette hym into the castell.
>
> (352/23–32)

---

[64] See above, Chapter 1, 23.

[65] See, e.g., 562/8, 570/16, 595/25.

[66] *On the Properties of Things: John Trevisa's Translation of Bartholomaeus Anglicus De Proprietatibus Rerum*, ed. M.C. Seymour, 3 vols (Oxford: Clarendon Press, 1975) 549–50, spelling slightly modernised.

[67] See Introduction, xix.

The time of isolation is more prolonged, and the weather far more noteworthy than usual, but still everything progresses towards a social and military
end. Gareth's need for lodging in the castle becomes the occasion of a long
conversation with its chatelaine, 'passynge good chere' in its hall, where
Gareth displays his 'knyghtly' eating, and, eventually, a fight with its owner,
the Duke de la Rouse, met 'by fortune' on 'a mountayne' (356/5). The period
of solitude exists only in anticipation of displaying the hero in various social
contexts and functions, of which fighting is the chief and culmination.
When, after the fight with the Duke, Gareth again stands 'alone', immediately another knight on horseback (Gawain) comes to challenge him
(356/31–33). Then, through this honorific fight with Gawain, which Lyonet
leads to a happy ending, Gareth is soon re-united with Arthur and his
family, and the festive conclusion can commence. Only then can he rest from
combat, and readers, within and beyond the text, perfect their judgements.

Fights as Single Combats

There is no single method of fight description in Malory, and his style varies
somewhat according to the different sources which informed each section
of the work. Still, with some exception of *Arthur and Lucius*, which has more
pitched battles, and more influence from an older 'chronicle' battle style in
the source, Malory tends to treat all fights as a series of individual conflicts
between opposed groups, usually opposed pairs, of knights.[68] Although
there are wars and prolonged military campaigns in *Le Morte Darthur*, the
text as a whole has a subdued interest in narrating logistics and military
strategy,[69] preferring to split up a battle into a series of discrete single

[68] See Vinaver, xxxiii, on Malory's predilection for single combat, and also N. Denholm-
Young, 'The Tournament in the Thirteenth Century' in *Studies in Medieval History Presented
to F.M. Powicke* (Oxford: Clarendon Press, 1948) 255, for this preference as a feature of
Arthurian stories. See also Stephen Knight, *Arthurian Literature and Society*, 125–26. The
depiction of large scale battles and tournament mêlées as parallel single combats is
common in art of the fourteenth and fifteenth centuries. See the illustrations in Richard
Barber and Juliet Barker, *Tournaments* (Woodbridge: Boydell Press, 1989) 113, 117; H.W.
Koch, *Medieval Warfare* (London: Bison Books, 1978) 165; E. Hallam, ed., *The Chronicles of
the Wars of the Roses* (London: Weidenfeld and Nicolson, 1988) 263; Viscount Dillon and
W.H. St John Hope, eds, *Pageant of the Birth Life and Death of Richard Beauchamp Earl of
Warwick KG, 1389–1439* (London: Longman, 1914) Plate VII. Illustrations of formal jousts
and lists from these sources show even more bilateral symmetry in the paired competing
figures. See, e.g., Barber and Barker, *Tournaments*, 5, 127; Hallam, *Chronicles*, 171.
[69] A major exception involves aspects of Arthur's campaign in Europe in *Arthur and Lucius*.
See Vinaver, 1368ff. See also Arthur's scorched-earth policy in the war against Lancelot
(1211/15–17). Mordred's use of 'engynnes' and 'grete gunnes' (1227/25) and the reference
to pillagers (1237/32–1238/4) distinguish his campaign against Arthur. For a good account
of some parallels between Malory's wars and the fifteenth-century English situation, see
Knight, *Arthurian Literature and Society*, Chapter 4.

combats. Where much medieval battle literature describes whole armies, and virtually personifies the fight itself, as well as its participants,[70] Malory nearly always tends to focus on named individual combatants, usually on horseback. This is a partial view,[71] and by no means universal in Malory's time. A contemporary soldier wrote:

> As for spearmen, they are only good to ride before the footmen and eat and drink up their victuals, and many more such pretty things they do. You must hold me excused for these expressions, but I say the best, for in the footmen is all the trust.[72]

The narration of Mordred's campaign against Arthur is exceptional in its use of anonymous description. The last battle achieves its stark effect partly through the surprise value of this technique in the *Morte:* [73]

> And never syns was there seyne a more dolefuller batayle in no Crysten londe, for there was but russhynge and rydynge, foynynge and strykynge, and many a grym worde was there spokyn of aythir to othir, and many a dedely stroke. (1235/30–33)

Elsewhere, Malory rarely includes the impersonal mass description of battle which can be so effective in other later medieval military romances:

> There was many pensel good
> Quyk ybathed in hote blood;
> Many heued a-two yslytt,
> Many lyme from body kytt,
> And also many gentil cors
> Was fouled vnder feet of hors.
> There laien on grounde moo than ynowe,
> Summe steruande and sume in swowe.[74]

Instead of the catalogue of injuries, the chilling, anonymous tour of the battlefield we see here, Malory's war is normally only a series of single 'deeds' attributed to named heroes.[75] Both the horror and the relish of battle

[70] See, e.g., Layamon's *Brut*, ed. G.L. Brook and R.F. Leslie, 2 vols (EETS OS 250 and 277, London: Oxford UP, 1963 and 1978) Caligula lines 766ff, 874ff, 2585ff (spelling slightly modernised): 'Heo smiten to-gaedere. helmes there gullen./ breken brade sperren; bordes ther scaenden./ redde blod scede; rinkas feollen./ ther wes muchel gristbat; ther wes cumene fael./ weoren tha hulles and tha daeles iwriyen mid the daeden.'
[71] Malory does not, however, join Lamerok in his contempt for foot combat, 667/21–28. He values Lancelot 'bothe on horsebacke and on foote' (745/25), and describes innumerable foot combats with full enthusiasm. See also 466/10–30.
[72] Quoted from William Gregory's Chronicle, in A.W. Boardman, *The Battle of Towton* (Gloucester: Alan Sutton, 1994) 65.
[73] See also 1229/29–32 (Mordred again) and 31/23–25.
[74] *Kyng Alysaundir*, ed. G.V. Smithers (EETS OS 227, London: Oxford UP, 1952) vol. 1, B, 2703–10.
[75] This point of difference in Malory from other fifteenth-century combat writers seems to be overlooked by Lambert, *Malory*, 43–45.

are diminished by this method, which relies on general epithets of intensity – 'grete', 'full', 'sore' – more than graphic detail.[76] (Again, the horrific physical details of Arthur's, Mordred's and Lucan's deaths are something of an exception to this rule.) No knight in Malory carries a permanent disfigurement, though this was a feature both in life and in other romances. A veteran of Agincourt, Thomas Hostelle, who petitioned Henry VI with a catalogue of his ills, reminds us of real war injuries:

> smyten with a springolt [missile] throughe the hede, lesyng his oon eye and his chek boon broken; . . . withe a gadde [bar] of yrene his plates smyten in to his body and his hande smyten in sondre, and sore hurte, maymed and wounded.[77]

Similarly, *The Legend of Fulk Fitz-Warin* is clinically direct about mutilation:

> A sa premere venue, fery Godard de Bruz . . . de sa hasche, e ly coupa leschyne del dors en deus meytes.
>
> Les uns de chevalers aveyent perdu la nees, les uns le menton; et tut furent desolees.[78]

By contrast, Malory's narrative tends to act in the manner of his best knights, suppressing the most unpleasant consequences of fighting. Amputations and cripplings may occur, but not to the knights of 'name', in whose combats the style is more honorific, the weapons are lance and sword, and the equal exchange of strokes is stressed.[79] Sometimes the fight description takes a summary form, when the narrative object is principally to praise one figure, without an interest in particulars. The formula ritualises the action, emphasising an accumulation of success in the field, crowding the incidents of a whole 'day', or part of it, into a short space:

> sir Trystram rode thorow the thyckyste prece and smote downe knyghtes on the ryght honde and on the lyffte honde and raced of helmys, and so passed forthe unto his pavelouns. (737/5–8)

---

76 Lambert, *Malory*, 28ff.
77 *Letters and Papers Illustrative of the Wars of the English in France During the Reign of Henry the Sixth, King of England*, ed. J. Stevenson (London: HMSO, 1861; Lichtenstein: Kraus Reprint Co., 1965) vol. 1, 295. I am grateful to Charles Acland for this reference.
78 Ralph of Coggeshall, *Chronicon Anglicanum; [etc.]*, ed. J. Stevenson (London: HMSO, 1875; Lichtenstein: Kraus Reprint Co., 1965) 299: 'At his first entry he struck Godard de Bruz . . . with his axe, and cut his spine in two'; 330: 'Some of the knights had lost their noses, some their chins, and all had been roughly treated.'
79 See below. There are very violent scenes, of course, such as 262–63, but these are carefully regulated. The knights who sustain the worst injuries on this occasion – death and broken backs – are anonymous. Others of name – Mador, Mordred and Gahalantyne – are sorely injured, but not killed or permanently maimed.

This is the method designed to praise one above many, especially suitable for tournaments. It emphasises Tristram's ability to take on all comers, to bring opponents to a symbolic death ('smote down'; 'raced of helmys')[80] and to maintain himself helmed in the field until a pause signalled by his temporary 'passing forth'. Frequently these more generalised descriptions are quantitative (as in Chaucer's description of the Knight in the *Canterbury Tales*) especially with reference to tournament mêlées, but also, on occasion, to the cavalry battles which earlier tournaments must have resembled.[81] The names take their turns to dominate the field, with their exploits registered and accredited, so that great importance is placed both on length of endurance and on the visible signs of honour in the combat.

Identifying Detail

Horseback fighting in tournament, joust or casual 'rencountre' has an inevitable sameness – the rushing together, the breaking of lances, the bearing of 'horse and man' to the earth. The degree of intensity but not the essential quality of these fights may be varied by greater detail, e.g., the breaking of girths and saddles as well.[82] These features provide visual signals of valour, such as might have been apparent to informed onlookers, and are specifically noted in Tiptoft's Ordinances of 1466. The breaking of strong spears 'all to pecis' (559/31) displays the courage needed to ride 'at large' directly at the other horseman, very different from the snapping of light lances at a safe angle in the lists, a common practice in later jousts.[83] Also important in Malory are clear colour differences, rather than coats of arms, making identification easier for an audience 'looking on', with or without an intermediary spectator in the text.

Malory is sometimes thought of as a bloodthirsty writer, and if one

---

[80] Pulling off the helm is a preliminary to beheading in tournments and jousts *à outrance*. See Cherewatuk, 'Sir Thomas Malory's "Grete Booke" '. See also 1057/31–32 (Lancelot and Mador).

[81] See Keen, *Chivalry*, 85; Denholm-Young, 'The Tournament', 240. A chronicler of 1273 called the tournament of Châlons 'non torneamentum sed parvum bellum Chalonii'; see F.H. Cripps-Day, *The History of the Tournament* (London: E. Quaritch, 1918) 43.

[82] Barber and Barker, *Tournaments*, 110 comment on the rather limited possible outcomes in the narrative of *pas d'armes*.

[83] For Tiptoft's rules, and others', see Gravatt, *Knights at Tournament*, 25. For the safe angle of the lists, see Denholm-Young, 'The Tournament', 240, and Peter J. Begent, *Justes Royale: The Tournament in England* (Begent: Maidenhead: 1984) 10: 'The tilt had a threefold purpose; it prevented the horses from colliding; it assisted the knight to keep a straight course, and, by increasing the incidence between the lance and the oncoming knight to about 30° it provided that the lance would snap rather than pierce the armour.' See also Cripps-Day, *The History of the Tournament*, 93–94: 'As we proceed in the [fifteenth] century the object of the jouster is to splinter a lance and not to unhorse his adversary, and hence the decreasing weight of the lances used.'

considers the many mortal fights he describes, this must be so. But the conception of what there is to *see* in a Malory fight owes little to the epic sense of spectacle.[84] Vinaver (1369–71) points out Malory's 'consistent . . . omission of some of the gruesome details of the battle-scenes' in revising the alliterative *Morte Arthure* for his *Arthur and Lucius*. Instead, the normal emphasis is on clear observation and identification, more in the style of a herald's report on a tournament: 'And all this was marked with noble herrodis, who bare hym beste, and their namys' (347/18–19).[85] Even when describing pitched battles, Malory often might as well be describing a tournament. In tournament descriptions there is more prominence given to the charging with lances, the breaking of lances and the unhorsing of opponents. But in all horseback fights this is the standard opening. Knights drop the contingent and more complex identities which might limit or distract from their participation in favour of a new role as object of vision, and briefly become only 'the knight with the red shield' or 'the black knight'. Identified only by externals they enjoy the freedom of pure combat display.

Through this temporary erasure of the past and the creation of a refreshed self, the pageant of the favoured hero's recognition and reward can be endlessly cancelled and renewed, rather as in a daydream, permitting massive dilation of the narrative.[86] Tristram, a prince of Cornwall and a rich man, tells Arthur that he is a 'a poure knyght aventures' (492/6). Arthur himself is willing to 'putte hys person in adventure as other poure knyghtis ded' (54/19–20) and to ride 'pryvaly as a poure arraunte knyght' (745/27). 'Poure' might seem to suggest a buried economic motive, a vestige of the supposed origin of these stories amongst younger sons anxious to found their own patrimonies.[87] But in its sense of depreciation and insufficiency[88] – a knight and nothing more, only a knight – 'poure' also suggests how Tristram, Arthur, Lancelot and Lamerok, like other 'stablysshed' figures of high rank, must return to the basic narrative role to recapture the attention of spectators within and beyond the narrative. To remain 'good' they must continue to co-operate with the text's major evaluative process – combat.

---

84 P.J.C. Field, *Romance and Chronicle*, 98, remarks on 'the general lack of sustenance for the visual imagination' in Malory.

85 For the growing importance of heralds' narratives in the fifteenth century, see Anglo, 'Archives', 154; Keen, *Chivalry*, 136–42; Richard Firth Green, *Poets and Princepleasers: Literature and the English Court in the Later Middle Ages* (Toronto: University of Toronto Press, 1980) Chapter 6, esp. 168ff. By the end of the fifteenth century, Henry VII's heralds were script-writers and stage-managers of tournament theatre. See *The Receyt of the Ladie Kateryne*, ed. G. Kipling (EETS OS 296, London: Oxford UP, 1990) Introduction, xxiv–xxix, esp. xxvi.

86 See Patricia Parker, *Inescapable Romance: Studies in the Poetics of a Mode* (Princeton: Princeton UP, 1979), 8, 10, 63, 220ff, for this term.

87 See Duby, 'Youth in Aristocratic Society' in *The Chivalrous Society*. See also Chapter 1, above, 9.

88 *OED*, 'poor' 4b; 5.

Pageant, Display and Vision

It is tempting to apply to this celebration of combat 'proof' Auerbach's famous comment on the *Yvain* of Chrétien de Troyes, that 'the feudal ethos . . . no longer has any purpose but that of self-realisation',[89] or Vinaver's remarks on the French Arthurian Cycle:

> They were no longer concerned with the practical business of warfare; they still wore their glittering armour and were eager to use their spears and swords; but their battles seemed to be fought in the void, and there was no discernible object in their exploits. (xxxiii)

The prominence of tournament-style battle descriptions, the long skeins of sketchily motivated fights between knights errant, often lend Malory's text an appearance of recreation, of play and self-display, which can be linked with some ceremonial and non-functional aspects of tournaments in Malory's day.[90] On occasions these notions of display overtly enter the discourse. Sir Palamides is said to 'play his play' and Tristram to 'play his pageants';[91] the possessive pronoun is telling: the knight is staging himself, serving as producer, performer and spectacle. The concurrence of phrases also shows that play here is not only 'sport' as it might mean in other contexts, such as Lancelot's 'play and game' (253/20), but like 'pageauntes' a development of tournament and the concept of fighting itself in the direction of theatre.[92] Whether we are speaking of massed battle, knight errantry or tournament, the term 'pageant', originally related to Latin 'pagina' ('page'),[93] aptly describes Malory's textual theatre of chivalry; the manuscript or printed page functions as a public arena where exploits are enacted and witnessed. His paratactic narrative is a succession of illustrative 'pageants' in verbal form, matching its contemporary pictorial text, the Earl of Warwick's *Pageant*. There, just as in Malory, the hero's appearances in fighting, especially single combat, are heavily privileged.

Warwick's *Pageant*, carefully structured by his descendants, and the meticulously staged feats of Lord Scales, discussed above,[94] remind us that there *is* always one clear and 'practical' object in these knightly arms, whether or not they had a further military or diplomatic purpose. It is to be *seen* to do well, as a uniquely prestigious means of advancement for the

---

[89] Eric Auerbach, *Mimesis: The Representation of Reality in Western Literature*, trans. Willard R. Trask (Princeton: Princeton UP, 1954) 134.

[90] See Keen, *Chivalry*, 206.

[91] 759/18, 748/09.

[92] Keen, *Chivalry*, 206: 'Theatre and décor as it were expanded to fill the gap left by the declining relevance of chivalrous sport to martial activity'. For 'play' in Malory, used of fighting, see also 444–45.

[93] *OED*, 'pageant'. Malory is cited under 1.b.

[94] See above, Introduction.

chivalric stars, their families and adherents. (Real battles still needed to be won, of course, but the obscure Thomas Hostelles who fought in them are not acknowledged in Malory's pages.) His 'tournament' style combat description is fundamentally a celebration of merit recognised and rewarded; it offers a model that could apply directly to men of arms in the service of the King or a great lord, but could also be transferred to other areas. (At times, such as in Henry VI's reign, the royal household had not been chiefly composed of men of arms, but the need for patronage was still as strong.)[95] Rather than maintaining a firm distinction between Tristram as a 'worshipful' feudal knight and Lancelot as a 'true' knight,[96] Malory tends to treat all success in knighthood as a route to royal preferment and approval. Arthur is a great king, unlike Mark, mainly because he 'establishes' and 'maintains' good knights for their deeds. Arthur's chief merit is, and remains to the end, the true vision of others' chivalric worth, which his own nobility helps him to recognise. This function carries great importance in itself.[97] When that is understood, assessments of Arthur as 'weak' in the *Tristram* and later books of the *Morte* are better contextualised.[98] And the importance granted to Arthur's vision of Lancelot's greatness (1174/12–13, 1192/28–33), even when the two are politically at odds, shows us that Malory's highest conception of knighthood still involves making a good impression on powerful judges. (In the *Sankgreal*, the main difference is that this judging function is transferred from Arthur to God and his clerical witnesses.)

At the core of an important fight will often be, therefore, a moment of vision, in which the action is assessed from a point of vantage within the text, rather than offered directly as a spectacle to readers:

> 'A, Jesu!' seyde kynge Arthure, 'se where rydyth a strong knyght, he wyth the rede shylde.'
> And there was a noyse and a grete cry:
> 'Beware the knyght with the rede shylde!'
> So wythin a lytyll whyle he [Tristram] had overthrowyn three bretherne of sir Gawaynes.
> 'So God me helpe,' seyde kynge Arthur, 'mesemyth yondir is the best juster that ever I sawe.' (607/4–11)

The incident typifies Malory's preferred 'tournament' style, in that it gives as much prominence to the story of recognition and approbation as to the

---

[95] See D.A.L. Morgan, 'The House of Policy: The Political Role of the Late Plantagenet Household, 1422–1485' in David Starkey, ed., *The English Court: From the Wars of the Roses to the Civil War* (London and New York: Longman, 1987) Chapter 2, 34.

[96] See Kennedy, *Knighthood*, 148ff.

[97] See Keen, *Chivalry*, 153ff, on the vital role of kings as patrons of 'poor knights'.

[98] See, e.g., Ginger Thornton, 'The Weakening of the King: Arthur's Disintegration in *The Book of Sir Tristram de Lyones*' in Hanks, *Sir Thomas Malory*, 3–16.

deeds of arms themselves. This episode (606–07) is stuffed with phrases such as 'he loked aboute and saw hym'; 'ryght so was kyng Arthure ware'; 'in the syght of kynge Arthure he smote downe twenty knyghtes'; 'all this aspyed kynge Arthure, for his yghe went never frome hym'. Attention is diverted from the participants as subjects to their existence as objects of the judicious spectator, who is made co-principal agent. The functional and strategic aspects of fighting are often less important 'needs of meaning' than these repeated moments of recognition and praise. The greater the onlooker, the greater is the honorific effect. Arthur's singular vision of Tristram, above, becomes magnified into a general 'crye', showing how powerful is his 'voice'. The incident also foreshadows the multiplication of honour that a single text, like Malory's, can offer through its many readers and hearers.

These shifts of attention from the plot of fighting to the celebration of prowess may occur even when local cause and effect are crucial. When Lancelot escapes from Guenevere's chamber, killing thirteen of Arthur's knights, the king's first reaction to the news is ' "Jesu mercy! . . . he ys a mervaylous knyght of proues" ' (1174/12–13). Arthur's role as judge of knightly deeds predominates here.[99] Just as the traitor Mordred can still do his 'devoure' in battle, so the narrative has its own chief duty, to record who did well, as if no more than a tournament prize were at stake. The combatants are honoured by the beholders, the beholders by what they see. A fight, therefore, whilst it may seem to us to display the social discord evident in Malory's world, paradoxically offers his chief vision of the common good. In the next chapters, I examine the narrative articulation of this combat vision in more detail.

[99] See also 1192/28–33.

3

The Thematics of Combat

White was made red their triumphs to disclose
(John Lydgate)[1]

. . . no more intellectual interest in those slashings, and staggerings, and buffetings, and piercings than in an account of prize-fighting in Bell's Life
(Edward Russell, 1889)[2]

As we have seen, Roger Ascham and many others since his time have considered Malory's knights as mere manslayers, and the *Morte* as a book of killings. One can easily see why this is so. Killings are common occurrences,[3] and in terms of plot developments nothing is more operative in the overall story than the violent deaths of important figures, such as Lot, Lamerok, Gareth and Arthur. Marginal notations in the Winchester Manuscript show the importance of the text's deaths to early readers.[4] Nevertheless, many episodes in Malory involve important fights without loss of life, especially in the great tournament encounters and set-piece single combats between knights of name. And just as a fight in Malory has its own structural integrity, a beginning and ending independent of plot causes and effects, as I have shown above,[5] so even in the description of mortal combat death does not necessarily receive a dominant emphasis. The conduct of the narrative privileges several other 'needs of meaning' to which the modern reader must be alert. Not all the descriptive factors I now turn to are necessarily stressed in every important fight, but the presence of most

---

1 *The Minor Poems of John Lydgate: Part II: Secular Poems*, ed. H.N. McCracken (EETS OS 192, London: Oxford UP 1934) no. 63, line 110. This well-known line refers to Christian martyrs, but seems, especially in its context, related to martial rhetoric.
2 Parins, *Malory: The Critical Heritage*, 242.
3 See, e.g., 600/8–9: Lamerok kills four out of twelve knights in a joust.
4 Pointing hands are drawn in the margin of the Winchester MS to mark a number of deaths, including 77/14 (Pellinore kills Lot); 81/10 (Garlon kills Peryne); 116/7 (Pellinore speaks to Outelake before killing him).
5 Chapter 2, 41–42.

of them is usual. Instead of a comparative typology of knightly conduct in Malory, one might more appropriately construct a typology of fights, with the most noble including the greatest elaboration of these honorific elements.

The Need for Prevision

I have discussed above[6] the status of Malory's fights as visual events for their spectators both within and beyond the fiction. 'A fayre felde' (127/3) – the term combines ethical and aesthetic preoccupations – presupposes a fight without unfair advantage, in which both combatants are 'ware' of each other. The ability for each knight to see and be seen by the other, as well as by any third party, is of great importance. Hence the horrific treachery of Garlon, who 'rydith all invisyble' (82/26) and the unbecoming behaviour of Palamides, who unhorses Arthur 'unwarely' (744/26) and 'unknyghtly'. To be 'unaware' is dangerous, tragically so when Lancelot kills Gareth and Gaheris, 'for they were unarmed and unwares' (1177/33–34) and 'sir Launcelot saw them nat' (1178/3). To see and be seen is to accept and have others accept the risk of the fight, the 'aventure', and so, normally, to be free of blame for ill consequences. A fight is prefaced with an account of the knights' seeing each other, either in isolation, or, more strikingly, against a significant background, as when Tristram sees Marhalt beside the ships that have brought him from Ireland to fight for the tribute:

> 'Sir', seyde Governayle, 'se ye hym nat? I wente that ye had sene hym, for yondir he hovyth undir the umbir of his shyppys on horseback, with his spere in his honde and his shylde uppon his sholdyr.'
> 'That is trouthe,' seyde sir Trystrams, 'now I se hym.' (380/24–28)

The background may also be an incident in battle, or an adventure, requiring action:

> Than sir Lucas saw kynge Angwysschaunce that nyghe had slayne Maris de la Roche; and Lucas ran to hym with a sherpe spere that was grete, and he gaff hym suche a falle that the horse felle downe to the erthe. (30/8–11)

> Whan sir Launcelot herde this he arose up and loked oute at the wyndowe, and sygh by the moonelyght three knyghtes com rydyng aftir that one man, and all three laysshynge on hym at onys with swerdys; and that one knyght turned on hem knyghtly agayne and defended hym.
> (273/7–11)

Malory is also expert in suddenly changing the point of view to permit the hero himself to be seen:

[6] Chapter 2, 53–55.

And as sone as he come thydir the doughter of kyng Bagdemagus herde
a grete horse trotte on the pavymente, and she than arose and yode to a
wyndowe, and there she sawe sir Launcelot. (261/4–7)[7]

Such moments of prevision seem necessary to the story to make sense of
the action, providing an evaluative frame for adventure. By contrast, 'suddenness' – a frequent occurrence – is associated with misfortune, treachery
and craft, events in which the fulness of prevision is impaired.

'Sudden' events and actions are often precipitated by 'prevy' feelings,
hence they are usually contrary to the collective ethos. Their occurrence
reveals a narrative tension between the accretion of new events, the lust for
incident, and the equally strong impulse to bind all new events into the
pre-existing ideological framework, where all can be seen and judged. To
prevent forethought and knightly judgement is dangerous behaviour. 'Suddenness' does not imply only speed of reaction, for which the normal
adverbs are approbatory – 'lyghtly and delyverly' – but applies even to a
premeditated act which goes beyond what can be foreseen and approved,
for example Gaheris's beheading of Morgawse:

> So whan sir Gaherys sawe his tyme he cam to there beddis syde all armed,
> wyth his swerde naked, and suddaynly he gate his modir by the heyre
> and strake of her hede. (612/9–11)

Almost the only thing a good being is able to do suddenly without loss of
worship is to part company, as Igrayne and Gorloyse, Lancelot, Tristram,
Galahad's soul and the Holy Grail all do.[8] Their suddenness is justified by
fear of guile, anticipation of a reappearance, or a rebuke of the place or
company left behind. Otherwise, suddden acts are usually the sign of
cowardice (Mark, Andret)[9] or of treachery (Mark, Phelot, Pedyvere,
Brewnys, Gaheris).[10] Suddenness characterises the ill manners of churls or
dwarves[11] and assassination by poison.[12] In the last and perhaps most
frightening occurrence of the term, Arthur 'suddenly' falls from the wheel
of Fortune (1233/18). Ambushes and grossly unfair tactics are 'sudden'
(518/11), and so are inglorious runnings away, like Marhalt's (382/30).
There are some exceptions,[13] but the markedly pejorative use of the term

---

7 Cf. 1251/29–31: 'And at the laste he cam to a nunry, and anone quene Gwenyver was
   ware of sir Launcelot as he walked in the cloyster.'
8 See, respectively, 7/23, 1048/4, 1125/10, 363/7, 1035/14, 865/33.
9 586/26, 431/4.
10 547/3–11, 578/23, 283/4, 285/12, 562/22–24.
11 109/8, 271/8, 713/1.
12 373/25, 374/2, 1049/12.
13 Mainly in *Arthur and Lucius*: 228/3, 239/29. These occurrences in pitched battle seem less
   culpable.

shows Malory's preference for *confirmatory* actions, those which are *seen* to fit a pre-arranged evaluative scheme. The linear thrust of the story, which might seem to threaten strict interpretative control, is ideally a measured, repetitive demonstration of the status quo and its hierarchies. In effect, the role of 'adventure' as *chance* is strictly limited. Yet because the appearance of chance is necessary to the narrative, to provide more opportunities for display, and to let interesting situations arise without implicating the great knights' personal motivation, suddenness often impacts on the norm of steady significance.[14]

The Need for Reciprocity

In all fighting, but especially fighting on foot, *Le Morte Darthur* stresses symmetry and reciprocity, the feeling of *sharing* in combat that Jill Mann has remarked on.[15] Each knight is like an equal half of a good fight, giving and receiving blows. In this phase of the narrative, names and individual-ising issues (e.g., moral and political alignments) are submerged into a collective 'they', and the action proceeds as if in a mirror exercise, or the more ceremonial later tournaments in which knights exchanged a fixed number of strokes. The fierceness of the encounter is conventionally at-tested by damage to armour, in a way that briefly defers damage to the body itself:

> and eyther com unto other egirly and smote togedyrs with hir swerdys, that hir sheldis flew in cantellys, and they bresed their helmys and hawbirkes and woundid eyther other. (161/2–4)

As in horseback fights, attention is held on visible signs of intensity, such as the pieces flying from hacked shields and armour. Other favourite *topoi* of intensity include mention of long duration, of exhaustion, comparisons with wild animals, and the reactions of spectators:

> Than lyghtly and delyverly they avoyded their horsis and putt their shyldis afore them and drew theire swerdys and ran togydyrs lyke two fers lyons, and eythir gaff othir suche two buffettys uppon their helmys that they reled bakwarde bothe two stredys. And then they recoverde bothe and hew grete pecis of othyrs harneyse and their shyldys, that a grete parte felle in the fyldes.
>
> And than thus they fought tyll hit was paste none, and never wolde stynte tyll at the laste they lacked wynde bothe, and than they stoode waggyng, stagerynge, pantynge, blowynge and bledyng, that all that

---

[14] The suddenness of a bad action may be mentioned to clear onlookers from blame for not preventing it, e.g., 285/12, Pedyvere and Lancelot.

[15] Mann, 'Knightly Combat', esp. 337–39.

behelde them for the moste party wepte for pyté. So whan they had rested them a whyle they yode to batayle agayne, trasyng, traversynge, foynynge, and rasynge as two borys. And at som tyme they toke their bere[16] as hit had bene two rammys and horled togydyrs, that somtyme they felle grovelynge to the erthe; and at som tyme they were so amated that aythir toke others swerde in the stede of his owne.

And thus they endured tyll evynsonge, that there was none that behelde them myght know whethir was lyke to wynne the batayle. And theire armoure was so forhewyn that men myght se their naked sydys, and in other placis they were naked; but ever the nakyd placis they dud defende.
(322/36–323/22)

A small zoo of animals here, but with no conscious humour, nor any Chaucerian hint of moral reprobation[17] and, unlike in Chaucer, the knights are always each the *same* animal. The fierce and equal maintenance of the fight without recreance is a good in itself, part of knightly 'truth'; the two combatants continually 'come together'[18] and do not 'fail' each other, a term which can be used equally of allies or opponents in a fight.[19] The narrative converts their conflict into a close bond of 'naked' bodies disvested by the ardour of fighting.

The Value of Blood

Blood is the basic currency of fights and quests, their operative factor as much as their issue, and often unrealistically prominent in fights that end without a death. Gareth says to Lyones, in a phrase redolent of Christian redemptive tradition, ' "well I am sure I have bought your love with parte of the beste bloode within my body" ' (327/15–17), and Pellinore says of the Questing Beast ' "othir I shall encheve hym othir blede of the beste bloode in my body" ' (42/30–43/1). The text acts consistently in a way that literalises blood as the seat of goodness and nobility. Gawain signs his last letter 'with parte of my harte blood' (1232/8), whilst Lamerok loves Morgawse's blood in more than a metaphorical sense, as becomes clear when Gaheris kills her:

Whan sir Lameroke sawe the blood daysshe uppon hym all hote, whyche was the bloode that he loved passyng well, wyte you well he was sore abaysshed and dismayed of that dolerous syght. (612/11–15)

He rebukes Gaheris for not respecting his own 'blood' (family): ' "Fowle

16 I.e., 'gathered impetus by a run', Brook's Glossary, *bere*, sb. in Vinaver's Malory.
17 *The Riverside Chaucer*, *Knight's Tale*, 1655–60.
18 Mann, 'Knightly Combat', 337ff. For a further discussion of some fight details, including blood motifs, see Lambert, *Malory*, 41ff.
19 See, e.g., 35/24–31, 523/19–20 of allies, 429/17 of foes.

and evyll have ye done, and to you grete shame! Alas, why have ye slayne youre modir that bare you?" ' (612/17–19). Lamerok loves the nobility of Morgawse's 'blood' ('modir unto sir Gawayne and to sir Gaherys, and modir to many other' (579/23–25)). But since Lamerok is also the son of Pellinore, killer of her husband, King Lot, Gaheris recasts Lamerok's love as an aggressive act to her children, reversing the other's benign, and very Malorian, view, in which Morgawse's noble progeny makes her all the more loveable. 'Love' and 'heart' were hackneyed words for political good will in Malory's day,[20] but his story reinvests them with erotic charge: love sheds blood[21] and blood 'buys' love, as Gareth says. But the expense of blood, whilst necessary, is sometimes dangerous, for it can also buy enduring hate.

An episode in Malory's *Noble Tale of Launcelot* shows how careful the good knight is to respect the blood of an opponent. In a comic error, Lancelot has mistakenly got into bed with and kissed another knight, Belleus, who was sleeping in a pavilion. In the ensuing fight, Belleus is badly wounded, but Lancelot manages to show him a 'love' he finds more acceptable:

> 'That me repentyth,' seyde sir Launcelot, 'of youre hurte, but I was adrad of treson, for I was late begyled. And therefore com on your way into youre pavylyon, and take youre reste, and as I suppose I shall staunche your bloode.'
> And so they wente bothe into the pavylyon, and anone sir Launcelot staunched his bloode. (260/8–13)

In another sense, Lancelot also respects Belleus' 'blood', by helping to make him a knight of the Round Table, and so elevating his social position (287/19–23), a happy ending of Malory's own invention. In the *Tristram* book, a noble fight between Tristram and the invading Saxon knight, Elias – 'the hoote blood ran freyshly uppon the erthe' (625/10–11) – displays the same respect, although this time Malory chose an unhappy conclusion:

> than he [Tristram] dressed hym unto sir Elyas and gaff hym many sad strokys, twenty ayenst one, and all to-brake his shylde and his hawberke, that the hote bloode ran downe as hit had bene rayne. Than began kynge Marke and all Cornyshemen to lawghe, and the other party to wepe.
> And ever sir Trystram seyde to sir Elyas, 'Yelde the!'
> And whan sir Trystram saw hym so stakir on the grounde, he seyde,
> 'Sir Elyas, I am ryght sory for the, for thou arte a passynge good knyght as ever I mette withall excepte sir Launcelot.'
> And therwithall sir Elyas fell to the erthe and there dyed.
> 'Now what shall I do?' seyde sir Trystram unto kynge Marke, 'for this batayle ys at an ende.' (625/30–626/7)

---

[20] See Du Boulay, *An Age of Ambition*, 135.
[21] Cf. *On the Properties of Things*, 294: 'The mater of the childe', described as 'digest blood of the fadir and of the modir', 'is isched in the place of conceyuynge abrood'.

Mark and the cowardly Cornishmen, like the Saxons before (625/20), display in their laughter not only the pleasure of victory, but also a lack of nobility, in that they will not respect the sight of a good knight's blood. But Tristram, impressed by the issue of wounds he himself has made, is as sorry for the expense of Elias's blood as he had been eager to shed it in the first place. As we see often in Malory, the proper evaluation of his opponent's prowess may be as important to a combatant as bringing the battle to its 'end', and Tristram's disappointment, partly achieved by Malory's alterations to the French original (1495/n.626/5–7), is palpable, all the more so as Mark is an unworthy spectator and judge. To 'see' the blood in its true meaning means as much as to be able to inflict the wounds, and in the best knights the one ability is the natural complement to the other. In this way also, good readers of Malory and his good knights share intimately in moments of recognition. His implied audience resembles in this the reading figures sometimes pictured in fifteenth-century illustrations, who are transported through meditation on their text into a direct vision of its sacred events.[22]

Blood and the Problem of Nobility: Gareth

Nobility of deed means nobility of birth in Malory, so that the display of blood is also a matter of genealogy. The word 'blood' is synonymous with 'kin', and remains a chief preoccupation of most of the knights, referred to more frequently by them than the more abstract 'order' of knighthood.[23] Criticism has made much of a thematic opposition between a loyalty to the Round Table and knighthood, as displayed by Lancelot and Gareth, and a loyalty primarily to kin, seen in Gawain. Nevertheless, one cannot deny the positive importance of kinship and heredity to all the leading personages in the story. The Lot–Pellinore family feud is a dark thread throughout the text, and such affairs must have been perfectly familiar to a man of Malory's experience.[24] But the 'blood of sir Launcelot de Lac' receives many references also, and Lancelot's many kinsmen frequently accompany him

---

[22] See, e.g., the illustration of Duke Humphrey of Gloucester kneeling before the Man of Sorrows, c.1420–1430, in BL, MS Roy, 2 BI., f. 8r, printed in Hallam, *Chronicles*, 293.

[23] See the references in Kato, *Concordance*. The standard format of inquisitions post mortem at this period was to find the 'consanguineus et heres' of the deceased. For 'blood' or 'consanguinity' as 'kin' in wills of armigerous men in the fifteenth century, see, for example, the wills of Henry Noon of Shelfhanger in Norfolk (1487; Norwich and Norfolk Record Office, A. Caston, 235–36) and Sir Thomas Ilketshale (1416; Norwich and Norfolk Record Office, Hyrnyng, 26–27). I am grateful to Philippa Maddern for these last references.

[24] See Michael Bennett, *The Battle of Bosworth* (Gloucester: Alan Sutton, 1985) 25: 'Indeed there can be no doubt as to the crucial importance of personal antagonisms and family rivalries in the civil strife which afflicted England from the reign of Richard II onwards.'

throughout the *Morte*. They will eventually head the list of twenty-two knights who promise 'to do what he wolde' after the rift with Arthur develops (1170/11–26), and follow him into the hermit's life after Arthur's death (1254–55).

Malory insists or assumes that the combatants in a fight are 'jantyll'. Gareth's opponents take this for granted (303/11–35). Gentility of birth, at least, goes without saying, and even royalty may be stipulated (379/15–36).[25] Noble blood cannot be fully hidden. Gareth, in disguise (295/25–35), is spurned by the aberrant Kay, but attracts the attention both of Gawain because of his consanguinity – 'that proffer com of his bloode, for he was nere kyn to hym than he wyste off' – and of Lancelot, through his equally sensitive 'jantylnesse and curtesy'. Fighting in a fair field ideally moves towards the display of that 'manhode and worship' which 'ys hyd within a mannes person', as Balin says (63/25). Yet the emphasis on 'proof' is not an argument for the idea of a nobility established by deeds alone, but rather a sign of the belief that worthy fighters must first be 'of jantill strene of fadir syde and of modir syde', as Balin is himself (62/23). Even the meritocrat Sir Torre,[26] whom King Pellinore has fathered on a peasant woman, still lacks something in Arthur's view:

> 'I know none in all this courte, and he were as well borne on his modir syde as he is on youre [Pellinore's] syde, that is lyke hym *of prouesse and of myght*' (131/29–31)

Arthur simply cannot separate the idea of physical strength and courage from nobility of birth. Naturally, Torre gets all his prowess from Pellinore.

Not surprisingly, then, Malory keeps his important combats only for knights. Giants are rarely encountered, and are distinguished as ignoble by their use of clubs, like other commoners.[27] Churls are unwelcome intruders into the Malorian scene, unable and unwilling to share in the economy of honour: 'Gyeff a chorle rule and thereby he woll nat be suffysed' (712/23–25). As Riddy has shown,[28] their deaths are not of importance to the narrative. Whilst noble birth does not guarantee good conduct, nothing noteworthy can be expected without it.

Yet fighting, though it supposedly functions as a sure indicator of class, has a disruptive, levelling-down social potential. For in order to benefit from the declarative power of combat, the 'proof' inherent in victory, the nobleman must temporarily put off the prestige of blood and rely on his

---

[25] Keen, *Chivalry*, 203, mentions that heralds discreetly enquired into the lineage of *chevaliers mesconnus*. See also Begent, *Justes Royale*, 11: 'Heralds had to certify that the combatants were "gentle".'

[26] See also Chapter 1, 10.

[27] For giants using clubs, see 175–76, 202–05, 220–21. For common people and churls using clubs, see 19, 271.

[28] See above, Chapter 2, 38.

'hands'. The risk remains that through another's greater success he and his kin will be disparaged:

> all the noyse and brewte felle to sir Trystram, and the name ceased of sir Launcelot. And therefore sir Launcelottis bretherne and his kynnysmen wolde have slayne sir Trystram bycause of his fame. (785/1–4)

By such means, one of the most socially conservative of Malory's narrative conventions, that noble deeds declare the noble man, becomes a point of pressure for chivalric ideology.

In the light of this attitude to nobility, the story of Gareth, great lord employed as kitchen servant, presents an interesting problem. Dame Lyonet's scornful discouragement of Gareth as 'Beaumains' can be seen as both properly conservative and merciful. Her instincts are sound. It would be unacceptable for a kitchen knave to fight, let alone defeat, knights. *The Tale of Sir Gareth* toys with the idea of true valour in a churl, in order to deny it. Gareth's disguise is a delaying device that makes his recognition more prolonged and more splendid.[29] His opponents are rebuked for presuming that he is base-born, but the presumption that the churl cannot partake in chivalry, although 'a full lykly persone, and full lyke to be a stronge man' (303/31–32), is not challenged. Prowess can only be converted into worship when it is known that the winner is 'gentle'. Otherwise, his victory over real knights will be regarded as ' "by mysseadventure and nat by proues of thy hondys" ' (302/31), a kind of treachery, and an offence against the fragile but important principle that the outcome of fights preserves the social hierarchy, and maintains an ideal order of worth within the knightly ranks. Lyonet and the Black Knight both use the odd phrase 'man of worshyp borne' (303/27–32), which conflates within one view the ideas of worship gained by deeds, and nobility conferred by birth, in an attempt to naturalise their connection.

Yet read in another way the *Gareth* story amusingly shows how the exclusion of the base-born from power and worship is itself maintained by force of arms, and can, apparently, be reversed by arms. The Green Knight at first regards the kitchen-knave Beaumains as a 'traytoure' for slaying his brother, 'a full noble knyght' (305/15–18). But when defeated and at the point of death he is understandably less keen to maintain this class position, whilst Lyonet, looking on, remains unmoved:

> 'Fye upon the, false kychyn payge! I woll never pray the to save his lyff, for I woll nat be so muche in thy daunger.'
> 'Than shall he dye,' seyde Beawmaynes.

---

29   See Jeanne Drewes, 'The Sense of Hidden Identity in Malory's *Mort Darthur*' in Hanks, *Sir Thomas Malory*, 7–23, 23: 'remaining nameless allows a knight freedom within the hierarchical society to reassert his position and thus maintain the power that is one with the name'.

'Nat so hardy, thou bawdy knave!' seyde the damesell, 'that thou sle hym.'
'Alas!' seyde the Grene Knyght, 'suffir me nat to dye for a fayre worde
spekyng. Fayre knyght', seyde the Grene Knyght, 'save my lyfe and I woll
forgyff the the deth of my brothir, and for ever to becom thy man, and
thirty knyghtes that hold of me for ever shall do you servyse.'

'In the devyls name,' seyde the damesell, 'that suche a bawdy kychyn
knave sholde have thirty knyghtes servyse and thyne!' (306/16–28)

The Green Knight later rationalises his change of heart:

'Damesell, mervayle me thynkyth . . . why ye rebuke this noble knyghte
as ye do, for I warne you he is a full noble man, and I knowe no knyght
that is able to macche hym . . . For whatsomever he makyth hymself he
shall preve at the ende that he is com of full noble blood and of kynges
lynage.' (307/16–23)

The Green Knight is required to believe this (at least, to act on this principle)
or else to suffer shame: ' "Truly . . . hit were shame to me to say hym ony
dysworshyp, for he hath previd hymself a bettir knyght than I am" '
(307/26–27). Unless he adopts this arbitrary but entrenched position, that
victory 'proves' nobility of blood, contrary to the informed witness of
Lyonet, who 'knows' that Beawmaynes is a kitchen servant, he must confess
himself guilty of begging mercy from a churl. Beawmaynes *must* become
Gareth, or ruin the economy of honour.

Read from within the chivalric mystique, the Green Knight's decision
offers a model of how Malory's textual conduct requires new events to fit
within the same loose ideological framework. If Beaumains is big, strong
and successful, he must be a nobleman. But if we step aside a little, the
declarative process can easily be reversed: success in fighting, like power
of any kind, gives the right to control social evaluations, and therefore to
transform knaves into knights, and to compel the service of lords. The
knights who fill Arthur's hall at the great feasts, who serve him for the
'establishment' he gives them (120/11–27), made visible in the food and
drink of the Round Table, are not radically different from those lower
servants in the kitchen, where there is also good supply of food
(294/12–295/7). *Gareth* seems anxious about the potential in this comparison, but in moving to quell it reveals more similarities than it could have
intended between the creation of knights and of churls. Particularly, it
shows a connection between Gareth's 'knyghtly' eating (354/2), his big
build and 'lykly persone', his strength in battle and his political importance,
although a younger brother. In fifteenth-century political life, one can
compare the advantage Edward IV enjoyed in his height and good looks,
at a time when so much public business was transacted face to face.[30] To be

---

[30] See Charles Ross, *Edward IV* (London: Eyre Methuen, 1974) 10–11, 232, 423.

fed at court was likewise an important political sign: it meant that one had a place there. In Malory's time, for instance, it was a pressing concern for young John Paston's family that he was

> not takyn as none of that [the King's] howse, fore the cokys be not charged to serue hym nore the sewere to gyue hym no dyche, fore the sewere wyll nat tak no men no dischys till they be commawndyd by the controllere.[31]

Power is the power to eat well at court: the story of *Gareth* ends in a great feast, with 'all maner of plenté' (362/20). The year-long kitchen transformation which Gareth makes from the weakness of symbolic starvation – 'he fared as he myght nat go nothir bere hymself' (293/32) – to immense physical power – 'so bygge that he [Lancelot] mervayled of his strengthe . . . passyng durable and passyng perelous' (298/35–299/3) – shows what superior diet does to establish a ruling class, and how permission to eat the king's food can make 'noble' rulers out of the man or clan who can obtain it. Overtly, the story denies Gareth's need for special nurture, by insisting that his natural nobility of 'blood' will always overcome. But a subversive counter-fable also persists, in which nobility of *food* takes precedence of blood in making the good knight and the nobleman.[32]

There is a medieval scientific basis for this alternative reading. Sperm, the bearer of male qualities from generation to generation, was considered in the later middle ages to be a highly refined form of blood, itself a refinement of the grosser matter of food.[33] As John of Trevisa puts it, 'blood is freend of kynde'. When an animal is fed 'mete' (food) with blood, i.e., flesh:

> he waxith and is in good disposicioun by the effect of the foode of such mete. And if the blood of the whiche the mete is imaad is clere and good, the body is hool.[34]

To the scientific mind of Malory's age, Gareth's noble 'blood', with its issue both in fighting and potential for procreation, has a plain source in his noble diet. So Gareth's need to eat meat, or at least the 'fatte browes' (broths) made from the water in which meat has been boiled (295/6), whilst it functions as a disguise of his social identity, can also be understood as a prerequisite for his own and his descendants' 'nobility'. A strange double effect is

---

31 *Paston Letters*, vol. I, no. 116, pp. 199–200.
32 Riddy, *Sir Thomas Malory*, 60–83, sees table manners, rather than sheer nutrition, as crucial to ideas of 'nobility' in *Gareth*.
33 See Aristotle, *De Generatione Animalium*, trans. D.M. Balme (Oxford: Clarendon Press, 1972) 45–49, 145–51; D. Jacquart and C. Thomasset, *Sexuality and Medicine in the Middle Ages*, trans. M. Adamson (Cambridge: Polity Press, 1988) 52–60; Joan Cadden, *Meanings of Sex Difference in the Middle Ages: Medicine, Science and Culture* (Cambridge: Cambridge UP, 1993) 22, 37, 133.
34 *On the Properties of Things*, 151.

created, for reading from inside Malory's ideology of class, the logic of this analysis becomes reversed: it is only natural that food, like those who eat it, should have its hierarchy, and therefore fitting that the noble man should have the most excellent diet (and appetite):

> Than was he sette unto souper and had many good dysshis. Than sir Gareth lyste well to ete, and full knyghtly he ete his mete and egirly.
> (354/1–3)

Since 'heat', the typically masculine quality, serves not only to concoct food into blood, but blood into semen, Gareth is therefore 'hote and corragyous' (the two things go together) in the sexual as well as the military sphere.[35] Lyonet, a good magician, uses her skill to regulate the hero's blood and preserve her sister's honour. First she forestalls any premature sexual encounter between Gareth and Lyones, 'for savyng of hir worshyp' (333/9–10). Gareth's 'hoote lustis' are purged by a sexually disabling wound 'thorow the thycke of the thygh . . . And than he bled so faste that he myght not stonde' (333/24–334/3).[36] Gareth recovers to feel 'lyght and jocounde' again (335/1) but the wound is renewed in a reprise of the adventure. On both occasions the uncanny knight who wounds Gareth is killed by him, but is restored to wholeness by Lyones, even when Gareth hews his head in a hundred pieces and throws them out the window into the castle-ditch (335). The function of the fights is purely to let the young hero's blood, saving his energies for the field and the procreation of legitimate offspring. It is not until Gareth has planned the tournament on Assumption Day (in hot harvest-time) that Lyones uses her magic ointment to make him ' "as hole and as lusty as ever ye were" ' (342/17–18), so that his 'hote and corragyous' (335/15–16) person may be directed towards arms. Just before the tournament, Lyones gives Gareth a magic ring 'for grete love' (345/14–24). The ring has a triple function: it makes her more beautiful; it changes the colour of the wearer's appearance; and it prevents the wearer from losing any blood. Through the gift, Lyones converts her beauty in Gareth's eyes, which has previously led him out of his reason (331/19–24), into an influence that is now, as he says, 'passynge mete for me' (345/26), co-operating with the wish to win more tournament worship incognito, and preserving for that good purpose the blood which her sexual appeal had earlier threatened with waste. The ring is returned *after* the tournament, as if to show the correct priorities (352/6–13).

Through the recurring wound in his thigh, the story of Gareth speaks of a deep patriarchal fear as well as its reassurance. Whilst no knight is actually

---

[35] See Aristotle, *De Generatione Animalium*, 145–50. Cadden, *Meanings*, 133, points out that the father's capacity to concoct seed resides in his *heart*, a frequent word for knightly bravery in Malory.

[36] Perceval wounds himself in the thigh to punish his 'fleyssh' (919/10–17).

castrated in a battle in Malory, there is a further suggestive thigh wound in
the Grail story (990), and the Giant of St Michael's Mount is defeated after
Arthur 'swappis his genytrottys in sondir' (203/5–8), thereby punishing his
rapes of noble women and symbolically eliminating his line, as well as his
individual existence. If fighting can demonstrate the equation of noble birth
with noble deeds, defeat and mutilation can also render one's race forever
disparaged and unmanned.[37]

Class and gender anxieties in relation to combat can be seen also in
Malory's *Tristram*, with whose original *Gareth* shares some features.[38] In an
incident at the Tournament of Surluse (669/24ff), Lancelot disguises himself
as a damsel and overthrows Dynadan. Then strong 'coystrons' ('kitchen-
servants', 'base-born fellows')[39] carry off Dynadan into the forest,

> and there they dispoyled hym unto his sherte and put uppon hym a
> womans garmente and so brought hym into fylde . . . and whan quene
> Gwenyver sawe sir Dynadan ibrought in so amonge them all, than she
> lowghe, that she fell downe; and so dede all that there was.
> 'Well', seyde sir Dynadan, 'sir Launcelot, thou arte so false that I can
> never beware of the.' (669/30–670/4)

The tension of tournament ranking, now in its seventh day, is relieved by
this burlesque scene, like an antimasque. Nevertheless, the episode betrays
the source of the tension – an anxiety that defeat in battle will forfeit one's
place in the company of the 'gentle' and even one's maleness, transforming
the loser into a woman and one of the servile class. (As we have seen, it has
been part of Gareth's period of servitude to be so much under the power of
Lyonet, and her 'crafts' are again employed later to cool his 'hoote lustis'.)
Furthermore, if the well-nourished 'grete coystrons' are strong enough for
Dynadan, then the story of Gareth's prowess as a kitchen knave contains a
class fear as well as a jest uncomfortably close to truth. A further suspicion
that even one's knightly opponent may be 'false', wishing one ill under
cover of class solidarity – a frequent theme in the *Tristram* book – is also seen
in Dynadan's remark to Lancelot, the man who has symbolically deprived
him of class and gender power by putting him under the rule of servants
and dressing him as a woman.

---

[37] Other references include Alexander's remark (643/23–25) that he would rather 'kut away
my hangers' than have sex with Morgan.
[38] See Vinaver's comments in 1432ff.
[39] Brook's Glossary, 1712, *coystron*.

Holy and Unholy Blood: the Sankgreal and Balin

The discursive preoccupation with the vision of noble blood finds its overt religious expression in the story of the *Sankgreal* (Holy Grail/Royal Blood):

> 'I woote full well,' seyde sir Ector, 'what hit is. Hit is an holy vessell that is borne by a mayden, and therein ys a parte of the bloode of Oure Lorde Jesu Cryste. But hit may nat be sene,' seyde sir Ector, 'but yff hit be by a parfyte man.' (817/6–10)

Lancelot's imperfection is revealed on the Quest when he is granted ' "no power to stirre nother speke whan the holy bloode appered before me" ' (896/8–9), so that 'aftir that many men seyde hym shame' (895/1–2). The shame is all the greater, since one can consider this a failure to respect his *own* blood, as a direct descendant of Christ's family. In another sense, his fault is a kind of military defeat in that 'he had no power to ryse *agayne* the holy vessell' (894/36–895/1). One can compare Uwayne's defeat by Gawain: 'the knyght had no power to aryse *agayne* hym' (944/14). Lancelot's pseudo-sleep (894–895) approximates to Chrétien's Perceval's stupid tongue-tiedness before the Grail, and to his Erec's recreant complacency in marriage. Elsewhere in Malory, Palamides rides away from the sleeping King Mark, declaring proudly ' "I woll nat be in the company of a slepynge knyght" ' (591/1–6). As Trevisa explains, sleep withdraws the body's potential for action:

> whanne a man slepith is litil blood. And no wondir, for thanne kinde drawith it inward to helpe the vertu of kinde to worche by helpe of blood; and for the blood is fer withinne, the uttir parties beth bloodles anon.[40]

Like Chrétien's Perceval, Lancelot must repent of his sin, but like Erec, he understands his fault in terms of the loss of worship, and even of the knightly function itself:

> And whan sir Launcelot herde thys he was passyng hevy and wyst nat what to do. And so departed sore wepynge and cursed the tyme that he was bore, for than he demed never to have worship more. For tho wordis wente to hys herte, tylle that he knew wherefore he was called so.
> Than sir Launcelot wente to the crosse and founde hys helme, hys swerde, and hys horse away. And than he called hymselff a verry wrecch and moste unhappy of all knyghtes. (895/29–37)

Sin is punished in and through worldly shame as a knight: ' "myne olde synne hyndryth me and shamyth me" ' (896/1–9). Sin, specifically adultery, temporarily ranks Lancelot with the 'advoutrers' (adulterers) whom he

---

[40] *On the Properties of Things*, 151.

himself has said ' "be nat happy nother fortunate unto the *werrys*" '
(270/28–271/4). Although in an ideal sense the Grail story contrasts Lancelot's earthly worship with the shame of his spiritual delinquencies, the
text's method of working out his humiliation and redemption effectively
meshes the concepts of spiritual and secular prowess.

Galahad, last vessel of Christ's blood, is a human version of the Grail
itself. Significantly, he accomplishes his healing of the Maimed King by
anointing him with blood from the spear that has killed Christ (1031/8–15).
The blood of a spotless victim is necessary for such a miracle. Perceval's
virgin sister must bleed to death before the lady of a castle can be cured
(1002–05). But the theme of healing through blood has its darker side. In an
episode of the tale of *Balin*, linked to the *Sankgreal* book through many
prolepses and parallels, a knight requires some of the blood of the traitor
Garlon to heal his wounded son (82/20–27). Balin obtains it by killing
Garlon in King Pellam's castle – ' "Now may ye fecche blood inowghe to
hele youre son withall" ' (84/16–18). The episode occurs immediately
before, and as a thematic prelude to, the Dolorous Stroke, in which Balin
wounds the King with the Grail spear (shedder of Christ's blood) that
Galahad will use to heal him (84–85). In its crudeness, the act recalls Balin's
beheading of the 'Lady of the Lake' in Arthur's court (65–66), and appears
highly contrastive to the healings by blood performed by Perceval's sister,
and by Galahad on Pellam. The Dolorous Stroke is framed by allusions to
these solemn occasions in the later *Sankgreal* (82/9–14, 85/21–30). Balin's
casual invitation to 'fecche blood inowghe' is uttered in a place which holds
'parte of the bloode of Oure Lorde Jesu Cryste, which Joseph of Aramathy
brought into thys londe' (85/24–25). Balin, or rather Balin's *story*, is rebuked
by this comparison, as by others. Unlike Galahad, he prevents his damsel
from bleeding to death (82/6–8). But she is then killed in the destruction of
Pellam's castle by the Dolorous Stroke (85), in a manner proleptic of the
destruction of the sick lady's castle in the *Sankgreal*, where sinners will also
feel 'the vengeaunce of Oure Lorde' (1005/8–9) which Balin is told to expect
(86/3–6). As I have said above,[41] Balin's 'unhappiness' is communicated by
recurrent formal features of this kind, rather than through any analysis of
a faulty moral character. To be 'Balin' is to shed blood, or to staunch it, at
the wrong time or in the wrong way.

Balin's long series of misadventures culminates in the battle with his own
brother Balan, with its surfeit of wounds and blood:

> Soo they went unto bataille ageyne and wounded everyche other dole-
> fully, and thenne they brethed oftymes, and so wente unto bataille that
> alle the place thereas they fought was blood reed. And att that tyme ther
> was none of them bothe but they hadde eyther smyten other seven grete

[41] See Chapter 1, 21–22.

woundes so that the lest of them myght have ben the dethe of the
myghtyest gyaunt in this world.

Thenne they wente to batail ageyn so merveillously that doubte it was
to here of that bataille for the grete blood shedynge; and their hawberkes
unnailled, that naked they were on every syde. (89/26–36)

The honorific nature of combat discourse, which matches the praise heaped
on the brothers in more abstract terms (68/8–15, 92/13–15), is mutated here
by a sense of its misapplication. The blood is marvellous but also fearful
('doubte') to contemplate, and for once the praiseworthy reciprocity of the
fight, with its naked intimacy, parallellism and repeated 'either/other', is
overshadowed by the readers' unusual alienation from the fighters, in that
we know, and they do not, of a further intimacy, making this an 'unkyndely
werre' (973/28), setting brother against brother, blood against blood, almost
self against itself – Balin/Balan. The stasis of an honourable tomb is the only
end for such excess, and although it provides no absolute closure, further
adventures that arise must be for others: Gawain, Lancelot and Galahad
(58/13–59/10). For the end of this tragic story is the end of Balin's 'blood'
(family line): ' "We came bothe oute of one wombe, that is to say one moders
bely, and so shalle we lye bothe in one pytte" ' (90/26–28).

The story of Perceval's sister reveals a similarly strong connection between 'worship' and a true vision of noble blood. The maiden's blood, of
royal lineage, which alone can heal the sick gentlewoman through its
anointment, is imaginatively resembled to the holy oil of coronation and of
the last sacrament (1004/5–7). It seems a feminised counterpart to Galahad's healing of the Maimed King (1031/8–15). To bleed as Perceval's sister
does is to win or display many things: the highest heavenly honour –
salvation through martyrdom (1005/11ff); the highest earthly nobility - 'all
were of kyngys bloode' (1005/16–17); and a worship comparable to that of
the knight who bleeds in battle:

'Now', seyde sir Percivallis sister, 'fayre knyghtes, I se well that this
jantillwoman ys but dede withoute helpe, and therefore lette me blede.'
'Sertes', seyde sir Galahad, 'and ye blede so muche ye mon dye.'
'Truly,' seyd she, 'and I dye for the helth of her I shall gete me *grete
worship and soule helthe, and worship to my lynayge*; and better ys one harme
than twayne.' (1002/25–32)

In the semi-allegorised world of Malory's *Sankgreal*, the world of *holy* royal
blood, Perceval's sister's action is a new version of noble combat that does
not quite forsake the old, and although its effect is to prevent 'mortall warre'
(1003/4), the model of male secular fighting with its testimony to earthly
nobility is still apparent, and enhanced rather than discredited. One is
reminded of Caxton's Preface, with its easy juxtaposition of good fame and
the joy of heaven:

al is wryton for our doctryne, and for to beware that we falle not to vyce
ne synne, but t'exersyse and folowe vertu, by whyche we may come and
atteyne to good fame and renommé in thys lyf, and after thys shorte and
transytorye lyf to come unto everlastyng blysse in heven. (cxlvi)

The evil custom of this castle recalls others where all comers must fight
an inmate.[42] Perceval's sister is confronted with the sick lady who is
'brought forth' as if an opponent in combat (1003/9), and Galahad and his
fellows attempt to staunch her blood as if after a fight (1003/17–20).[43]
Tellingly, the episode is detached from any causal function in the story. For
the castle is destroyed and its entire population, including the healed lady,
struck 'dede by the vengeaunce of Oure Lorde' 'for bloode-shedynge of
maydyns' (1005/7–10); that is, for the very action which Perceval's sister
has determined to undergo. One might argue that in the mode of the
Sankgreal narrative such access to the symbolic confers greater honour, in
the way that Galahad is honoured by the allegorical significance of fights
which the sinful Gawain can only undertake in a worldly sense
(891/3–892/21). Certainly, this virgin receives much more honour than
Balin's damsel, who bleeds less, and without healing effect, and who is
destroyed herself through the Dolorous Stroke (81/19–82/14, 85/8–20). In
this respect, Perceval's sister is to Balin's damsel as Galahad is to the
'unhappy' Balin. But the combination of symbolic and fully 'transitive'
action, as seen in Galahad's later healings, is still denied the woman.[44] The
point of the incident, therefore, is vested mainly in its iconic properties,
amongst which the copious display of noble blood, as in a combat, is
foremost.

An episode such as this ideally invests the representation of blood-shed-
ding with a sacramental power that rebukes the carnal combats of earthly
chivalry. We remember that only Galahad can bear the shield on which
Joseph has shed some of his own (and therefore Christ's) blood (881/1–13).
But in the detail of narration the ideal distinction is blurred, and the traffic
of significance is reversible, so that the sign of blood can be lent a quasi-
religious force within the discourse of earthly knighthood. It is not surprising to find holy men like Evelake/Mordrains 'full of grete woundys'
(908/3–5), or Galahad served communion by Christ, 'that had all the
sygnes of the Passion of Jesu Cryste bledynge all opynly' (1030/2–5); these
figures are highly reminiscent of wounded Christs in contemporary English

---

42 Specifically, it may recall the island-castle in 'The Tale of Balin', 88ff.
43 For references to similar occasions, see Lancelot and Belleus, 200/8–13 and above, 61;
Brastias and Lancelot, 1076/9–13.
44 This point is made by Philippa Beckerling, 'Perceval's Sister: Aspects of the Virgin in the
Quest of the Holy Grail and Malory's *Sankgreal*' in Hilary Fraser and R.S. White, ed.,
Constructing Gender: Feminism and Literary Studies (Nedlands, W.A.: University of Western
Australia Press, 1994) 39–54, esp. 49–51. See also Chapter 6, 147–50.

devotional art.[45] But even Lionel, the 'murtherer', 'the rotyn tre', 'dry withoute vertu' (968/8–22), is epiphanised like the Man of Sorrows:

> So he [Bors] mette at the departynge of the two wayes two knyghtes that lad sir Lyonell, hys brothir, all naked, bowndyn uppon a stronge hakeney, and his hondis bounden tofore hys breste; and everych of them helde in theyre hondis thornys wherewith they wente betynge hym so sore that the bloode trayled downe more than in an hondred placis of hys body, so that he was all bloodé tofore and behynde. But he seyde never a worde as he whych was grete of herte. He suffird all that they ded to hym as thoughe he had felte none angwysh. (960/21–31)

This appreciative vision is no part of Bors' deceiving temptations, but a true occurrence to which Lionel later refers (969/11–19). In the French text, the point is that Bors chooses to save a virgin from rape rather than rescue Lionel, and in doing so 'must sacrifice (apparently) his blood relations'.[46] In Malory, the description looks like straightforward and heartfelt praise of Lionel, and we remember that this 'blood' is also Lancelot's, and therefore Christ's. As often, the discourse sets its own terms, with a disregard for the context of plot or allegorical value. There is no strict allegorical purpose in Malory here, nor even the conscious recurrence of a motif, but a strong ideological value is achieved through association and repetition, reliant on this text's cult of blood, and probably encouraged by its contemporary prominence both in genealogy and in religious art. Upon the temporal narrative of moral and political consequences, Le Morte Darthur superimposes the omnitemporal, sublime icon of the noble, wounded body.

The true vision of 'blood' was a crucial topic for Malory's century, in military, genealogical, medical and religious contexts,[47] and his story venerates in its blood-saturated combats and visions the prowess, nobility and piety of his heroes. And yet the prevalence of the theme also complicates Le Morte Darthur in several ways. While there can be no doubt that in the

---

[45] See Douglas Gray, Themes and Images in the Medieval English Religious Lyric (London: Routledge and Kegan Paul, 1972) 34 and Plate 2, 'O man unkynde' (British Library MS Additional 37049, f. 20r). See also Plate 5, 'The Charter of Christ' (British Library MS Additional 37049, f. 23r) and p. 130.

[46] Pauline Matarasso, The Redemption of Chivalry: A Study of the Queste del Saint Graal (Geneva: Droz, 1979), 157ff. For an English translation see The Quest of the Holy Grail, trans. Pauline Matarasso (Harmondsworth: Penguin, 1969) 187–88.

[47] For the religious motif of blood, see Gray, n. 45 above. A sumptuous genealogy of the period is that of Edward IV in BL MS Harl. 7353. See also Alison Allan, 'Yorkist Propaganda: Pedigree, Prophecy and the "British history" in the Reign of Edward IV' in C. Ross, ed., Patronage, Pedigree and Power in Later Medieval England (Gloucester: Alan Sutton; Totowa, NJ: Rowman and Littlefield, 1979) 171–92. It is interesting that a medieval reader has added blood to the illustration of Richard Beauchamp's fight with Sir Pandolf Malateste, in Pageant, Plate XIV. After celebrating Warwick's military career, including many single combats, the Pageant ends with two genealogical illustrations (Plates XXXIII and XXXIV).

consciousness of the *Morte* 'worshyp in armys may never be foyled' (1119/27–28), the theme of blood, as I have tried to demonstrate, points incidentally to the destructiveness and the waste, as well as the 'worship', of chivalric combat, Balin's fate as well as Lancelot's. It unconsciously opens to question the automatic connection of military success and power with noble birth, and accompanies with gruesome parody the holiest religious mysteries. Rather than functioning as a thematic grid or pattern, this volatile textual preoccupation always keeps the potential to 'prove' double and dangerous meanings in Malory. Rather than a conflict between or within individual knights, the discourse of blood contains a conflict between some of the text's major symbolic systems.

Wounds, Vision and Healing

Malory often expresses a practical acquaintance with wounds and their treatment: 'For as yett my woundis bene grene, and they woll be sorer hereaftir sevennyght than they be now' (624/13–14).[48] Even in his more religious contexts, wounds possess narrative importance through their corporeality rather than as abstracted symbols, in keeping with a text which calls the Holy Grail 'the rychyst thynge that ony man hath lyvynge' (793/32–33), and the beatific vision 'the spirituall thynges' (1034/22). The incurable physical wound becomes a potent recurring theme of malice, ignorance or spiritual blindness. Melyot, Tristram and Urré carry unhealed wounds through sorcery, while Balin, Balan and Uwayne (944–45), die of wounds they have received while unrecognised. To heal great wounds, conversely, requires a corresponding good will, and clear sight.[49] In the story of blind King Evelake, the *Sankgreal* provides a model of the link between true vision and healing, comparable in its loftier way to the religious faith Lancelot must possess to cure Urré. Evelake's blindness is caused by God – he has come too near the Grail (908/21–24) – but his wounds are from 'many persecucions the whych the enemyes of Cryst ded unto hym' (908/17–18). The two punishments, with their mixture of good and evil causes, will be cured simultaneously when the type of the true Judge appears:

> 'Fayre Lorde, lat me never dye tyll the good knyght of my blood of the nyneth degré be com, that I may se hym opynly that shall encheve the

---

[48] See details of the treatment of wounds in, e.g., 52/4–7, 234/18–21, 473/29–32, 1076/9–13. Wine is used to wash wounds and drunk to counteract blood-loss. See *On the Properties of Things*, 1078: 'drynke of wyn filleth soone the veynes ful of blood'.

[49] Gray, *Themes and Images*, 126–27: 'The author of the [Pseudo-Bonaventura] *Meditations* is always exclaiming "observe", "see", "behold", and insists that we should carefully regard each particular [of the Passion]'.

Sankgreall, and that I myght kysse hym.'

Whan the kynge thus had made hys prayers he herde a voyce that seyde, 'Herde ys thy prayers, for thou shalt nat dye tylle he hath kyssed the. And whan that knyght shall com the clerenes of youre yen shall com agayne, and thou shalt se opynly; and thy woundes shall be heled, and arst shall they never close.' (908/25–34)

In the specific allegorical terms of this passage, the beginning of the beatific vision means the end of earthly punishment, the one opening as the other closes, but the power of similar reference is more general in the *Sankgreal* and in the rest of Malory. The convention of sin as wounds inflicted on Christ, and of Christ and confessors as spiritual physicians, is common in later medieval religious writing.[50] The *compunctio* of a penitent sinner is a stinging wound, which must be healed by grace.[51] The confessor 'searches' (probes) wounds, the penitent 'discovers' (uncovers) sins. Lancelot's confessor urges him to ' "hyde none old synne frome me" ' (897/10). Nacien's presumption in drawing the Sword with the Strange Girdles, against his better knowledge of the writing on it, causes both the breaking of the sword and his own wounding (988–89), and 'Pelles" knight is maimed for too great 'hardynes' (989–90) in this connection. Such wounds come from a kind of blindness – wilfulness or ignorance – and sins cause spiritual blindness, as a hermit tells Lancelot:

'Well', seyde he, 'seke ye hit ye may well, but thoughe hit were here ye shall have no power to se hit, no more than a blynde man that sholde se a bryght swerde. And that ys longe on youre synne, and ellys ye were more abeler than ony man lyvynge.' (927/12–16)

True vision of the noble blood is, therefore, more a matter of the 'herte' and spiritual inclination than of ordinary sight or knowledge.[52] The Holy Grail is eventually taken from the sight of Logres for this reason:

'Therefore thou must go hense and beare with the thys holy vessell, for this nyght hit shall departe frome the realme of Logrus, and hit shall nevermore be sene here. And knowyst thou wherefore? For he ys nat served nother worshipped to hys ryght by hem of thys londe.'

(1030/23–27)

To see with the eyes is the outward accompaniment of an interior

---

[50] See Gray, *Themes and Images*, 133ff; *The Riverside Chaucer*, *Pardoner's Tale*, 472–76, 709; *Parson's Tale*, 59ff. For Christ as knight, confessor and physician, see R.T. Davies, *Medieval English Lyrics* (London: Faber, 1963) no. 51: 'I am Jesu that cum to fight'.

[51] See Catherine La Farge, 'The Hand of the Huntress: Repetition and Malory's *Morte Darthur'* in Isobel Armstrong, ed., *New Feminist Discourses* (London: Routledge, 1992) 263–79, esp. 270.

[52] See also Chapter 6, 145.

'observance' of the heart, whose importance I discuss at length in a later chapter.[53] The obvious paradigm is attendance at religious worship, and the Grail visions are like intensified moments of eucharistic liturgy, but the process also resembles the 'worshipping' (honouring) of knightly prowess very closely.[54] It is the best who 'serve and worship' the best. And the best are given an authoritative judging role that resembles God's. Arthur is 'sette on hyght uppon a chafflet to beholde who ded beste' (1069/8–9),[55] like Chaucer's Theseus, 'right as he were a god in trone'.[56] A happy closure depends on a clear vision that sees 'opynly'.[57] The perfection of this vision comes at Galahad's death: ' "thou shalt se that thou hast much desired to se" ' (1034/19–20). Galahad sees God because God looks openly at him in the beatific vision.[58] And all Malorian greatness is registered in this way, as either subject or object of sight. Lancelot's death, we remember, is also a moment of special sight: the bishop sees it in sleep, while the dead Lancelot's face bears the sign of his own vision, 'he laye as he had smyled' (1258/16). This, in turn, is celebrated in the eyes of others, with an amplification of the original singular vision similar to the expansion of honorific speech and writing about knightly greatness:

> And ever his vysage was layed open and naked, that al folkes myght beholde hym; for suche was the custom in tho dayes that al men of worshyp shold so lye wyth open vysage tyl that they were buryed.
>
> (1258/30–33)

Healing and Wounding: Closure and Renewal

At the beginning of his reign, the 'Lady of the Lake' gives Arthur a sword to inflict wounds, and a scabbard that prevents them bleeding (52–54). These two objects might stand as images of the opposed yet complementary tendencies in Malory's narrative of fights. The ability to heal is often the more important: Excalibur is mighty, but of less worth than its scabbard (54/1–6). The gift of a sword alone, as in Balin's story, can mean 'grete harme' (68/8), and even a sword may serve more to heal than to wound, as in the Chapel Perilous. Wounds are noble, but to make knights ready to fight again, healings are essential, and given sacred status in major incidents at the Chapel Perilous, the Grail Castle and Camelot, whilst the broad

---

53 For further discussion of the 'herte' see Chapter 6, 145–47.
54 See above, Chapter 2, 53–55.
55 See also 518/24–26.
56 *Riverside Chaucer, Knight's Tale*, 2528–29.
57 See, e.g., 866/11, 908/27, 948/12.
58 This seems to me to be the implication in Malory, 1034–35. Matarasso, *The Redemption of Chivalry*, 198ff, is not sure if in the French *Queste* Galahad sees the face of God quite openly.

course of plot events towards the end of the *Morte* becomes increasingly governed by a pattern of woundings and healings. The Grail story contains several cases of divinely-inflicted wounds awaiting their cure, as we have seen. In *Launcelot and Guinevere*, Lancelot is wounded and healed four times himself, and then achieves a miraculous healing of the wounds of Urré. In the last book, Gawain, wounded twice in the head by Lancelot, dies of a third wound on the same spot sustained in the first battle against Mordred. And Arthur, although apparently fatally wounded by Mordred in the last battle, still tells Bedivere: ' "I wyll into the vale of Avylyon to hele me of my grevous wounde" ' (1240/32–34). The narrative impulse to the end is to undo or defer for as long as possible the consequences – political and bodily – of fighting, while still demanding the occurrence of noble 'deeds' and the wounds that prove them noble.

As earlier critics have noted, this cycle of openings and closures, whose paradigm is the wound, exists in another form in the recurrent departures and reunions of the Round Table and of individual knights errant.[59] Arthur lives in a state of tension, desiring his knights to win worship, yet anxious for their return, reluctant to see them go. As Mann puts it, commenting on the double sense of 'departe' as 'leave' and 'separate':

> we feel the poignancy of separation as an emotional pressure behind even the most routine of knightly departures. It also creates in us a corresponding yearning for that which negates separation, for 'wholeness' – both the wholeness of the individual person, and the wholeness of the Round Table in itself.[60]

The state of being 'holé togydirs' (864/5ff), as Arthur loves his company to be, is a version in the body politic of how the private body is made 'whole', i.e., 'healed' of its wounds. The same incident may comprehend both impulses towards unity. Lancelot undertakes the healing of Sir Melyot at the Chapel Perilous 'for he is a felow of the Table Rounde', and the outside of the Chapel is hung with the reversed shields of dead knights of Lancelot's acquaintance. The Arthurian ambience is strong. Conversely, Hallewes the Sorceress offers an unbalanced travesty of the healing impulse in her confession to Lancelot:

> 'and sytthen I myght nat rejoyse the nother thy body on lyve, I had kepte no more joy in this worlde but to have thy body dede. Than wolde I have bawmed hit and sered hit, and so to have kepte hit my lyve dayes; and dayly I sholde have clypped the and kyssed the, dispyte of quene Gwenyvere.' (281/15–20)

The wish to save and heal can go too far, just as one can bleed too much,

---

[59] See Lambert, *Malory*, 63ff.
[60] Mann, 'Knightly Combat', 332.

like the dead Gilbert, or Melyot, ' "that is sore wounded and never styntyth bledyng" ' (279/16–17). Hallewes wishes Lancelot dead, so as to 'keep' his body, in what appears a grim parody of Arthur's and Guenevere's wish to 'rejoyse' (possess) him as knight and lover. By contrast, the true 'making whole' of Melyot is accomplished because Lancelot obtains from the Chapel both the 'fayre swerde' (280/23) and a piece of the 'blody cloth that the woundid knyght was lapped in' (279/23–24), as if to signify the right balance between inflicting and staunching wounds.

So the ideal narrative episode in Malory envisions both the noble pleni- tude of bleeding and the joyful closure of 'wholeness' that permits new adventures, whereas either impulse taken singly brings an excess leading to stasis and death. In the latter books, the process seems seriously thrown out of balance. Lancelot's growing passion for Guenevere brings him several wounds both difficult to heal and worryingly misfortunate in their consequences: from Bors (1072), the lady huntress (1104–05) and even himself, when he cuts his hand on the bars of Guenevere's bedroom window (1131). Commensurate with that, his growing need to 'save' Gue- nevere wounds some he would not have wished to harm, especially in the great 'unhap' of Gareth's death. More and more, as the story continues after the Grail Quest, it is only in the marvellous and unmotivated episodes, such as the healing of Sir Urré, that the full redress for wounds and recovery of wholeness can be properly found.[61]

Yet before the healings of the *Sankgreal* and *Launcelot and Guinevere*, and before the unhealable wounds of the dolorous last book are inflicted, *Le Morte Darthur* introduces a massive section – *The Book of Sir Tristram de Lyones* – in which the joys of combat are celebrated almost beyond limits. My next two chapters turn to that work.

---

61 See Robert L. Kelly, 'Wounds, Healing and Knighthood', who contrasts one pattern of knightly deterioration in Lancelot's wounds with another of his knightly perfection, culminating in the healing of Urré.

4

Good and Ill Will (1):
The Book of Sir Tristram

'. . . hit sleyth myne harte to hyre this tale.' (699/28–29)

As I have argued in the preceding chapters, Malory's deepest narrative interest and his most important discourse are centred on combat prowess. It is a paradox, then, that the *Book of Sir Tristram de Lyones* should articulate most fully the many issues relating to combat, yet be amongst the least studied sections of Malory's work. This notable critical neglect indicates the disappointment of modern readers' search for a unifying *conjointure* and explicit *sen* in the paratactic mass of *Tristram* episodes. Simply because *Tristram* is mainly preoccupied with descriptions of fighting, and offers relatively little in the way of an explicit master-theme, a good third of Malory has met with limited critical appreciation. Even Vinaver, its most learned reader, sees the book as more or less a failure:

> As for the *Book of Sir Tristram* as a whole, it remains true that in reinter-
> preting the story in his own way, as each medieval writer had done before
> him, Malory failed to give it a meaning, a *sen*, capable of supporting its
> complex and delicate narrative frame. He failed above all to grasp and
> bring out the tragic theme . . . Mark is Tristram's overlord whom he
> respects, as he respects the bond of feudal service . . . Without this notion
> of an involuntary breach of a sacred tie the traditional *données* of the
> legend cannot survive. (lxxxviii)

I will not argue here that Malory does provide a tightly organised narrative or thematic *structure* for his Tristram book. As I have suggested above,[1] the demand for structure in Malory has looked in the wrong places, expecting novelistic connections, formal patterns and explicit themes, whereas discursive formulations and the often unstated ideological as-sumptions behind them – 'what goes without saying' – provide what is most structured in Malory. One could even say, especially in the case of the *Tristram*, that these are more important cohesive elements than ordinary

---

1 Chapter 2, 39.

notions of plot. Malory's 'patterns', and even much of his intrigue, are like the tracks of strong habit, articulated more tellingly in practice than in the idealist utterances his practice sometimes follows, sometimes contradicts. The *Tristram* as Malory tells it is interconnected mainly by the sheer regularity of its narrative preoccupations and their language. It has the consistency of the successive 'days' of a particular, professional life and its outlook, rather than of a book conceived as totalising artistic statement. This is not to say, of course, that his *Tristram*, so obviously a fabulation, 'mirrors' any life, only that it seems to reveal piecemeal the confused but distinct mind-set which would prompt its writing in the first place.

Of the named sections, the eight 'books' in Vinaver's edition of the Winchester manuscript, this is by far the longest and the most loosely episodic. The kindest overall judgement, Larry D. Benson's, is 'lively and leisurely'.[2] Others have been less patient: the young Vinaver, speaking of Caxton's version, referred to 'the ponderous jumble of blindly transcribed stories'.[3] Even Malory may have felt his material excessive at times, especially when it related to lesser figures: in his own words, 'for to tell batayle by batayle hit were overmuche to reherse' (647/31–32). Indeed, in the Aristotelian sense of a plot as a connected action of a length to be taken in by the memory, with a beginning, a middle and an end, *Sir Tristram* definitely disappoints. Few modern readers would remember the story in detail without laborious notation, and if the beginning seems orthodox enough, its middle and end are a surprise, especially to those familiar with other versions. Malory's original, the French prose *Tristan*, had, in Vinaver's words, 'shifted the emphasis from the original story of tragic love to the protagonist's adventures in the service of the Round Table' (1443). Malory mainly concurred in this. Relatively few of his pages deal with the love between Tristram and Isoude, and though their deaths are mentioned often, they are never directly narrated. Instead, after the christening of Sir Palamides, an event about halfway through the French source, he announces:

> Here endyth the secunde boke off syr Trystram de Lyones, whyche drawyn was oute of Freynshe by Sir Thomas Malleorré, Knyght, as Jesu be hys helpe. Amen.
> But here ys no rehersall of the thirde booke. (845)

The manuscript moves on to the Holy Grail story, and we get almost no more of Tristram.[4]

The form of the book is therefore elusive, and, in any case, since the

---

2 Benson, *Malory's Morte Darthur*, 109.
3 E. Vinaver, *Le Roman de Tristan et Iseut*, 20: 'ses [Malory's] procédés littéraires qui . . . per cent à travers le lourd fatras des récits aveuglément recopiés'.
4 Vinaver, 1443–44 and 1531–32 explains that Malory's source for the 'thirde booke' contained another version of the Grail story, to which Malory preferred the French *Queste*.

Winchester manuscript has some of the characteristics of a fifteenth-century miscellany,[5] what constitutes a 'book' in Malory is hard to define. Some, like Book III (of Lancelot) or Book IV (of Gareth), cohere around the adventures of an individual. The *Sankgreal* (Book VI) is easily seen as a separate quest-tale. Books I and II deal with the foundation and extension of Arthur's rule, as Book VIII deals with its end. All these have some temporal or thematic unity. But *Tristram* (Book V), which the Winchester manuscript calls two books (following the French originals) and Caxton five, is unlike all of these. Although Tristram is its protagonist, many other figures – Palamides, Lancelot, Lamerok, La Cote Mal Tayle and Alexander – challenge him for attention. His adventures and life story are certainly foregrounded, but scarcely dominant and often lost to sight. After one of the long tournament descriptions Malory even seems forced to re-emphasise just who is his main subject:

> Now turne we from this mater and speke of sir Trystram, of whom this booke is pryncipall off. And leve we the kynge and the quene, and sir Launcelot, and sir Lamerok. (670/28–31)

In consequence, when we look for something to bind the *Tristram*'s many episodes together, we find not one quest but a plethora of quests, conversations, casual passes at arms, tournaments and rescues, overlapping and intertwining with each other, and all with little sense of a shaping chronology. As Elisabeth Pochoda says, narrative events occur in a kind of timeless 'aevum', replacing the apocalyptic time and eternity of St Augustine with 'a sense of the infinite continuity of the world', an 'endless sempiternity with past and future'.[6] The time of narration, the time taken to read, establish principally a sense of duration rather than progress. In Aristotelian terms, *Tristram* seems to aspire to the condition of an endless 'middle' without thought of closure. For instance, we see the story pass smoothly over much the same words (426/7–11) that later signal the end of the more time-conscious *Launcelot and Guinevere*. The narrative spills over its potential divisions, in a victory for the 'proairetic', the 'code of actions', over the 'hermeneutic', the 'code of enigmas and answers' which permits the assessment of story event as meaningful within given structures.[7] In Malory's fundamentally paratactic style, made of a potentially endless series of 'ands', foregoing the privileging and subordination of the periodic sentence, something *more* can always happen. Barthes' 'dilatory space', in which hermeneutic control is anticipated but suspended, seems to extend

---

5   See Cherewatuk, above, Chapter 2, 43.
6   See Pochoda, *Arthurian Propaganda*, 38.
7   For 'proairetic' and 'hermeneutic' and their definitions, see the discussion in Peter Brooks, *Reading for the Plot* (Oxford: Clarendon Press, 1984) 18ff, relating to Roland Barthes, *S/Z: Essai* (Paris: Seuil, 1973) 81ff.

without limits.[8] The *Tristram* well resembles Patricia Parker's view of romance as

> a form which simultaneously projects the end it seeks and defers or wanders from a goal which would mean among other things the end of the quest itself [9]

though in this case the projected end, whilst theoretically important to the evaluation of events, seems less powerful than the need to prolong and divert the adventures far beyond what can reasonably be called a 'quest'. As Parker adds, 'the Questing Beast of Malory . . . is in many ways a subtle parody of the quest itself'.[10] Corinne Saunders has brilliantly shown that hunting in *Tristram* is an emblem of its 'continuous movement, repetition and circularity' and helps create a book 'not of conclusion, finality and death, but of process, continued action and lack of closure'.[11] The attempt to make a meaning out of this theoretically interminable and apparently unperfected series is therefore fraught with unusual difficulties. And yet for all this, the *Tristram* is not basically unlike the rest of Malory; in the most important things it is very much the same. It is only that we must read it without the help offered elsewhere by a more cohesive (at least a shorter) intrigue, which can more easily be summarised and thematised in the way modern critics like. Instead, the reader of *Tristram* must discover the book's moods and tendencies, prejudices and principles, by living with it, as if with a household, over its long duration of 'days'.

Larry D. Benson's concept of a 'thematic structure', 'proving' the hero's attainment of full knighthood, remains the simplest and most attractive of the unifying readings of *Tristram*. For Benson, the story moves in 'elegant' fashion towards the ending of each of its two books, the meeting of Tristram with Arthur and the eventual christening of Sir Palamides, simultaneously testing and displaying, in both a courtly and Christian context, the excellence of its protagonist. The story is seen as part biography, part thematic pattern, with an interlacing of themes. The bracketing episodes and structural parallels serve to establish a sense of significant analogies to Tristram's progress, so that the adventures of a single knight are extended to comprehend the adventures of every knight in one coherent work.[12] Benson's

---

8   See Brooks, *Reading for the Plot*, 18; Parker, *Inescapable Romance*, 220–21.
9   Parker, *Inescapable Romance*, 173. See also Jill Mann, *The Narrative of Distance, The Distance of Narrative in Malory's Morte Darthur* (The William Matthews Lectures, London: Birkbeck College, 1991) 2: 'the sense of movement *away from* is always stronger than the sense of movement *towards*; we know what the knight is leaving but are not sure what he is going to'.
10 Parker, *Inescapable Romance*, 173.
11 Corinne Saunders, 'Malory's *Book of Huntynge*: The Tristram Section of The *Morte Darthur*', *Medium Aevum* LXII, 2, 1993, 270–84, see 280–81.
12 Benson, *Malory's Morte Darthur*, Chapter 6, esp. 114–28.

analysis is truly elegant, but seems to filter the rambling narrative very selectively. Read like this, few stories would lack a unitary structure. It is hard to see how the subtraction or addition of material would alter Benson's assessment, since all conflicting episodes could be described as contrasts, and all similar ones as buttressing parallels.[13] The theme required to be 'proved' is very general – Tristram's worthiness in knighthood. No one could deny that it is proved. What may confuse us is that it should need to be proved so often, and that so many other things are proved in this text that rejoices in plenitude – restatement, repetition, and, as I discuss below, negation of former incident.

There have been several attempts other than Benson's to supply *Sir Tristram* with a controlling order, for instance those of the Lumiansky school, with their misguided appeal to a unity dependent on a self-enclosed plot, coherent motivation, and naturalistic and consistent presentation of character – the premises, in other words, of the usual criticism of the realist novel. Beverly Kennedy, much more helpfully, stresses the comparative element in the episodes, and assesses differences in knightly behaviour by the codes of conduct drawn from contemporary chivalric manuals.[14] Within the *Tristram*, as within the other books of the *Morte*, there are many behavioural inconsistencies, and these elicit a wide variety of modern critical opinions. The same text which Benson sees as demonstrating Tristram's full knighthood Kennedy sees as implying his inferiority to a true knight such as Lancelot.[15] The critical variance shows us, perhaps, that 'knighthood' is a broad term in Malory, even a 'clean' knighthood like Tristram's (760). This is a 'practical' chivalry, as Vinaver said, not well suited for exemplary purposes, especially in the highly moralised terms of writers like Ramon Lull. (It is sometimes forgotten how much the emphasis on individual good conduct in the manuals is a distraction from the material political and economic basis of knighthood.[16] Men did not become knights simply to obtain opportunities for doing good to society.) Just as the *Tristram*'s knights are not displayed in a unitary, organic narrative structure, but in a vast collation of stories, its knighthood is not presented as a pure, elemental thing, but as a pragmatic compound of varying political, economic and military requirements. My reading acknowledges the co-existence of many apparent contradictions in knightly behaviour, but treats these more as requirements of the story's 'needs of meaning' than as exemplary studies of misconduct in individuals. In the interpretation that follows, I have tried to analyse the habitual structures of 'proof' in the text, the discursive

---

[13] See also above, Chapter 1, 15–16; Riddy, *Sir Thomas Malory*, 86–87.

[14] Kennedy, *Knighthood*, Chapter 4.

[15] For further discussion, see above, Chapter 2, 33.

[16] See, for instance, the consensual fantasy of 'the begynnyng of cheualry of knychthed' in *The Book of the Ordre of Chyvalry*, 14–16.

revelation of those features of ideology that keep it going, rather than to
concentrate on character, or to construct an overarching thematic structure.
If, as I think, 'theme' is too broad, and the ideal of chivalric conduct too
narrow a guide to Malory, it is even more necessary to describe those other,
smaller features which continue independently to leave their traces in the
text. Rather than trying to fit the rambling narrative (implicitly seen as
deficient) to the structures of a unifying theme or code, we can better
understand its effects of discontinuity and inconsistency as moments which
highlight the gap between these fields of discourse and the story-events,
and therefore as moments in which the inadequacy of normal 'chivalric'
interpretations is often revealed.

The *Tristram*'s non-apocalyptic view of time, its relatively slight 'sense of
an ending' (Benson has identified all there is) seem to co-exist with a
narrative desire to prolong, even to resist, the process of getting there. In
major part, the idealising and moralising response of most *Tristram* critics
arises from their wish to compensate for the story's lack of progress either
towards closure or the building of a clear *sen*.[17] There are two possible
reactions to this narrative feature: our difficulty, as modern readers, in
keeping track of the story and in finding its shape may involve us even more
closely in seeking an idea of its unifying ethos. In searching for the connec-
tive principle of these many episodes, even as an apparently neutral quest
for the story's aesthetic form, one may easily begin to repair the chivalric
themes that at first sight have seemed so ragged. Another approach, and
the one I take here, is to accept the massive dilation of event and the strong
resistance to closure as irreducible features of the *Tristram*, distinctive
narrative achievements rather than evidence of structural failure. The repeated narrative situations, including the means by which their renewal is
achieved, can then become in themselves the chief object of study. Such an
approach will lead us immediately back to the book's dominant subject-
matter, which its repetitive structure was born to serve – knightly combat.
In the previous chapter, I have discussed some of the principal thematics of
combat discourse. Now I emphasise the specific importance to *Tristram* of
a further set of issues fed by and clustered around the continually reiterated
narrative 'proof' of the difference in military power between individual
knights. Amongst these issues are the economic and political implications
of fighting, the need to cope with defeat as well as success, and prudent
ways of behaviour towards military superiors and inferiors. The *Tristram*
demonstrates the power of knightly 'means' in many contexts – military,
political and social – and the power of fellowship and good will. Equally,
however, the narrative continually introduces episodes displaying envy, the
ill will knights hold towards each other as hostile competitors. The problem
of envy will come to provide the central topic of the ensuing discussion.

[17] For related discussions of Malory reception see Introduction, xvi–xvii; Chapter 2, 36–37.

The Resistance to Closure (I): Economics and Politics

David Aers has usefully reminded us that later medieval English knights were more given to amassing property and the exploitation of surplus capital than to fighting,[18] and it is clear that land and money are as strong a motive throughout the *Tristram* story as they were in the lives of established and aspiring fifteenth-century families.[19] Young Tristram comes to prominence through his decision to fight Marhalt for the 'trwayge' of Cornwall (376). For this, he is horsed, knighted and armed at Mark's expense 'on the beste maner that myght be gotyn for golde othir sylver' (379/29–31). He keeps Marhalt's sword and shield as trophies. In Ireland, La Beale Isoude offers him horse and armour to participate in a tournament at which the prize is a lady: 'And what man wanne her, foure dayes after sholde wedde hir and have all hir londis' (385/22–24). Isoude is impressed by Tristram's prowess, and eventually offers him what is ostensibly the wardship of her marriage, but implicitly herself as betrothed (392/13–16). Back in Cornwall, Tristram revisits his family 'And than largely kynge Melyodas and his quene departed of their londys and goodys to sir Trystrames' (393/7–9). He immediately begins an affair with another woman, the wife of Sir Segwarides. A good knight's reward in this tale is much more than an appreciation of his 'worthiness'. It is political and financial security, with other incidental perks, achieved through inheritance, patronage, military success and marriage. Many of the apparently playful narrative incidents make more sense in this social and economic light. Abductions of women occur, by worshipful knights like Bleoberis (396ff), as well as by scoundrels such as Sir Brunys Saunce Pité. Another interesting case is the forbidding of a female neighbour to marry, whether for love or some other reason.[20] 'Love' and enlightened self-interest are impossible to separate in this context. La Beale Alys, a prominent character, is described as 'passynge fayre and ryche, and of grete rentys', and frankly offers herself as a combat prize: ' "what knyght may overcom that knyght that kepyth the pyce of erthe shall have me and all my londis" ' (645). Tristram's passion for La Beale Isoude is strangely intermittent when other rewards are offered him.[21] Her love for him is stimulated by her sense of his military power and Mark's obvious lack of it, as much as by the love-potion and what it represents. We

---

[18] David Aers, *Chaucer, Langland and the Creative Imagination* (London: Routledge and Kegan Paul, 1980) Chapter 1, esp. 10–14.

[19] See, e.g., *Paston Letters*, passim.

[20] 640/7, where the blocked marriage is Malory's addition; 664, where the oppressed lady offers Palamides herself and all her current and heritable lands as an inducement to fight for her.

[21] See Vinaver, 1447. See also Dhira B. Mahoney, ' "Ar ye a knight and ar no lovear?": the Chivalry Topos in Malory's Book of Sir Tristram' in K. Busby and N.J. Lacy, ed., *Conjunctures: Medieval Studies in Honour of Douglas Kelly* (Amsterdam: Rodopi, 1994) 311–24, esp. 317–20.

see also the taking of prisoners for ransom,[22] and that the delivering of prisoners may involve intercession and treaty as well as force of arms.[23] Even great knights are thrifty: Lamerok disdains the gift of the 'Isle of Servayge', but still impounds the horses and saddles of beaten tournament opponents, unless they are knights errant (598–600). The economic element in 'worshipfulness' is inventive and subtle, and emphasised by the repetition of similar incidents. The frequency of disguise and incognito in tournaments and knight errantry always permits new combats, even between established Round Table knights; though they have sworn to avoid fighting each other, the text can avail itself of a handy exception: 'but yf hit were that ony knyght at his owne rekeyste wolde fyght disgysed and unknowyn' (377/17–18). Fellowship, even of the Round Table, is not allowed to prevent the incidence of combats. Nor, as I have noted already, does the economic theme end with a hero's initial successes. He is periodically renewed as a 'poure arraunte knyghte', so that the story of merit rewarded can recommence.[24] Given the immense costs of maintaining a knight in arms, costs which had done away with knight errantry before Malory's time,[25] one suspects the recurring poverty of the heroes was originally a realist feature also, and it must also have represented a live concern to the cash-strapped knights of Malory's day. The cycle of (assumed) poverty and renewed reward becomes another force driving the *Tristram*'s perpetual motion.[26]

Most of the action in *Tristram* takes place away from the court, and hence well away from Arthur, who is forced to seek out and ride after his favourites. Critics have particularly blamed Arthur for failing to keep Tristram and Lamerok within his ambience, due to his inability to restrain Gawain and his bad brothers.[27] There is some force in the accusation if we feel obliged to consider the king's behaviour closely. Thinking instead of the requirements of the story, we might decide that there had to be some means of keeping the knights away from court for their adventures to continue as long as they do, and that this was a plausible way of providing it. With Tristram mainly away from Arthur, the conventional ending of his adventures through return and reward is much delayed, and can easily be renewed after a brief pause. Arthur is present only when required, usually as a tournament witness. The overall effect is to foreground the hero's knightly autonomy, with Tristram himself, separate from both Arthur and Mark, assuming a quasi-regal rule over his band of tournament adherents. In the *Tristram*'s ethos, a knight's prowess is mainly for himself, and he

---

[22] E.g., 597: Palamides' objections to ransom seem based on the fact that Morgan is capturing her liege lord Arthur's knights, not to the practice itself.

[23] See, e.g., Darras and Tristram, 551–52.

[24] See Chapter 2, above, 52.

[25] See Denholm-Young, 'The Tournament', 240.

[26] On the economic interests of 'genuine' knights, see Keen, *Chivalry*, 230–33.

[27] See, e.g., Thornton, 'The Weakening of the King', 5–9.

carefully controls its reference to other centres of power. Tristram may want
to be with Arthur, but not until he is ready, for the essence of this story is its
wide scope for independent self-enrichment and self-promotion.[28]

The Resistance to Closure (II): Good Counsel Rejected

The text repeats on several occasions the following process: a knight re-
ceives or gives good counsel, then rejects it or is ordered to disregard it; he
then acts against the good counsel, yet suffers or causes no ultimate harm.
One is used to this event in chivalric romances when another's rejected
advice is purely a means of aggrandising the hero's eventual achievement.
So it may be when Governayle warns Tristram not to joust against two
Round Table knights, and the young knight is victorious (398/9–399/14).
But there are more troubling instances: Mark wants Tristram to encounter
Sir Lamerok at a tournament. Tristram is unwilling because 'hit were no
worshyp': Lamerok is too tired. But when Mark 'requires' Tristram, he
complies, and makes a temporary enemy of Lamerok by unhorsing him and
then refusing to fight on foot (428–29). Lamerok later sends Mark the
cuckold's horn, purely to spite Tristram. When they meet again, in a tight
spot on the Isle of Servayge, the two champions agree to 'forget' their
ill-will:

> 'But all youre malyce, I thanke God, hurte nat gretly. Therefore,' seyde sir
> Trystrames, 'ye shall leve all youre malyce and so woll I, and lette us assay
> how we may wynne worshyp betwene you and me.' (444/2–5)

One would think that this was to be a final narrative closure of reconciliation, but on the very next occasion they meet (quite typically of the
amnesiac Malory text) Tristram has changed again:[29]

> 'A, sir Lamerok!' seyde sir Trystram, 'well be we mette! And bethynke the
> now of the despite thou dedist me of the sendynge of the horne unto
> kynge Markis courte, to the entente to have slayne or dishonourde my
> lady, quene La Beall Isode. And therefore wyte thou well,' seyde sir
> Trystramys, 'the tone of us two shall dy or we departe.' (483/4–9)

Needless to say, neither dies, because they rediscover each other's virtues
as fighters and settle for a draw, in a flood of compliments, swearing never
to fight again (483–84).
What drives incidents like these is the need to negate closure so that the
same knights' encounter can occur an indefinite number of times, with the
same opportunities for combat display followed by reconciliation in fellow-

---

[28] Kennedy, *Knighthood*, 150–51, sees Tristram's desire to join Arthur as more pressing.
[29] For a discussion of this sequence, see Mann, 'Knightly Combat', 336–38.

ship. Paradoxically, in order to permit such opportunities, the narrative is incidentally required to make its worshipful characters deny their better instincts, or, if the reader prefers, to reveal the competitive violence under their veneer of fellowship.[30] So Malory must include both the Tristram who acts sportingly and the Tristram who is unsporting, both Lamerok the peacemaker and Lamerok the spiteful, envious man. To be worshipful, the knights must think of honour. But to have the fights in which they win it, they must first forget their own honourable misgivings. Once more, there is a problem here, if we consider the psychology of individual characters: Tristram, for instance, will seem untrustworthy, even deceitful.[31] If we consider the story's requirements instead, things look differently: some aggression between the great is needed to set up their combats. This is clearly exemplified at the Tournament of Lonezep, where the same process of 'requiring' permits an otherwise impossible fight between Lancelot and Tristram. Arthur asks Lancelot, out of anger and revenge, to encounter with an unknown knight (Tristram) on a black horse (735). Lancelot demurs, as Tristram had before when Mark made a similar request, because the unknown knight is tired, but he is commanded to fight. The encounter sets up another occasion on which the two great knights can encounter each other, and combine to prove each other's prowess. In the process Arthur, otherwise so unlike Mark in 'conditions' (see 1173/21–25), is made to resemble him. Later in the same tournament, Lancelot fails to recognise Tristram again (through Palamides' treachery) and they fight 'longe togyders' until the moment comes:

> 'A, Jesu! what have I done?' seyde sir Launcelot, 'for now am I dishonoured'; and seyde, 'A, my lorde sir Trystram, why were ye now disgysed? Ye have put youreselff this day in grete perell. But I pray you to pardon me, for and I had knowyn you we had nat done this batayle.'
> . . . So all the peple on that one syde gaff sir Launcelot the honoure and the gre, and all the people on the othir syde gaff sir Trystram the honoure and the gre. (753/24–754/2)

As the symmetry of the result suggests, these narratives of mistake or forced rejection of one's better judgement are designed to produce a friendly outcome, leaving both combatants with equal honour and further narrative potential. The greatest fights, such as between Tristram and Lamerok, or Lancelot and Tristram, are unfinished and involve no deaths, as Merlin has earlier prophesied (72/5–11).[32] Those who carry out to the death hostile

---

[30] This effect of necessary inconsistency is evident elsewhere in Malory also. For example, Sir Damas is so evil and cowardly that he can find no champion, yet he has 'many a knyght' to lay in wait with him to capture others, and Arthur agrees to fight for him rather than to die in prison (138–40).

[31] See Maureen Fries, 'Indiscreet Objects of Desire' in Spisak, *Studies in Malory*, 87–108.

[32] See Chapter 1, 23.

intentions against good knights are, in fact, the murderers: Gawain, Mark, Andret. Their closure of another's potential for more adventures is the worst crime such a narrative can imagine, especially when the potential is great. Tristram's or Lancelot's incidental killing of some also-ran can be overlooked, but Gawain's killing of Lamerok can not be. A special quality of Lamerok, Lancelot and Tristram is their frequent (not constant) attempt to win worship without causing ultimate shame or harm to others of 'name' (excluding invading enemies like Marhalt and Elias). The text seems to have sought in these knights' adventures a way of continuance, a knightly mean between the equal respect and hatred spawned by the competitive evaluations of chivalry. No doubt this is also connected with the practical need not to offend the powerful families of opponents. Tristram's long imprisonment by King Darras for killing his sons, in however 'knightly' a fashion, carries an obvious warning, and Tristram acknowledges the political realities involved: ' "ye have done to us but as a naturall knyght ought to do" '. (552/30–32)

The Resistance to Closure (III): Proverbs and Repetition

Along with the wish to keep the story open-ended goes a feeling for relativity of values and practical wisdom, expressed in many proverbs: 'he that hath a prevy hurte is loth to have a shame outewarde' (396/15–16); 'that knyght nother horse was never fourmed that allway may endure' (429/22–24); ' "here may a man preve, be he never so good yet may he have a falle; and he was never so wyse but he myght be oversayne, and he rydyth well that never felle" ' (516/2–6); ' "hit is ever worshyp to a knyghte to refuse that thynge that he may nat attayne" ' (581/24–26); ' "manhode is nat worthe but yf if it be medled with wysdome" ' (700/18–19). The ideal of surpassing prowess is alloyed with this more canny set of values, enabling knights to cope with losing, as well as winning, and above all to permit continuity. There can always be another 'day' for the losers.[33]

One can also note in the *Tristram* a marked tendency towards repetition and recapitulation of the same incidents, as if the text were regretful that the time for narrating them had gone. Lamerok's death, the great crime of the book, is recounted many times in conversation, and with additional details, fixing Gawain's 'name' henceforth.[34] Tristram's fight with Marhalt receives similar treatment, as if Malory were unwilling to let go for very long of Tristram's definitively worshipful action.[35] We see enacted here the

---

[33] See the further discussion of proverbs below, 112.
[34] 688, 691, 698, 699, 716 and, later, 1190.
[35] See in Kato, *Concordance*, under 'Marhalt/Marhalte'.

self-renewing reputation the *Morte* attaches to deeds of arms: '[he] dud passyngely well, that dayes of hys lyff the worship wente never frome hym' (75/29–30). With its undirected path, and copious adventures, the idea of progress in the *Tristram* is always qualified by the wish to restate the past, either directly, or in the generation of new events that resemble the old. There may be inconsistency, but there is little growth in chivalric character or outlook, only additional and more complex chances to display what is clear enough already in terms of theme.

The narrative structure that serves such an end is therefore not one of thematic closure, but of opportunistic prolongation. A perfect instance of this is the role of Sir Brunys Saunce Pité, sporadically reintroduced into the action. Not so much a single person as a commonly observed feature of the forest wildlife, Sir Brunys, disguised under his many spellings, never functions for longer than one episode at a time, but always gets away to prepare for his next appearance.[36] He pushes to reprehensible extremes the *Tristram's* penchant for guile, anonymity and reckless aggression, so removing scrutiny from worshipful knights' actions, which occasionally resemble his own. Sir Brunys' function as a common enemy also usefully links otherwise separate groups of knights errant into temporary fellowships. He is a perfect instrument both for linear narrative extension and for cross-linking, and it is this above all that seems to determine his very patchy career.[37]

The love of repetition sometimes extends into dialogue, where in particular speeches knights will labour a single word like 'custom', 'play' or 'adventure', offering thematic stress and acknowledging their shared viewpoints. At such times, one almost gains the impression that the incidents occur mainly so that the characters can talk about them.[38] A single broad conclusion can be drawn from all these related narrative features: what structures Malory's work is not a series of fixed outcomes corresponding to a probative pattern, but a number of related narrative practices and tendencies which either prolong the story, or effectively unmake it as fast as it is made, so that it can be told again. Instead of keeping the characters' actions within the limits of consistent chivalric values, Malory is prepared to deny the apparent requirements of those values (at the cost of many apparent 'inconsistencies') in order to permit the same story to continue. So great is this need, apparently, that when the strategies of disguise, accident and feudal obligation are not available to achieve it, the text is willing to tolerate the incidental admission of malice, envy and ill will, even in its most worthy personages. An irony lies in the effect this produces: for in order to

---

36 His last appearance, 820, is, characteristically, in flight.

37 See, e.g., 560ff, where Brunys' attack on Palamides is encountered by Tristram; 683–87, where, through Brunys, three separate groups meet and lament Lamerok's death: Palamides/Bleoberis/Ector, Perceval, Harry.

38 See 417/11–22, 445/13–25, 798/33–799/16.

prolong the narrative for the sheer pleasure of celebrating 'clean knight-hood' Malory was unconsciously led to testify to the flaws in the chivalric ethos. The *Tristram* releases multiple possibilities, several Tristrams, several Palamides,[39] not often simultaneously, in the manner of the psychological novel, but sequentially, or alternately, in its sequence of episodes. In his remarking of the alternation of good and evil in Malory, it may be that the shrewdest critic of *The Book of Sir Tristram* is its first, William Caxton, who wrote in 1485 'herein may be seen noble chyvalrye, curtosye, humanyté, frendlynesse, hardynesse, love, frendshyp, cowardyse, murdre, hate, vertue, and synne.' In finding the unrestricted narrative means to celebrate the virtues of knighthood, the *Tristram* was forced to display its vices also. Amongst these, the chief is envy.

Envy

Ideally, 'worshyp in armys may never be foyled' (1119/27–28), but envy always lurks behind the military pageant of the *Tristram*. There is the treacherous hatred of Mark and his satellites for Tristram, and the Orkney brothers' hatred of Lamerok. Ill will, whether possessed by rival kin-groups, treacherous lords and vassals, or merely competitive fellow-knights, continually bursts out. More than the other books of Malory, this one shares its attention amongst many great figures: Tristram, Lancelot, Lamerok, Palamides, La Cote Mal Tayle, Alexander and others. *Tristram* is often a book of 'communitas' and fellowship,[40] or at least of knights keeping company, and is studded with collective occasions, especially tournaments. But it is also for that reason, and all the more powerfully, a story of singular, 'prevy' yearnings.[41] In theory, treachery should exist only amongst the bad – ' "evermore o good knyght woll favoure another, and lyke woll draw to lyke" ' (527/5–7). But in habitual narrative practice – and in such a long book there is always the stream of habit to erode individual narrative assertions – envy and hatred find a place almost routinely in courts and chivalric fellowships. Tristram's step-mother, though daughter of Howell of Brittany (373/15), tries to poison Tristram 'because her chyldir sholde rejoyse his londe' (374/12). Two of Isoude's ladies have 'ordayned for hate and envye for to distroy dame Brangwayne that was mayden and lady unto La Beale Isode' (419/28–29). Malory has altered the French story here, in which Isoude is behind the plot (1464/n.419.27–28), but still left in the

---

[39] See Riddy, *Sir Thomas Malory*, 56–59 for a view of multiple identity in Lancelot's adventures.

[40] Ibid., 111. Archibald, 'Malory's Ideal of Fellowship', 317ff, contrasts 'fellowship' with the less bonding notion of 'company'.

[41] See Riddy, *Sir Thomas Malory*, Chapter 4, esp. 94ff.

impression that jealousy and envy easily lead to acts of malice. We might think of Palamides' envious behaviour, including killing his opponent's horse (739/5–9) and riding over a fallen knight, as attributable to his jealous nature. But even figures such as Galahalt and Bagdemagus arrange a tournament in Cornwall 'to the entente to sle syr Launcelot other ellys uttirly to destroy hym and shame hym, because sir Launcelot had evermore the hygher degré' (675/5–7). Vinaver's note (1508) partly explains how a condensation of the French original provided Malory with the materials for this treachery of two normally worshipful figures, but cannot do away with the impression the text gives that envy and malice are normal, the expected outcome of a 'name' like Lancelot's. (Malory's story may touch on history here: it has recently been suggested that 'we cannot be sure that the long list of notables killed in the lists does not include some well-concealed murders'.[42]) The division between the envious and the 'well-willers' amongst knights seems about equal, and not only in this section. In the final book, we are to learn that 'Whan they harde that kynge Arthure and sir Launcelot were at debate many knyghtes were glad, and many were sory of their debate' (1178/16–18).

Ill will is so common, even necessary, in Malorian representation, that it does not always need a strong motive, though some figures certainly have them. Mark has a well-founded personal grudge against Tristram, one would think, but his ill nature alone is motive enough for Malory. Mark's followers, such as Andret, have economic ambitions: 'he wolde have had sir Trystramys londis' (499/3–4). The vengefulness of Gawain and his bad brothers comes partly from the inherited family feud, partly from their apparently inherent 'conditions'. But the motive for ill will may be comparatively trivial, and, in keeping with Malory's love of a public ethos, is more likely to be so when the holder of a grudge is a surpassing figure, like Lamerok, Tristram or Lancelot. Lamerok sends the magic horn to Mark's court, which will prove Isoude's adultery (429ff), only in order to avenge a tournament fall, and Tristram responds in the same spirit: 'welle he [Tristram] knew that hit was done in the dispyte of hym, and therefore he thought to quyte sir Lameroke' (430/28–29). It is always unwise to annoy the great: when Sir Castor queries Lancelot's incognito, he is told ' "wyte you well, and ever hit lye in my power, I shall greve you, and ever I mete with you in my way!" ' (826/24–32).

Palamides also suffers from others' ill will and his own. He considers himself (whether justly or not Malory does not reveal) the victim of 'falsehod and treson' practised by Bors and Ector (528), and for his own part often shows 'hate' to Tristram, alternating between envy and admiration of the better knight's prowess. Burdened with this complex consciousness, Palamides is the most modern-seeming of Malorian figures, and becomes

---

[42] Barber and Barker, *Tournaments*, 146–47.

the principal focus for the study of envy where it is most acutely problematical, within the ranks of the worshipful themselves:[43] ' "mesemyth that ye ar a good knyght; and that ony other knyght that namyth hymselff a good knyght sholde hate you, me sore mervaylyth" ' (697/15–18). It may be marvellous, but it happens regularly. In his *Arthur and Lucius*, Malory had even laid it down as a principle that envy, at least in the sense of fierce competition, was inherent in the system,[44] and a source of bravery in battle, albeit a dangerous one:

> for oftetymes thorow envy grete hardynesse is shewed that hath bene the deth of many kyd knyghtes; for thoughe they speke fayre many one unto other, yet whan they be in batayle eyther wolde beste be praysed.
>
> (223/9–13)

If the urge to shine in battle causes envy, then battle is sometimes able to remove it. Tristram's own 'despite' and envy of Palamides (385/14–19) can be resolved by conquering him in a fair fight. He is relieved of ill will, but only by transferring the problem to his defeated opponent. Palamides is totally humiliated in tournament combat, first given a fall with the spear, then, as he shamefacedly leaves the field, engaged in a horseback combat with swords and again knocked from the saddle. He is forced, under threat of death, to forsake his suit to La Beale Isoude for ever, and to bear no armour or weapons for a year. For that period, Tristram effects on Palamides what Galahalt and Bagdemagus will seek for Lancelot, 'uttirly to destroy hym and shame hym' (675/5–7): ' "Alas," seyde sir Palomydes, "for ever I am shamed!" ' . . . So for dispyte and angir sir Palomydes kut of his harneyse and threw them awey' (388/19–22).

For the lesser fighters, since combat cannot purge them, anger, envy and hate are hard to lose. Consequently the very best knights always remain their targets. Reviewing Malory's notable figures of treachery or malice, the majority have a position by birth greater than their fighting prowess, and suffer from the disparity. Most are from royal families: Mark, Mordred, Aggravain, Gaheris, Gawain (whose fighting is frequently devalued in Malory), Galahalt, Bagdemagus, Meleagant. The defeat of Lot by the 'boye' Arthur (17/17–38) and the 'wytche' 'dreme-reder' Merlin (18/11–37) creates and emblematises a subsequent imbalance in Lot's descendants between birth and 'name' which only Gareth resolves worshipfully, by arms. The other brothers are driven into murder and 'prevy hate' (1161/12).

How to cope with being a lesser knight in such a competitive society,

---

[43] Southey, *The Byrth, Lyf and Actes of Kyng Arthur*, xv–xvi, was shocked by the behaviour of knights in the Tristram story: 'The characters also are in many respects discordant with themselves; and the fault, so frequent in such books, of degrading one hero to advance another, is carried here to great excess.'

[44] See Stephen Knight, *Arthurian Literature and Society*, 122–26.

where at each encounter one man must conquer and another 'have the worse', provides a deep social and psychological problem. The text tries to control it by asserting a supposed consensus that envy is only the property of the bad. Guenevere and Arthur, most fit to speak for the worshipful, sharply rebuke the envy of Palamides (749/15–19) and see him as 'false' for turning against a knight of his own side. Guenevere's universalising insistence shows how seriously the issue is perceived:

> 'for and hyt happyn an envyous man onys to wynne worshyp, he shall be dishonoured twyse therefore. And for this cause all men of worshyp hate an envyous man and woll shewe hym no favoure, and he that ys curteyse and kynde and jantil hath favoure in every place.' (764/27–31)

This statement is like many others in Malory, in that it is expressed as a permanent general truth, but really relates especially to the case in hand, and has limited applicability elsewhere. For Palamides cannot be written off as bad or merely 'hated', even by those to whom his envy has done most wrong. Instead, Lancelot and Tristram very often show him favour, and seem to battle to rescue his honour. And so does the text, which also likes to honour him as the 'good' or 'noble' knight:[45] 'And though he were nat crystynde, yet he belyved in the beste maner and was full faythefull and trew of his promyse, and well-condyssyonde' (717/11–13).

So we must perceive a contradiction here: Palamides can be sometimes envious yet stay 'good'. On the other hand, Tristram and Lancelot, though 'curteyse and kynde and jantil', do not find 'favoure in every place', nor can they, logically, given that the 'envyous man' apparently exists, and they are his most obvious targets. Guenevere's affirmation is self-contradictory, a benign wish covering a well-grounded social fear. The text says calmly elsewhere that 'sir Trystrams was nat so behated as was sir Launcelot, nat wythin the realme of Ingelonde' (675/31–33), that is, where Lancelot most resides. Tristram is more hated in Cornwall and Ireland. The most that courtesy can achieve is to *lessen* envy. The problem is in practice betrayed as systemic, the down-side of the economy of honour, rather than just a question of individuals' 'prevy' malice, whatever Guenevere (and Malory) prefer to think.

Analysis of an incident of treachery in the *Tristram* will illustrate this contention. Lamerok finds two knights 'hovyng undir the woodshaw', 'in a wayte uppon a knyght that slew oure brothir' (485–86).

> 'What knyght was that,' seyde sir Lamorak, 'that ye wolde fayne mete withall?'
> 'Sir,' they seyde, 'hit ys sir Launcelot that slewe oure broder, and yf ever

---

[45] E.g., 385/13, 401/8, 603/32.

we maye mete with hym he shal not escape, but we woll slee hym and he com thys way.'

'Ye take uppon you a grete charge,' seyde sir Lamorake, 'for sir Launcelot ys a noble proved knyght.'

'As for that, sir, we doute nat, for ther ys none of us but we ar good inowghe for hym.'

'I woll nat beleve that,' seyde sir Lamerok, 'for I harde never yet of no knyght dayes of oure lyff but sir Launcelot was to bygge for hym.'

(485/17–28)

Lancelot then appears, but the two knights take no action,

and sir Lamorake rode ayen thereas he leffte the two knyghtes, and than he founde them hydde in the leved woode.

'Fye on you!' seyde sir Lamerak, 'false cowardis! that pité and shame hit ys that ony of you sholde take the hyghe Order of Knyghthode!'

(485/34–486/3)

The brothers' grievance against Lancelot is not considered as an issue in its own right; we do not hear of the rights and wrongs of the stronger knight's behaviour. What matters is the disparity between the brothers' will to take redress and their ability to do so. Lacking the force of arms that can maintain ill will openly, aggressive feelings, which would be acceptable if they found issue in fighting, especially successful fighting, are shamefully internalised as cowardice and falsehood, hidden within the brothers as they are hidden at the edge of the wood, and, metaphorically, on the fringes of the Order of Knighthood. In Malory, to be envious is to have a *talent* (desire) which prolongs itself as *mautalent* (Malory's 'evil will') mainly because it cannot be expressed openly in arms. The major factor in assessing these grudges, as Lamerok shows here, is which knight will be 'to bygge' for the other. It is that which precedes and governs the more abstract reference to shameful conduct and the Order of Knighthood. The prowess that has presumably enabled Lancelot to commit the offence also converts the offended party's relative weakness, a matter of physics, into moral deficiency – 'false' behaviour and cowardice. By extension, Lancelot's physical superiority is *in itself* offered as right, in the face of which their only honourable choices seem, in effect, to fight (and lose) or to forgive. The prize of great prowess is the ability to take and defend every action according to the dominant public modes. Tristram, leaving Ireland, 'opynly' says:

'yf there be ony man that woll proffir me wronge other sey me wronge, other shame me behynde my backe, sey hit now or ellys never, and here is my body to make hit good, body ayenste body!' (392/25–28)

For the weaker figures, aggressive intent is easily represented as singular and malicious. By this method, Malory's discourse attempts to police in moral terms the unpleasant consequences his narrative of fighting intermittently reveals.

There remains always the considerable problem of reconciling the mayhem of the field, in which anger is a knightly and kingly virtue, with the friendly fellowship supposed to obtain elsewhere. How is the reconciliation, or its illusion, to be achieved? One method favoured in the *Tristram* (and in its associate *Gareth*), as we have seen, is the honourable draw with the 'forgiving' of ill will. One can also note that the very best knights, Lancelot, Tristram and Lamerok, sometimes practise a forbearance in their quest for worship which permits others to partake of some worship too, providing an outlet for rival ambitions and defusing political enmity. Also, good knights encourage and nurture younger men: Lancelot with Gareth, Tristram, Lavayne and Urré, Tristram with Hebes. In knight errantry and tournament, they frequently break off encounters to preserve the honour of both sides, share the 'prise' or even give it to another. By such means, prowess in arms is converted into political goodwill. So Tristram, fighting in lists on behalf of Isoude's father, King Angwysshe of Ireland, nevertheless finds a way of sparing his opponent, Lancelot's kinsman Bleoberis:

> 'For, my fayre lordys,' seyde sir Trystrames, 'hit were shame and pyté that this noble knyght that yondir lyeth sholde be slayne, for ye hyre well, shamed woll he nat be. And I pray to God that he never be slayne nother shamed for me. And as for the kynge whom I fyght fore, I shall requyre hym, as I am hys trew champyon and trew knyght in this fylde, that he woll have mercy uppon this knyght.' (410/8–14)

The scene ends with Bleoberis and Blamoure, his brother, kissing Angwysshe in sign of reconciliation, and Tristram and the brothers swearing never to fight again. 'And for that jantyll batayle all the bloode of sir Launcelott loved sir Trystrames for ever' (411/6–7). Tristram's knighthood is further attested, and another compliment is paid to the bravery of Lancelot's blood.

The friendly outcome of battle is a frequent enough event in the *Tristram* to suggest itself as a theme: conflicting political forces resolved by a hero's 'means' of prowess and wisdom. This characteristic of Tristram has been apparent since his youth, when he begged for his treacherous step-mother's life and permitted her reform (374–75). But what must also strike us about the *Tristram* is the impermanence of resolutions like this. They are amongst many things in Malory which are said to apply 'for ever' but can still suffer change and reversal. The summary and homogenising trend in the discourse is eroded by the necessity to recount so many varying details of the story, with complex effects. Change – 'no stabylité' (1119/19–20) – is abhorrent in theory yet not necessarily to be noted as a bad thing when it occurs. A completely permanent state of affairs is rare in Malory, and may even involve dangerous 'instability' in other ways. Lancelot's love for Guenevere

– 'unmesurabely and oute of mesure longe' (897/16) – provides one instance. Despite its praise of constancy, the *Morte's* preference in practice is
subtly different. It celebrates fervently what is unchanging ('ever'), but the
narrative situations can silently alter and develop in changed contexts,
without attracting charges of falseness or inconsistency. Concluding this
incident of Tristram and Bleoberis, the happy outcome of eternal 'love' is
shadowed by another in which Lancelot's kin retain their envy:

> sir Trystram enchevyd many grete batayles, wherethorow all the noyse
> and brewte felle to sir Trystram, and the name ceased of sir Launcelot.
> And therefore sir Launcelottis bretherne and his kynnysmen wolde have
> slayne sir Trystram bycause of his fame. (784/33–785/4)

Unfailingly, the flaw in the system asserts itself against individuals' good
will, and Lancelot has to forbid his kin from killing Tristram, as he must
later forbid Bors to kill Arthur. The narrative interpretation of this instance
of envy is as a proof of Lancelot's nobility of spirit (785), but more than that
is proved. In the honour economy, kinsmen and supporters of the great are
like shareholders[46] whose stocks are devalued when another centre of
worship – for 'worship' read 'power' – grows stronger. In consequence, the
'love' of the great, ultimately even that of Lancelot and Arthur, is often
under threat from the interests of lesser knights, who see others' gain as
their own loss. Only a few think of 'wealth creation' in honour, and they
find the idea difficult to sell, sometimes even to themselves. (One might
compare the extreme unpopularity of the newly honoured Wydevilles in
Malory's day, enriched as they had been at others' expense.[47]) Tristram says
to Palamides 'ye ar nat so fayne to have worship but I wolde as fayne
encrease youre worshyp' (728/23–24), but remains fiercely competitive and
sometimes deliberately causes Palamides to lose face. From an analysis of
the relation of competing knights, two conflicting factors emerge in the
narrative: recognition of the political need to share the fruits of power and
so attract personal support, but also the impossibility of achieving this fully
while the will to dominance of mighty individuals is also legitimated.

---

[46] The process also works in reverse. See 526/20–24: ' "Now, Jesu," seyde sir Trystram, "well
    may he be called valyaunte and full of proues that hath such a sorte of noble knyghtes
    unto hys kynne. And full lyke ys he to be a nobleman that ys their leder and governoure."
    He mente hit by sir Launcelot du Lake.'
[47] See M.A. Hicks, 'The Changing Role of the Wydevilles in Yorkist Politics to 1483' in Ross,
    ed., *Patronage*, 60–86.

Co-existence: The Model of Dynadan

Much of the *Tristram* articulates or betrays the problems of fellowship, and attempts to celebrate the ways in which good knights manage to co-exist with equals, with inferiors and with betters. When this ability is absent, the story soon darkens into envy and treachery – the killings of Lamerok, Alexander and Tristram by lesser knights. The text prefers to deal in terms of the reputations of individual figures either for 'gentle' or 'envious' conduct, but the deeper issue is the credit of the signifying processes vested in military competition, without which a narrative of fighting will lose its attachment to ideas of 'goodness' and face a severe moral critique. Malory's text labours to keep in repair an ideology in which might is seen to be right mainly because to be mighty is also to be righteous. Therefore his best knights must be accepted as such 'by right' (521/25), and co-operation with these great figures is represented as an important kind of goodness, as well as prudence.

Dynadan's agency offers us a model of this worshipful co-existence, the antithesis of envy. His ability, as one of the 'meane knyghtes' (668/18), to get on with the great, is his true role in Malory, more than that of a 'skoffer and a gaper' (665/7). His scoffs are a means partly of coping with his relative lack of prowess, partly of asserting the true worth of others, good or bad:

> 'Well, well,' seyde sir Dynadan to sir Launcelot, 'what devyll do ye in this contrey? For here may no meane knyghtes wynne no worship for the. I ensure the,' sir Dynadan seyde to sir Launcelot, 'I shall no more mete with the, nother with thy grete speare, for I may nat sytte in my sadyll whan thy speare hittyth me. And I be happy, I shall beware of thy boysteous body that thou beryst.' . . .
> Than lowghe the quene and the Haute Prynce, that they myght nat sytte at their table. (668/17–23)

Vinaver's change, following Caxton, of the Winchester manuscript's 'boyteous' (beauteous) to 'boysteous' (rough) tones down a jest in which Dynadan sexualises his opponent's tournament prowess, and implicitly feminises himself as swooning victim of the 'grete speare'.[48] The speech prefigures Lancelot's dressing Dynadan as a woman, on the seventh day of the tournament.[49] In his role as japer, Dynadan is permitted to touch on truths about chivalric rivalry. He bridges the gap between field and table – competitive and collective impulses – by dissipating through jest the anxieties it generates. In a book overshadowed by the murder of Lamerok, partly owing to envy of his tournament success (688/6–10), Dynadan's

---

[48] Vinaver has also reattributed the second part of the speech, beginning 'I ensure thee', from Lancelot to Dynadan.

[49] See Chapter 3, 68.

jesting shows a way of converting defeat at a better knight's hands from shame into a mode that acknowledges pleasure at so closely experiencing the other's prowess. Though Lancelot's excellence threatens to debar Dynadan from winning worship, or even practising knighthood at all ('I may nat sytte in my sadyll'), it also delights him; he is a fellow knight, even if a 'meane' one. In a more solemn mode, but in similar spirit, Gawain, much later, writes to Lancelot

> 'I was hurte to the dethe, whych wounde was fyrste gyffyn of thyn honde, sir Launcelot; for of a more nobelar man myght I nat be slayne.'
>   (1231/21–23)

This death-bed confession, signed in his heart's blood, shows Gawain accepting at last and for good the 'right' attitude to Lancelot's superiority.[50]

Dynadan may grumble about the thirst for worship of Lancelot and Tristram, but always in a manner that singles them out as the best, and so fits in with the text's own evaluative processes. His humour is very far from subversive. He is himself 'a good knyght on horsebacke' (583/25) and does well enough in tournaments, though he dislikes fighting on foot with the sword (524/4–7) and thus has no claim to be an all-rounder like Lancelot ('take hym bothe on horsebacke and on foote' (745/25)). The issue of just how good a knight Dynadan is is complicated by an apparent tendency to make him into more than a 'meane knyght' in prowess because he is good in other ways, displaying the naturalised association between the two areas.[51] So Dynadan is, rather confusingly, an ordinary knight, a 'good knyght' (665/7) and a 'passynge good' one (615/7–8). Were he really a coward, like his French original (1448), the textual attitude to his other qualities would be untenable, or rather, he could not be conceived of as a 'good' knight in any way (605/19–20, 615/7–8). He would be a Meleagant or a Mark.

Dynadan is not at all an *habitual* scoffer or japer. That is more the role of the mocking Kay, 'a good knyght, but . . . unfortunate and passyng overthwart of . . . [his] tunge' (488/20–21). Dynadan is by contrast expressly presented as a knight unusually gifted with words, a wonderful 'maker' even in Tristram's eyes (626), and a man of 'jantyl' conduct. His jests are eloquence, closely associated with his worship – 'a grete bourder and a passynge good knyght' (615/7–8), and his career is marked by intelligent conversation, in most of its senses, with others. When he finds Palamides alone lamenting (591/21ff, 595/6ff), he comforts him with remarkable courtesy and tact, falls in fellowship with him, skilfully elicits his name, proposes his worship and in every way seeks his good:

---

[50] See also Chapter 1, 15; Chapter 5, 120–21.
[51] See Chapter 2, 43–44; Chapter 6, 139.

'Sir, I thanke you,' seyde sir Dynadan, 'for I am glad that I knowe your
name. And by me ye shall nat be hurte but rathir avaunced, and I may,
on my lyff. For ye shall wynne worshyp in the courte of kynge Arthure
and be ryghte wellcom.' (597/1–4)

Dynadan then joins Palamides in an adventure against Morgan. ' "I shall
nat fayle you," seyde sir Dynadan, "unto my puyssaunce, uppon my lyff!" '
(597/32–33). His fair speech is praiseworthy both in itself and because it
opens up the avenues to worship for others.

Although Dynadan likes verbal skirmishes, he has them only with
knights at their best or worst, either with Tristram and Lancelot, or with
Mark (most notably) and Palamides in his worse moods (537/1–5). His
speech, whether solemn or jesting, must always be seen in conjunction with
his role as chivalric judge, in which he virtually represents a principle
contrary to envy and ill will:

> For sir Dynadan had suche a custom that he loved all good knyghtes that
> were valyaunte, and he hated all tho that were destroyers of good kny-
> ghtes. And there was none that hated sir Dynadan but tho that ever were
> called murtherers. (614/27–31)

Dynadan's 'love' (or political good-will) towards good knights is made
clear in his seeking them out (693/22) and in his attempts to bring them to
Arthur's court (Palamides, Lamerok). This part of his role outweighs his
occasional gripe that the chivalric way of fighting 'for love',' "with an harde
speare" ' (604/33, 605/1–3), is often irksome. A similar compensation can
be seen in his attitude to love 'paramours'. His proverbial 'sentence' – ' "the
joy of love is to shorte, and the sorow thereof and what cometh thereof is
duras over longe" ' (693/33–35) – is immediately converted into praise of
Bleoberis, who has ' "fought wyth three knyghtes at onys for a damesell" '
(694/3). Though he would not fight himself for that reason (694/10–18),
Dynadan's warm acknowledgment of ' "the noble knyghtes of the blood of
sir Launcelot de Lake" ' (694/6–9) binds him strongly into the judging elite,
here led by Isoude. She, at Tristram's command, makes him great 'chyre'
and offers him lodging (694/19–21), publicly demonstrating his worthiness, as well as his amusing social qualities. To judge by his whole career,
Dynadan is no enemy at all to love. Indeed, he is especially successful as
the companion of lovers – the chamber companion of Lancelot, virtually
playing Ami to Tristram's Amant, and especially hard on Mark as the enemy
of Tristram's and Isoude's love. He vilifies Mark both directly and through
his abusive 'lay'.

My reading of Dynadan, therefore, is that his apparently subversive role
causes just enough disturbing of the ruling ethos of 'worship' and 'love' to
permit its speedy and comforting reaffirmation. His jesting curses at the
burden of chivalry (706/1–5) always serve to unite the company of the
good. He gives them the pleasure of recognising that their group bond is so

strong that it can survive the 'outsider's' attacks he seems to make.[52] Superficially, Dynadan subjects chivalry to accusations that it is pointless violence, apparently aligning himself with both clerical censure and churlish incomprehension of the joys of fighting. In other contexts, his views might have more force.[53] As he presents them, they offer the pleasure of being conscious 'insiders' to the initiates that hear him. If his objections are unanswered, it is part of their function that they remind the hearers of a shared value-system which is beyond lay analysis. Dynadan comically elicits, in order to exorcise, the helplessness of the chivalric ethos before the unappreciative critic: 'Than there was lawghynge and japynge at sir Dynadan, that they wyste nat what to do wyth hym' (706/3–5).

Dynadan's career is also exemplary in that he makes no enemies except of the truly bad, and the bad are uniformly bad in his presence. He brings it out in them, as a good knight should. In Dynadan, the functions Malory gives to fighting itself – to display and to evaluate relative prowess – are so closely aligned that the one may serve for the other. So even his refusals to fight are credited to his worship, as signs of an understanding of others' chivalry. In declining to encounter with Lamerok (587/32–34, 591/21ff, 595/6ff), Dynadan matches him better than Mark does, who is willing to fight, but does not recognise who and what Lamerok is, and so seems to make a foolish self-comparison (580/22ff). Dynadan acknowledges, like a good reader, the presence of greatness, and wants to be its fellow rather than its opponent, whilst Mark does not know a good knight when he sees one:

'Thynke ye that a shame?' seyde sir Dynadan. 'Nay, sir, hit is ever worshyp to a knyght to refuse that thynge that he may nat attayne. Therefore youre worshyp had bene much more to have refused hym as I ded.' (581/24–27)

Were all knights to take Dynadan's attitude here, including Dynadan himself, who often does otherwise, the pace of tournaments and knight errantry would certainly slow down. His evaluative genius would destroy the impulse to 'take the adventure'. But, as I argue elsewhere,[54] other factors severely limit the scope of 'adventure' in Malory. Here, reaction takes precedence over action in a celebration of others' worth that becomes the main agenda of the narrative. In this sequence of adventures with Mark, Dynadan is revealed as a highly conservative force, restating the principle that to kill a better knight than oneself is an act of murder rather than prowess (585/1–7). He denies probative value to the chances of battle which have permitted the deed, because it is mainly through another's efforts that

[52] See Benson, *Malory's Morte Darthur*, 112–13.
[53] See, e.g., *The Works of John Clanvowe*, ed. V.J. Scattergood (Cambridge: D.S. Brewer, 1976) 69–70; Keen, *Chivalry*, 227–37.
[54] Chapter 1, 22–25; Chapter 5, 120–23.

Mark gets the better of his opponent Berluse (583/26–32). 'Adventure' is by
no means all; it must respect in Dynadan's (and Malory's) eyes, the ideal
order of merit. Conversely, when the better knight kills the weaker, as when
Tristram kills the three sons of Sir Darras at a tournament (540/3–6),
although the father's anger is understood, the facts are represented as
inevitable, not to be helped:

> 'And as for the dethe of youre three sunnes, I myght nat do withall. For
> and they had bene the next kyn that I have, I myght have done none
> othirwyse'. (552/20–23)

As a staunch upholder of such views, Dynadan's unusual behaviour is
essentially a form of respect; if he employs 'raylynge langage' against a
knight like Tristram, it is only 'for to cause hym to wake hys speretes'
(742/7–13).

Fighting against Envy

Dynadan extends his awareness in the field of combat into other areas of
life also. In his intimate social relations with Tristram and Lancelot, skill
with words plays a prominent part. One important focus for it involves an
incident in which Mark sends an abusive letter to Guenevere:

> And whan quene Gwenyver rad hir lettir and undirstode hyt, she was
> wrothe oute of mesure, for the letter spoke shame by her and by sir
> Launcelot. And so prevayly she sente the lettir unto sir Launcelot. And
> whan he wyste the entente of the letter he was so wrothe that he layde
> hym downe on his bed to slepe, whereof sir Dynadan was ware, for hit
> was his maner to be prevy with all good knyghtes. And as sir Launcelot
> slepte, he stale the lettir oute of his honde and rad hit worde by worde,
> and than he made grete sorow for angir. And sir Launcelot so wakened,
> and wente to a wyndowe and redde the letter agayne, whyche made hym
> angry.
> 'Syr,' seyde sir Dynadan, 'wherefore be ye angry? I pray you, discover
> your harte to me, for, pardé, ye know well that I wolde you but well, for
> I am a poore knyght and a servyture unto you and to all good knyghtes.
> For though I be nat of worship myself, I love all tho that bene of worship.'
> (617/22–618/3)

Dynadan's literacy and his privileged access to Lancelot's chamber[55]
permit him to share the great man's reaction with personal directness, as

---

[55] On the political importance of access to the private royal apartments, see D.A.L. Morgan,
'The House of Policy', 58: 'Because they were so personally, and lastingly, the king's men,
it was those "which wait most upon the king and lie nightly in his Chamber" who could
represent their master and implement his will across the range of his concerns.'

described in a sentence whose syntactic sleight of hand hardly distinguishes Dynadan's reading of the letter, and his anger, from Lancelot's own. Dynadan's boldness to steal the letter and then feign ignorance is part of his service, and so 'true' that the narration seems to forget that Dynadan already knows what Mark wrote. The loyal intent of the speech and his closeness to Lancelot's 'harte' are what count (617/35). Dynadan's own verbal attack, the 'lay' abusing Mark, is communicated (with Tristram's help) by the harper Elyas. By its means, Dynadan once more vindicates the company of the good – Guenevere, Lancelot and Tristram – against an 'outsider', restoring the sense of corporate well-being. His achievement deflects the 'anger' caused by Mark's incursion back into Cornwall, but this time impacting in the public sphere: Mark is openly shamed in his own hall rather than by a private letter. The incident has been called typical of the minstrel's 'hand in the dissemination of court propaganda', although two 'men of letters', Dynadan and Tristram, are calling the tune.[56] This is the kind of action even a 'meane knyght' can perform on behalf of the great. In such incidents, Dynadan figures far less as a quirky individual 'character' than as a model for all of how to achieve benign symbiosis with greater figures. In sharing their triumph over King Mark, his loyalty is rewarded with a symbolic social promotion. In all, Dynadan is like a more responsible Pandarus, a man of vision, who is 'ware', 'privy with' the good and 'loves' them. In this he is implicitly contrasted with Mordred and Aggravain, whom he denounces for their 'prevy despite' and 'hate' of Lancelot and his kin (700/1–7) His death at the hands of the Orkney family, foretold in the *Tristram* (615/5–8), is a straw in the wind, as the Arthurian world edges closer to open factional warfare.[57]

Redeeming Ill Will

Envy or ill will in a 'good knight' is an affront to the Malorian habit of connecting combat prowess with other forms of goodness, and its converse, the belittling of the prowess of those knights who act badly, such as Gawain. It is a commonplace of Malory criticism that the surface of knightly solidarity covers deep hatred and divisions. This was certainly not news to the author: the most persuasive of his 'horizontal' chains of cause and effect are the treacherous kin feuds. These and other antagonisms must have seemed perfectly understandable to a man of his times, who expected, like John Paston, to have 'well willers' and 'ill willers'.[58] It is not as if Malory

[56] Richard Firth Green, *Poets and Princepleasers*, 169.
[57] With Malorian unconcern, Dynadan is revived in the great list of the Urré episode, 1148/13.
[58] See *Paston Letters*, vol. II, no. 631, p. 236.

overlooked the darker side of chivalric emulation. The murder of Lamerok, told and re-told, often eclipses his chivalric joys: 'Now, fye upon treson!' seyde sir Trystram, 'for hit sleyth myne harte to hyre this tale' (699/28–29). Malorian knights regularly acknowledge that they have 'evil will' towards each other, and though Vinaver reads this as 'anger', translating *mautalent*, Field's view is more persuasive: 'The only recorded Middle English sense of *evyll wyll* is "ill will" ' (1533). In Malory the phrase 'evil will' often comes in a context of a knight asking forgiveness. Since wishing to see another harmed or shamed is basically a deliberate political alignment, though sometimes with an emotional cast, it may be deliberately altered for good reason, and is therefore corrigible under certain conditions, as when Darras forgives Tristram (551–52).[59] Even the long-time enemies of 'good knights' can be redeemed, as Gareth has redeemed Sir Ironsyde, the Red Knight of the Red Lands, who has shamefully hanged many knights. He is made to ' "goo unto the courte of king Arthur and . . . aske sir Launcelot mercy and sir Gawayne for the evyll wylle he hath had ayenst them" '. There he is accepted: ' "God forgyff you and we do" ' (325/31–33, 337/22–34). It is an instance of good will redeeming ill, but one only made possible through Gareth's initial fighting prowess.

In the *Tristram*, with its multiple interlocking adventures, such incidents are common; the abundance of prowess naturally attracts enmity as well as good name. A favoured development of the redemption story is one involving both parties directly, in which an offended knight's hatred is purged in the course of the fighting itself. The narrative efficiently combines the overcoming of the vengeful figure with his re-acceptance into chivalric goodwill. Indeed, it seems that only in the 'playne fylde' (450/19) of knightly combat can such transformations be achieved. Cowardice, therefore, prolongs incorrigible envy, as we saw in the incident involving Lancelot and two brothers. King Mark clearly exemplifies this, as does Meleagant later on. One might easily add to the *Tristram*'s list of proverbs one concerning him: 'A good man ys never in daungere but whan he ys in the daungere of a cowhard' (1126/5–6). Prowess, by contrast, can achieve anything. The *Tristram*'s combats sometimes verge on the mystical in their operations; they can be transformed beyond any logic of individual conduct into a concept of fighting as the administration of a secular sacrament, which, like matrimony, is conferred by the recipients themselves. This proposition can only be illustrated through detailed analyis. I choose the conflict between Lamerok and Bellyaunce, occurring after Lamerok has killed Sir Froll, Bellyaunce's brother. Malory's telling of the story is typically obscure in terms of cause and effect; it seems, rather, designed to display the clash

---

[59] See also Chapter 6, 138–40.

between kin loyalty and chivalric 'love', and the possibilities of the redemption of 'hate' through arms:

And so he [Bellyaunce] horsed hym and armed hym, and within a whyle he overtoke sir Lamerok and bade hym turne, 'and leve that lady, for thou and I muste play a new play: for thow haste slayne my brother sir Froll that was a bettir knyght than ever was thou.'

'Ye may well sey hit,' seyde sir Lamerok, 'but this day in the playne fylde I was founde the bettir knyght.'

So they rode togydyrs and unhorsed eche other, and turned their shyldis and drew their swerdys, and fought myghtyly as noble knyghtes preved the space of two owres. So than sir Bellyaunce prayde hym to telle hym his name.

'Sir, my name is sir Lameroke de Galys.'

'A,' seyde sir Bellyaunce, 'thou arte the man in the worlde that I moste hate, for I slew my sunnys for thy sake where I saved thy lyff, and now thou haste slayne my brothir sir Froll. Alas, how sholde I be accorded with the? Therefore defende the! Thou shalt dye! There is none other way nor remedy.'

'Alas!' seyde sir Lameroke, 'ful well me ought to know you, for ye ar the man that moste have done for me.' And therewithall sir Lamerok kneled adowne and besought hym of grace.

'Aryse up!' seyde sir Bellyaunce, 'othir ellys thereas thou knelyste I shall sle the!'

'That shall nat nede,' seyde sir Lameroke, 'for I woll yelde me to you, nat for no feare of you nor of youre strength, but youre goodnesse makyth me to lothe to have ado with you. Wherefore I requyre you, for Goddis sake and for the honour of knyghthode, forgyff me all that I have offended unto you.'

'Alas!' seyde sir Bellyaunce, 'leve thy knelynge, other ellys I shall sle the withoute mercy.'

Than they yode agayne to batayle and aythir wounded othir, that all the grounde was blody thereas they fought. And at the laste sir Bellyaunce withdrew hym abacke and sette hym downe a lytyll uppon an hylle, for he was faynte for bledynge, that he myght nat stonde.

Than sir Lameroke threw his shylde uppon his backe and cam unto hym and asked hym what chere.

'Well,' seyde sir Bellyaunce.

'A, sir, yett shall I shew you favoure in youre male ease.'

'A, knyght,' seyde sir Bellyaunce unto sir Lamerok, 'thou arte a foole, for and I had the at suche avauntage as thou haste me, I sholde sle the. But thy jantylnesse is so good and so large that I muste nedys forgyff the myne evyll wyll.'

And than sir Lameroke kneled adowne and unlaced fyrst his umbrere [vizor] and than his owne, and than aythir kyssed othir with wepynge tearys. Than sir Lamerok led sir Bellyaunce to an abbey faste by, and there sir Lamerok wolde nat departe from sir Bellyaunce tylle he was hole. And than they were sworne togydyrs that none of hem sholde never fyght ayenste other. (450–51)

The history behind this fight, as Malory adapts it, is scanty,[60] but the honorific potential remains very strong, enriched by many markers of nobility. There is the emphasis on self-display – the 'playne fylde', 'play'; on the revealing of name; on duration – 'the space of two owres'; on bodily sign and gesture – bleeding, kneeling, kissing and weeping; the exclamatory speech-tokens of deep feeling – 'A' and 'Alas'; the dialogue of 'forgiveness'; finally the recovery to health of the opponent, and an outcome of 'love'. There is even a tender humour in Bellyaunce's dogged refusal to admit his 'male ease'. It is a scene, in short, much to Malory's liking, in which combat incarnates the psychic wounds of hatred, so that they may be first displayed then healed on the knightly body. The episode crowns Lamerok's adventures at this time in something of the way the Chapel Perilous does Lancelot's in his own book. Fighting, here, is a temporary narrative end, but principally a knightly *means*, a medium which invokes through its noble gestures the inner realignment which is their correlative. Bellyaunce's original attitude towards Lamerok – 'revenge' (450/12) and 'hate' (450/26) – is determined by historical consequences: the deaths of his brother and sons. But that impulse quickly reaches an impasse which threatens final unhappiness. Bellyaunce is unable to assuage his hatred by defeating Lamerok in a fair fight, and shame forbids him to accept any other conclusion. He simply fights until he is unable to stand (451/12). But Lamerok's prowess as a knight, the same prowess, of course, that has killed Froll for no very good reason (450/1–8), by withstanding Bellyaunce's initial 'quarell' permits a new transformative discourse to operate, eventually overcoming historical causality. Lamerok does not realise who Bellyaunce is until after their first bout of sword-play. He then converts his strength in arms into a controlled yielding: 'Wherefore I *requyre* you, for Goddis sake and for the honour of knyghthode, *forgyff* me all that I have offended unto you.' Bellyaunce refuses at first, again preferring his 'historical' knowledge of Lamerok, but is at last compelled, by the compound of superior force and 'gentleness', to forgive Lamerok 'myne evyll wyll'. The possessive pronoun shows how closely Bellyaunce has drawn to himself Lamerok's killing of his brother – the 'evyll wyll' Lamerok has seemed to show becomes a thing of Bellyaunce's own. He 'forgives' it, then, in a double sense, both giving up his own revenge and releasing Lamerok from the blame which motivated it.

It is a noble and exemplary way out for Bellyaunce, made possible under the double compulsion of Lamerok's prowess and 'jantyll' behaviour. Only this combination could save Bellyaunce from shame or death, and Lamerok from further enmity, and the misfortune of killing yet again in the same family. The 'tale' too is saved from unhappiness. The significance of combat,

---

60 See Vinaver, 1465–66. See also Mann, *The Narrative of Distance*, 3–8, esp. 6–7: 'Bellyaunce's revelation . . . is shorn of experiential context'.

clouded and imperilled by the desultory adventures immediately preceding this one, is brilliantly clarified through the discursive resources of a mighty combat between 'noble knyghtes preved' (450/22).

Caught between these self-redeeming heroes and the abhorrent man-murderers of the story we find the intriguing figure of Sir Palamides, with his long-term quest for the Questing Beast, the long deferral of his christening (until he has fought even more battles) and his constant oscillation between admiration for Tristram and malicious envy of him. His story of ill will and redemption is the subject of my next chapter.

5

Good and Ill Will (2):
Tristram *and the problem of* Palamides

'I wote nat what eylyth me' (697/15)

The Birth of 'Palamides'

Although we have seen, in Malory's *Tristram*, that combat is ideally the cure for its own effects, able to convert ill will into good, this process must always remain liable to reversal, with a sudden incursion of enmity stemming from former deeds of arms. The *Tristram* is full of those who 'hate' particular names they are only waiting to put faces to. Amongst all its personages, Palamides most registers the instability of chivalric culture, as a 'good knight' whose malevolent actions often belie his 'noble name'.

Palamides, much more truly than Dynadan, is a 'passing good' fighter, and therefore, perhaps, more likely to envy the handful who are better: Lancelot, Tristram, Lamerok, Perceval, Gareth, La Cote Mal Tayle. He has an extensive role in the narrative as a foil to Tristram, as an unsuccessful rival in arms and love.[1] Beyond that, his jealousy and anti-social behaviour serve to expose the dangers of chivalry and love 'paramours' much more than Dynadan's friendly jests. His unchristened, Saracen status, his hopeless love, his singular, endless quest for the Questing Beast, a penchant for solitary lament and a distinctive interior life, out of kilter with consensual wisdom, allow Palamides' story to make him more of a 'character' than other figures in the *Tristram*. Though 'noble' by blood and reputation, he is decidedly melancholy in humour (hence his habit of lamenting to himself) and frequently tormented by circumstances. Furthermore, his narrative significance is established by unusually mixed behaviour which both

---

1   See Robert Merrill, *Sir Thomas Malory and the Cultural Crisis of the Late Middle Ages*, American University Studies, Series 4 vol. 39 (New York: Peter Lang, 1986) 12: 'Palomides represents all those losers who through no fault of their own are caught in a system which simply needs failures to make its successes seem valid, and to make membership in the institution seem all the more desirable'; Mahoney, ' "Ar ye a knyght?" ', 321: 'He becomes a kind of cracked mirror to Tristram, reflecting the latter's chivalry, but always with some flaw that mars the line.'

departs from and asserts the public standard. He exhibits not so much a steady *degree* of worthiness, like other knights, as a series of achievements and lapses, something like Lancelot's career in the *Sankgreal*, but more erratic, with less sense of a continuing *voie*. More than others, Palamides seems a pure adventurer, with a predilection for marginality, staying away from courts, finding it hard to keep fellowship. He is a liminal figure – often leaving and rejoining company, praised as a true believer in Christ yet unchristened, and, though he often offends, remaining 'sir Palomides the good knight' (401/8, 401/19, 716/20).

The contradictory career of Palamides perfectly displays the conflict between the competitive basis of chivalry and its myth of collectivity. One naturally expects the association of ill will with Mark (548/34). It is his 'kind', and the good may blamelessly reciprocate (609/07). But Palamides poses far more complex issues in the textual consciousness. Most figures of ill will can easily be seen as actants pressed into the needs of the narrative from page to page, with the psychological issue largely discounted. Some other occasional 'ill-willers', like Lamerok, Tristram, Arthur and Lancelot, discussed in previous chapters, have a great 'name' that resists tarnishing by the occasional aberration in their behaviour required by the story to set up new adventures.[2] Palamides, by contrast, slowly accrues a personal *history* out of his contradictions, the more concentrated, perhaps, because his adventures are related in detail only within the *Tristram*, and are therefore not subject to generic variation. (Beyond its bounds 'Palomides' is a much lesser figure – a tournament 'name' and a 'dedely' knight of Lancelot's party in the war against Arthur (1192/7).) In this chapter, I consider Palamides as a figure whose potential as a psychological subject eventually comes to challenge and complicate the norms of Malory's narrative. In analysing him, a problem of strategy arises, because the story of Palamides is strung out over many episodes and interspersed with many others. Since it is basic to my critical approach to discuss Malory's narrative discourse in some detail, I choose to concentrate on a selection of events mainly involving the troubled relations of Tristram and Palamides. The aim is to provide a manageable, though substantial, *Tale of Sir Palomides*, 'briefly drawn out of' *Tristram*, to focus on the problem of envy and its resolution which is the theme of these chapters.

Being 'Palamides'

In good part, a secondary knight, as Palamides is to Lancelot, Tristram and others, exists as a living monument to those who have 'won' him and (by extension) all those he has beaten. Bleoberis, keenly following the form of individuals and families, understands Tristram by this method:

---

[2] See Chapter 1, 5–6; Chapter 4, 87–88.

'Also ye overcom sir Palomydes, the good knyght, at the turnemente in
Irelonde where he bete sir Gawayne and his nyne felowys.'
(401/7–9, cf. 408/16–19)

Tristram understands himself like this:' "I am he that bete sir Palomydes"'
(442/20–21). And Palamides also knows his place in the scheme of things.
His history and geography are comprised of occasions when Tristram has
beaten him:' "Onys in Irelonde sir Trystram put me to the wors, and anothir
tyme in Cornwayle and in other placis in thys londe"' (529/9–11). This
magic of the tournament marketplace creates an ideal order of value, but
has a dangerous effect if one thinks in terms of individual psychology.
Palamides can be driven by his shame at losing into unknightly deeds and
seeking unfair 'avauntage', then to further, demented shame at both his loss
and his departure from his better self. What can be explained from within
chivalric ideology as lapse and reform in the individual also tells, more
obscurely, of the narrative problems of reliance on military combat as an
adequate evaluation of the self. There is more to Tristram than his victory,
or to Palamides than his defeat. The story seeks to save the credit and
potential of both parties. Palamides cannot win, yet no one wants to see him
lose too badly. Isoude expresses the problem:

'Alas! that one I loved and yet do, and the other I love nat, that they sholde
fyght! And yett hit were grete pyté that I sholde se sir Palomydes slayne.'
(425/8–10)

She might be speaking generally for Palamides' ambivalent function in the
story. It is necessary that he should 'have the worse' but something else
contains that impulse, even more than we have already seen in Arthur's
war against Lot.[3] Vinaver lamented Malory's failure to perceive the importance of Mark in the Tristram story.[4] But in Malory's ideology, Palamides'
situation as second-best takes on something of the poignancy of Mark's as
Vinaver saw it. The 'sacred tie' is no longer that of feudal service but of
putative 'fellowship' in knightly society, and the new problem, inevitable
though not quite 'involuntary' in origin, is that to realise his own chivalric
destiny Tristram must cloud that of another good knight.

Palamides as Textual Object

He who loses must leave the field, while his opponent remains in possession
of it. Palamides' lonely career is studded with dismissals, in which he
becomes the object of another's intention: the bearer of defeat in his own

---

[3] Chapter 2, 39–41.
[4] See Chapter 4, 79.

person, and the victor's messenger. Tristram dictates humiliating terms to Palamides in Ireland (388/13–22). Isoude banishes him with a message for Guenevere:

'and tell her that I sende her worde that there be within this londe but foure lovers, and that is sir Launcelot and dame Gwenyver, and sir Trystrames and quene Isode.' (425/27–31)

In love and in combat Palamides is thus made an exile and a figure of his rival's success. Isoude sends him to Guenevere as a kind of penance. This incident will recall others, in which Gareth has sent the Red Knight to Arthur, and Lancelot has made Pedyvere bear the head of the wife he has murdered to Guenevere, to seek forgiveness, and she sends him on a further pilgrimage to Rome. Such journeys of the defeated are acts which begin their chivalric or spiritual regeneration, in a way the text quickly signals (285/29–286/18, 325/22–33, 336/26–337/35). But Palamides' redemption is very long in coming, with ambivalent effects. The delay permits much dilation of the action, as if to allow maximum space to the theme of conversion, but it also indicates the difficulty of truly reconciling the warring pressures on the situation to which the name 'Palamides' is given. Until near its end, the story mixes his good deeds, for example the recapture of the Red City, undertaken as an enterprise granted by Tristram (702/5–12) with aberrant acts against better knights, such as cutting off Lancelot's horse's head (739/5–9), or beguiling Tristram (746–47).

Containing Palamides: Motivation and the Limits of 'Adventure'

On the fairly rare occasions when Palamides achieves independent combat success against better knights, the narrative works to limit his credit and to preserve the ideal order of merit. For instance, when he gives a fall to La Cote Mal Tayle (463/17–20), Mordred is present to explain that Palamides is only better on horseback, not on foot (466/10–30), and to advance La Cote Male Tayle by a comparison with Lancelot (466/23–30).[5] When Palamides gives a fall to Tristram and Lamerok 'with one speare' (484/11–22), an array of strategies immediately limits the 'proof' of the event: Palamides will not stay to fight on foot; a brevity *topos* ('to breff thys mater') is employed, very rare in Malory's combat description where an encounter between knights of name is involved, yet used twice of Palamides.[6] Finally, as in several other cases in the *Tristram* where the text needs to deprive an individual event of

5   That Mordred can do this as well as any one else shows, incidentally, the normal limitations on the importance of 'character' in Malory.
6   See also 663, where Palamides defeats three of Arthur's nephews. Arthur regards this as a 'grete dispyte', setting up Lamerok's payback of him.

declarative power, a proverb-like 'sentence' attributes the occurrence to chance rather than merit:[7]

> Here men may undirstonde that bene men of worshyp that man was never fourmed that all tymes myght attayne, but somtyme he was put to the worse by malefortune and at som tyme the wayker knyght put the byggar knyght to a rebuke. (484/18–22)

In a narrative medium in which sheer length characterises nobility of fighting, both as a descriptive technique and as a prize category,[8] the abbreviation of two of Palamides' fairly infrequent victories enacts his inability to convert his prowess into lasting supremacy, and shows again how limited is Malory's sense of 'adventure' when the prestige of a ruling hero is at stake.[9]

An incident at the Castle of Maidens, when Palamides unhorses Tristram 'at avauntage' (515/23–35), sees Tristram consoled by Dynadan with similar proverbs, but with a different result:

> 'Lo, sir Trystram, here may a man preve, be he never so good yet may he have a falle; and he was never so wyse but he myght be oversayne, and he rydyth well that never felle.' (516/3–6)

Not surprisingly, Tristram's response is an angry desire for revenge. As the best, he need not console himself with proverbs for the many, but can make the course of events prove his preeminence again. To adopt his own words, he is not so keen to win worship as Malory is to increase his worship. His decision to be against Palamides at the tournament (525/3–6), because it cooperates so well with this narrative goal, escapes scrutiny of motive, unlike Palamides' otherwise similar-looking refusal to be with Tristram at Lonezep (716/12–25), which is attributed to 'envy'. As is often seen in Malory, to be a 'character' with psychological motivation is incipiently discreditable and a potential sign of 'unhappiness'.

The question of motivation in Malory remains a subtle one, on which I have more to say below.[10] I have argued above,[11] following Mark Lambert, that the sense of a *private* inner life is slight, and that deeds declare their own value in the public arena. Obviously the *Sankgreal*, with its purpose of rebuking chivalry based on earthly pride and violence, has a deeper interest in *why* knights act. In most other contexts the best motivation is simply one like the text's own: 'he thought hymself to preve in straunge adventures'

---

7 For other proverbs in *Tristram*, see Chapter 4, 89–90.
8 E.g., 'the space of two owres' (450/22); 'lengyst durynge' (741/4). See also Chapter 2, 41–42.
9 See Chapter 1, 23; Chapter 4, 101–02; below, 120–23.
10 See Chapter 6, 144.
11 See Chapter 1, 14.

(253/21).[12] But in order to achieve better the ranking of combatants, who to the naked eye might seem only 'bigger' or 'weaker', a controlled focus on intention and psychology is sometimes necessary to the story, to preserve the key idea that fighting superiority is linked to other kinds of 'goodness' and 'right', such as legitimate political rule (521/25). Hence, I think, arises the unusual interiority of Palamides, which is originally a function of the need to represent some of his actions as unworthily motivated, to protect in turn the reputation of more dominant figures, and the means by which they have attained it. Motivation is essentially a political discourse here. Palamides, lacking the military power to represent his self-interest as the common good, is viewed as dangerously singular, a malcontent. On several occasions, he only maintains his worship through special pleading and even lies (754/28–30, 755/19–21), which are dependent on the sometimes grudging credit of his betters for their currency (697).[13]

It is clear, then, that Palamides exists as a foil for Tristram, more than in his own right, and that the text will 'rebuke' his attempts to be more.[14] Yet he is also fashioned to show the value of the chivalric fellowship which his envy threatens; though he frequently departs from Tristram's company, he is always restored to it at last. Spite, anger and envy force the two asunder, but their 'kind' as noble knights reunites them. Without a kin group he cares to claim, because of Mark's treachery, Tristram is preeminently the friend of all good knights – ' "evermore o good knyght woll favoure another, and lyke woll draw to lyke" ' (527/5–7). Read in this spirit, the frequent meetings of Palamides and Tristram, even as they rehearse their 'olde sorys' (840/22–23), also display a 'goodness' they hold in common. Their shared history enacts a strife for the Saracen's chivalric soul.

Tristram and Palamides: The Battle for Identity

Palamides' clouded chivalry can sometimes be redeemed simply by thinking of combat with Tristram (697), although in actual combat he sometimes acts in an unknightly way. As I have stressed above,[15] in Malorian fighting the act of beholding the opponent (and through him, oneself) as fighter is often as important as the giving and receiving of blows. So Palamides, even when he most 'hates' Tristram, must still behold his goodness in the field. To steal worship from him, he must suppress that knightly vision in unworthy acts: he strikes Tristram 'at avauntayge' (515), tries to ride over

---

[12] See Benson, *Malory's Morte Darthur*, 82.
[13] See also Chapter 1, 12–13.
[14] Perhaps Palamides' role as Tristram's chief antagonist may have arisen because Cornish knights are so despised in the *Tristan*. See 1460/n.398.26–27. Malory references include 398, 400, 581.
[15] Chapter 3, 62.

him (530/24),[16] and pretends weariness in order to gain all the glory (746ff). Envy is a 'perverse kind of loving', as Riddy states,[17] and Palamides' 'vision' is double, typically dependent on 'feeling' in combat as a corrective: the Tristram that fights *himself* he usually sees (and feels) as noble, but the sight of Tristram (or Lancelot) in combat against *others* arrests him in an envious dream (749). Consequently, Palamides cannot quite decide who 'Tristram' is, to the frequent confusion of his wits.[18] The text apparently likes to engineer moments in which Palamides must confront his envious idea of Tristram with a more considered consciousness of his worth, and even a third encounter with the man in person, unrecognised. And just as mixed feelings about Tristram seem to torment Palamides as complex 'character', they also make Tristram's narrative agency seem more complex. Their encounters refract 'Tristram' into different, though related, constituent roles.

Analysis of an episode at the Castle of Maidens will show what I mean. Tristram, unrecognised by Palamides, attempts to help him out of a fit of distraction:

> Than sir Trystram toke hys horse and hys swerde, and rode thyder, and there he harde how the knyght complayned unto hymselff and sayde,
> 'I, wofull knyght, sir Palomydes! What mysseadventure befallith me that thus am defoyled with falsehed and treson, thorow sir Bors and sir Ector! Alas!' he seyde, 'why lyve I so longe?'
> And than he gate his swerde in hys honde and made many straunge sygnes and tokyns, and so thorow the rageynge he threw hys swerd in that fountayne. Than sir Palomydes wayled and wrange hys hondys, and at the laste, for pure sorow, he ran into that fountayne and sought aftir hys swerde. Than sir Trystram saw that, and ran uppon sir Palomydes and hylde hym in hys armys faste.
> 'What art thou,' seyde sir Palomydes, 'that holdith me so?'
> 'I am a man of thys foreyste that wold the none harme.'
> 'Alas!' seyde sir Palomydes, 'I may never wyn worship where sir Trystram ys, for ever where he ys and I be, there gete I no worshyp. And yf he be away, for the moste party I have the gre, onles that sir Launcelot be there, othir ellis sir Lamerok.' Than sir Palomydes sayde, 'Onys in Irelonde sir Trystram put me to the wors, and anothir tyme in Cornwayle, and in othir placis in thys londe.'
> 'What wolde ye do,' seyde sir Trystram, 'and ye had sir Trystram?'
> 'I wolde fyght with hym,' seyde sir Palomydes, 'and ease my harte

---

[16] See Cherewatuk, 'Sir Thomas Malory's "Grete Bookes" ', referring to Titpoft's Ordinances: 'who so striketh a horse shall have no prize'.

[17] Riddy, *Sir Thomas Malory*, 111.

[18] See, e.g., 424, 529/13–15, 536, 762–63: Palamides is out of his mind at Tristram's greater success at Lonezep, yet 'sorowful aparte to go frome the felyshyp of sir Trystram. For he was so kynde and so jantyll that whan sir Palomydes remembyrd hym thereof he myght never be myrry' (763/22–25).

uppon hym. And yet, to say the sothe, sir Trystram ys the jantyllyste
knyght in thys worlde lyvynge.' . . .

And sir Trystram seyde hym such kynde wordys that sir Palomydes
wente with hym to hys lodgynge. (528–29)

Palamides' frantic behaviour reveals the identity crisis as knight which
Tristram's superiority causes, leaving him uncertain whether to cast away
his sword in despair or to take it up in revenge. (This description may
remind readers that in their first encounter Tristram forced Palamides not
to bear arms for a year (388/13–22)). The text's penchant for repetition
makes Palamides' story of reform and obsessive relapse peculiarly vivid
(cf. 388/13–19, 762/5–8). Here, one version of 'Tristram' is the bane of
Palamides' chivalric identity, while another is revered for his 'jantylnesse'.
And in the struggle to bring Palamides within his wits and within four walls
for the night, it takes a third Tristram – ' "a man of thys foreyste that wold
the none harme" ' – to rescue him from his mental conflict over the others,
one hated, one loved. In the wider struggle to bring him into fellowship,
and Christendom, Tristram also has a vital role, as we shall see below.[19]

As a surpassing 'jantyll' knight, Tristram has a complex agency, and none
of his roles can be separated from the others. So although his intervention
(an instance of like drawing to like) briefly stabilises Palamides' conflict,
nothing will long contain the narrative of prowess. On the very next day of
the tournament, Tristram again asserts an implacable superiority, and is
again met with foul tactics. The result is the same as usual, the abasement
and phantom death of Palamides: 'And sir Trystram smote downe sir
Palomydes, that he had a vylaunce falle and lay stylle as he had bene dede'
(533/7–8). Tristram's 'kynde wordys' and 'chere' as Palamides' unrecognised host (529) are closely related versions of the same chivalric agency
that dishes out blows and 'curtayse' speeches of another sort on the field:
'at every stroke that he gaff he seyde, "Have thys for sir Trystram's sake" '
(530/31–35). Acting this day as 'the knight with the black shield', another
temporary role that extends his capacity to win a new name, Tristram
re-articulates through a variety of blows and words his being as Palamides'
superior; this is also a part of his 'kynde' (natural) behaviour, though it is a
kindness which leaves the envious fallen and 'grovelynge' (530/36–37). The
point of this episode might seem that Palamides must learn to understand
the relation of these complementary aspects of Tristram, and that Tristram's
changing manifestation is merely the reflex of Palamides' own attitude. For
the present, in the grip of envy, Palamides can elicit the other knight only
as opponent. He steals away 'prevayly' (529/34) from the man who 'wold
[him] none harme' (529/4), without understanding who he is: 'in no wyse
sir Trystram myght nat be knowyn with sir Palomydes' (529/29–30). The

---

[19] See below, 129–32.

full vision is lacking. In not really 'knowing' Tristram, Palamides fails to realise his own chivalric potential. His misconduct, one sees, stems from a lack of faith ('belyeve') or chivalric grace, perhaps a fault supposed to parallel his delayed baptism. Lack of 'belief' is seen on another occasion when Palamides fails to 'know' Arthur in two senses – to recognise him, and to understand his style as knight-king:

> 'Sir, I may never belyeve,' seyde sir Palomydes, 'that kynge Arthure woll ryde so pryvaly as a poure arraunte knyght.'
> 'A!' sayd sir Trystrams, 'ye know nat my lorde kynge Arthure, for all knyghtes may lerne to be a knyght of hym.' (745/26–29)

Learning to know, and to be, a knight – the two processes are crucially linked (see Dynadan, Lamerok and Mark above)[20] – might suggest itself as a theme for much of Palamides' story, in which Tristram is the chief teacher. The alternation of different aspects of Tristram on Palamides continues throughout the tale. In subsequent scenes Palamides recovers his fellow feeling for Tristram only when Tristram falls sick and so loses his physical advantage (540). But he is further 'abaysshed' when Dynadan suddenly confronts him with the real Tristram, after he has been abusing a Tristram of his mind's eye (551). If it is treachery to appear what one is not, like Meleagant or Mark, there is also a shame in preferring a private 'imagination' over what is there for those of good will to see plainly.

Palamides' mixed behaviour gives him also a multiple identity for Tristram, and sometimes tempts Tristram himself to unworthy acts. Tristram alternates between frequent 'despite' at Palamides and a celebration of his noble qualities as a knight (728, 738). Initially, in Ireland, his ill will is the result of jealousy over Isoude:

> And wete you well sir Tramtryste had grete despyte at sir Palomydes, for La Beale Isode tolde Tramtryste that Palomydes was in wyll to be crystynde for hir sake. Thus was ther grete envy betwyxte Tramtryste and sir Palomydes. (385/15–19)

Its resurgence is usually the result of Palamides' own unworthy behaviour, but Tristram also is capable of failing his own best vision, as in the following episode:

> So sir Trystram rode by a foreyste and than was he ware of a fayre toure by a marys on the tone syde, and on that other syde was a fayre medow, and there he sawe ten knyghtes fyghtynge togydyrs. And ever the nere he cam, he saw how there was but one knyght ded batyle ayenst a nyne knyghtes, and that one knyght ded so mervaylousely that sir Trystram had grete wondir that ever one knyght myght do so grete dedis of armys.

---

[20] Chapter 4, 101.

And than within a lytyll whyle he had slayne halff theire horsys and unhorsid them, and their horsys ran into the feldys and forestes.

Than sir Trystram had so grete pité of that one knyght that endured so grete payne, and ever hym thought hit sholde be sir Palomydes, by his shylde. (560/24–36)

The pleasurable scopic enticement of this scene, with its slow approach to gaze on the valour of 'one knight', restores Palamides to the reader's view, as if cleansed of his misdeeds. An identity sullied by recent events is withheld until after its prowess is redisplayed; the episode serves to clear Palamides' 'name', matching in a small way how Chrétien's Yvain is redeemed as 'Knight of the Lion'. Tristram responds nobly to this sight, so long as the other's identity is unknown. Then, influenced more by past events than the present 'proof', he takes the less lofty course of 'knowing' Palamides by private intellection rather than seeing what he is in the 'field'. Hence *his* view is singular, and the ensuing narrative provides its corrective through Palamides himself:

> 'What is your name?' seyde sir Trystram.
> 'Sir, my name ys sir Palomydes.'
> 'A, Jesu!' seyde sir Trystram, 'thou haste a fayre grace of me this day that I sholde rescowe the, and thou art the man in the worlde that I moste hate! But now make the redy, for I shall do batayle with the!' (561/30–35)

Not for the last time, it is left to Palamides to point out the unseemliness of such a proposal, and to rescue Tristram from himself: 'for inasmuche as ye have saved my lyff hit woll be no worshyp for you to have ado with me; for ye ar freyshe and I am sore woundid' (562/4–6).

Checked in this way, Tristram recovers his equilibrium in the anticipation of another 'day' of combat that will bring him together with Palamides again. It seems that as a pair one can always make up any deficiency of worship in the other. As they repeatedly promise, neither will 'fayle' the other (564/4–5; 564/33–4; 663/35). At times, neither knight seems to know which of them is at fault. Palamides blames Tristram for his own treachery (762/3), and Tristram catches 'hate' from Palamides at moments when the other has lost it for him (840–41). Between them, however, there is always enough grip on the worshipful outcome for one to forebear the other until a new occasion arises. In this way, their relation is a patent means for prolonging and recapitulating combat incidents.

Where the text has less interest in articulating nuances, as in the less important Palamides/Lamerok relation, it finds an accord of near-equals much sooner (601–03). (We see affirmed a Malorian principle here – that the matters of highest importance are those which resist closure most strongly.) In their last fight (601ff), both Palamides and Lamerok begin with a disadvantage that protects their credit in the agreed draw that follows. The combat is long, and therefore seen to be equal. Palamides kneels, but Lamerok raises him again, and they swear 'love' for ever. One knows that the chances of tournament, knight errantry and non-recognition can easily lay aside this friendly conclusion if another combat is required. And one also knows by the fact that this relation requires less repetition and elaboration of textual 'proof' that its importance is limited in degree, though not in kind. In such moments of temporary closure knights are not on oath about relative merit: the ranking of value tacitly maintained by the narrative strategies I have mentioned is ignored: 'Sir Palomydes, the worthy knyght, in all this londe is no bettir than ye be, nor more of proues, and me repentys sore that we sholde fyght togydirs' (602–03). The truth of this speech is tied to its moment of utterance, celebrating the Palamides of this particular page. Their combat, as far as Lamerok is concerned, has made its own terms (603/3–10), even if one cannot elsewhere rank Palamides with a Lancelot or a Tristram, or with Lamerok himself. Malory's speeches, like his fights, as I have noted above,[21] have a tendency to respect their own moment, and to ignore much of what goes before and after, even when they seem to make universal claims.

As we have seen also in Tristram's verbal accompaniment to his strokes at Palamides, and in other cases,[22] courteous and noble speech forms part of combat, and combat itself is sometimes likened to a speech act.[23] Speech about the prowess of knights is also a way of participating in their worship.[24] Like Dynadan, Palamides is sometimes more honoured through attesting another's value than through trying to prove his own. He is one of the elite figures – Tristram, Gareth, Perceval and Lancelot are the others – who lament Lamerok's death (688, 691, 698, 699, 716, 1190), and typically is the one to begin, for others of more worship to supersede, as always happens in his tournament participation. If the goal of combat is union – 'coming together', as Mann says[25] – shared speech like this offers a clear parallel, binding Palamides more securely into Tristram's fellowship than he is either before or after. The direct exchange of speech with his betters is a thing of value for him. When Tristram is actually in his view, or truly in his mind's eye, then all becomes clear, and his ill will fades:

'I pray you, sir Trystram, forgyff me all my evyll wyll! And yf I lyve I shall do you servyse afore all other knyghtes that bene lyvynge. And thereas I have owed you evyll wyll me sore repentes. I wote nat what eylyth me,

---

21 See Introduction, xv–xvi; Chapter 4, 96–97.
22 See Chapter 4, 106–07.
23 See below, 130—31.
24 See Chapter 2, 30.
25 Mann, 'Knightly Combat', 338.

for mesemyth that ye ar a good knyght; and that ony other knyght that
namyth hymselff a good knyght sholde hate you, me sore mervaylyth.'
(697/12–18)

For a while, Palamides even fulfils the role of chief vassal at Tristram's
tournament court (727), with subsidiary adventures undertaken with his
approval, and Tristram even showing an Arthur-like concern that
Palamides should soon return (708/8–12). Now, at last, within this safe
containment, and fighting against a common enemy – the two churls who
have stolen the aptly named Red City – Palamides proves his worth without
the customary discursive restraints. He achieves a salvific victory for a
whole people, akin to Lancelot's freeing of Tintagel from churls and giants
in his own *Noble Tale* (271–72). The fight description underlines the class
motive in its details – 'grovelynge' (falling on all fours), kneeling, hanging
the head low (718-19). Publicly restored to his responsibilities, Palamides
then rejoins Tristram as, for the first time, a close companion:

> Than sir Dynadan wente unto sir Palomydes, and there aythir made othir
> grete chere, and so they lay togydirs that nyght. And on the morn erly
> cam sir Trystram and sir Gareth, and toke them in their beddis; and so
> they arose and brake their faste.
>   And than sir Trystram desyred sir Palomydes to ryde unto the fyldis and
> woodis, and so they were accorded to repose them in the foreyste. And
> whan they had played them a grete whyle they rode unto a fayre well.
> (720/14–22)

Palamides is for once an insider here, subsumed into an 'accord' affirmed
by the repeated collective pronoun 'they', also so prominent in fights. The
scene offers a model to subjects of the reward that follows legitimation of
monarchical rule, or, at a lower level, simply of the benefits of loyal service
and resulting 'good lordship'. In another privilege permitted to the well-
behaved, Palamides is able to invite Guenevere to dine with him, with the
sense of social integration and temporary closure that such occasions often
provide in the romance genre (666/32–5).

Lonezep: The Political Lesson

After the independent adventure of the Red City, the following sequence of
Tristram provides a corrective influence, to show the danger of the lesser
knight taking too much on himself. Palamides unsuccessfully tries to make
the little band of Tristram, himself, Gareth and Dynadan into one 'party'
against all comers in the forthcoming tournament of Lonezep:

> 'Nat be my counceyle,' seyde sir Trystram, 'for I se by their pavylouns
> there woll be foure hondred knyghtes. And doute ye nat,' seyde sir

Trystram, 'but there woll be many good knyghtes, and be a man never so valyaunte nother so bygge but he may be overmatched. And so have I seyne knyghtes done many, and whan they wente best to have wonne worshyp they loste hit; for manhode is nat worthe but yf hit be medled with wysdome. And as for me,' seyde sir Trystram, 'hit may happen I shall kepe myne owne hede as well as another.' (700/13–22)

'Manhode is nat worthe but yf hit be medled with wysdome' might stand as a motto for many of Tristram's actions. As Beverly Kennedy has shown, Tristram is a practical knight, turning his military prowess to his best advantage.[26] Tristram is not one to 'take the adventure' as pure chance, but a shrewder operator, less dangerous to himself and others than Palamides. He distinguishes the right degree of individuality from a foolish isolationism. Even so, an anxiety that good counsel may appear an excuse for slackness seems to motivate the vaunting conclusion of this speech.

When the long-awaited tournament at Lonezep arrives, Tristram behaves throughout in lordly style, anxious to place his party in the best light, and allowing others to shine as well as himself. The tournament offers, I suggest, something of an idealised Malorian political model, with the pre-eminent power of one supposedly validated by the opportunities thereby created for all. But a dilemma soon arises. In Dynadan's eyes, Tristram goes too far in permitting a lesser figure, Palamides, to gain glory, 'for well knew sir Dynadan that, and sir Trystram were thorowly wrothe, sir Palomydes shulde wynne no worship upon the morne' (742/7–13). Tristram *cannot* satisfy both his own and Palamides' ambitions; the sharing of 'worship' must be understood for what any honours system is – a disguise for inequalities of power. But how can an impression of Tristram's benevolence co-exist with the 'anger' necessary to dominance in the field? Only by constructing Palamides' actions on his own behalf as illegitimate – culpable ill will:

'wondir ye nat so uppon sir Palomydes', [says Gareth] 'for he forsyth hymselff to wynne all the honoure frome you.'
'I may well beleve hit,' seyde sir Trystram, 'and sytthyn I undirstonde his yevil wyll and hys envy, ye shall se, yf that I enforce myselff, that the noyse shall be leffte that is now uppon hym.' (747/23–28)

It seems that the story is not for long prepared to tolerate the rise of a notional inferior before this is represented as an affront to nature and morality, and the ruling class suspected of folly or cowardice (742/7–13). Just as Palamides revenges his class on the churls of the Red City, Tristram

---

26 Kennedy, *Knighthood*, 152.

is obliged to assert his prowess over the lesser man's. A Tristram does not simply *win* the lion's share: he alone has a right to it:

> 'So God me helpe,' seyde kynge Arthure to sir Launcelot, ' . . . I sawe never a bettir knyght, for he passyth farre sir Palomydes.'
> 'Sir, wyte you well,' seyde sir Launcelot, *'hit muste be so of ryght,* for hit is hymselff that noble knyght sir Trystram.'
> 'I may ryght well belyeve hit,' seyde kynge Arthure.
>
> (748/11–16)

So illusory is the sense of free 'adventure' that any change from the preconceived ideal ranking, such as the temporary triumph of Palamides, is constructed as an act of treason to be put down. Palamides' 'envy' has to be read as a legitimation of monarch-Tristram and the preservation of a mystique disguising the chances of military success with an appearance of law and right. Indirectly and unconsciously, Malory's tournament 'civil war' anticipates Shakespeare's – 'Well, God be thanked for these rebels – they offend none but the virtuous.'[27]

The early tournament was a small cavalry battle, a means of gaining horses, armour and money, and a training for military service. It was also a place to satisfy baronial ambitions, often conducted against regal objection and suspected as a pretext for rebellion.[28] In Malory's day it had become a safer, more formal pageant in which all or most competitors could 'do well',[29] and therefore pre-existing reputations were easier to keep. It had ceased to provide a field for baronial meritocracy, potentially subversive of monarchical claims, and become, especially under Edward IV, a controlled venue sponsored by the crown.[30] Malory's narration, using a text formed on the model of the earlier tournament to perform the conservative function of the later one, requires considerable partiality to achieve its ends. Palamides' tactics, although so deplored, closely resemble actions by Lancelot and Tristram at other times. The wayfaring Lancelot 'beguiles' knights to their doom with his covered shield,[31] and in tournaments he, Tristram and Gareth often fight disguised, fight against their normal side, or change sides. These ploys increase their honour, but not Palamides', because their military dominance (and special relationship with Arthur) ensures that only their self-interest is legitimated as right.

In terms of character, Palamides' explanation that he came to fight

---

27 *William Shakespeare: The Complete Works,* ed. P. Alexander (London: Collins, 1951), *Henry IV, Part 1,* III, iii, 189–90.
28 See Begent, *Justes Royale,* 2–4; Denholm-Young, 'The Tournament', 240–53; Keen, *Chivalry,* Chapter V; Barber and Barker, *Tournaments,* 146–47.
29 See Denholm-Young, ibid., 240.
30 See Barber, 'Malory's *Le Morte Darthur* and Court Culture', 143ff.
31 See above, Chapter 1, 5–6.

against Tristram by remaining with his original side is correctly decried as 'false' (749/19), an important ethical consideration. But it would be foolish to forget that Palamides' falsehood is *required* to cover up the process by which military success decides what is loyalty and what treason. Even a slight and self-imposed eclipse of Tristram's premiership must be represented as treachery. The whole incident exposes the thinness of the impulse towards an idea of 'fellowship' in the first place, unless it fully respects the hierarchies. Palamides must remain a kind of chivalric 'vassal' or 'subject' of Tristram. Tristram's temporary forbearance of him is mainly the text's delaying device to set off the hero's own prowess more clearly later on. Palamides, the spurious cause but real casualty of events, is cast out weeping 'for dispyte' and Gareth is advanced to take his place (746/34–747/4). Unlike Palamides', Gareth's changing sides is to be celebrated later, under similar circumstances, as 'grete worshyp' and 'goodnes' (1114). Gareth does not play to win against Tristram and Lancelot. He may be 'passyng perelous', but not to them, because he does not try to equal the holders of power or challenge the naturalisation of their rule as right.

Under these circumstances, the text's harping on Palamides' faults points to some serious pressures on the preferred self-image of chivalry; the fantasies of 'fellowship' and 'adventure' have to be shielded by the attribution of fantasies to their victims:

> 'But sir,' seyde sir Launcelot, 'ye may se how sir Palomydes hovyth yondir as thoughe he were in a dreame, and wyte you well he ys full hevy that sir Trystram doyth suche dedys of armys.'
> 'Than ys he but a foole,' seyde kynge Arthure, 'for never yet was sir Palomydes suche a knyght, nor never shall be of suche prowes.' (749)

My analysis is not offered in support of Palamides' behaviour, but to investigate the political discourse that results when the fact of success in military 'adventure' is translated into supposedly inherent and interior personal qualities. A 'shame' culture, with its stress on the 'proof' that earns outward reputation, is transformed into a 'guilt' culture, operating by internalised moral imperatives. The original 'signified' of prowess – the good name won in battle – becomes in turn a 'signifier' of 'right'. The oddly unresolved situation of Palamides, unable either to submit to his betters, or to be destroyed by them, seems to undermine the normal acceptance that there are two legitimate 'parties' in each fight. Could Palamides be killed, like Lot, Balin or Elias, he could, perhaps, be praised more consistently. But in his case, the value placed on Tristram's 'name' finally renders his persistent military competition, which must seek to destroy in order to oppose, under the all-or-nothing power-system represented by Malorian 'worship', both wicked and stupid. And yet, as a further and contradictory effect, the 'proof' in the struggle between these knights, if read without Malory's partiality, permits a deconstruction of its very partisan forms. The validity of these is purely conventional, and depends on Palamides' being as 'clene forgotyn' by readers as he is by the crowd after defeat by Tristram, and on our giving the 'cry' to Tristram alone (759/17–29). Otherwise the text will have power to prove more complex effects than Tristram's rightful pre-eminence, questioning, in the process, the real value of his 'fellowship'.

Palamides' impossibly double identity – noble yet envious, 'well-conditioned' yet a 'fool' 'full of despite', poses many problems to the discourse of prowess – 'Alas . . . so noble a man as ye be sholde be in this aray!' (762/23–24) – and threatens to damage its effectiveness. One potential solution is to cut him off with the ultimate sanction: 'A, sir, ar ye such a knyght? Ye have be named wronge!' (755/1), but this seems to be impossible, too dangerous a move against the power of 'name' from which all great knights benefit. Instead, Tristram reaccepts Palamides back into fellowship, despite his personal knowledge of his faults.[32] In so doing, Tristram saves not only the reputation of his associate, but, more importantly, the manner in which reputation is gained, important because Tristram's status (power) is derived in the same way; in addition, to support his own 'rule', Tristram requires Palamides as a worthy subject. So Isoude's direct knowledge of Palamides' unworthiness – 'I saw hym wyth myne yen' (756/2) – must be silenced in the higher interest: 'La Beall Isode hylde downe her hede and seyde no more at that tyme' (756/18–19). The authority of a Malorian voice always depends on what it wants to say. Palamides may not live up to his name, but no one can afford to forget it.

The last political lesson of Lonezep is actually delivered in a later episode. Though Palamides has been formally pardoned by Tristram, he is taken and tried by twelve knights for the slaying of their lord. Palamides testifies that his fate is a punishment for leaving Tristram's party:

> 'I ryde now towarde my dethe for the sleynge of a knyght at the turnemente of Lonezep. And yf I had not departed frome my lorde sir Trystram as I ought not to have done, now myght I have bene sure to have had my lyff saved. But I pray you, sir knyght, recommaunde me unto my lorde sir Trystram and unto my lady quene Isode, and sey to them, yf ever I trespast to them, I aske them forgyffnes.' (776/1–7)

The deeper offence, of course, is not the killing of a knight 'without any quarrel', but rebellion against a rightful superior. With his submissive confession, Palamides can be saved. Tristram will be too late, but Lancelot sees all:

> 'A, Jesu!' seyde sir Launcelot, 'what mysseadventure ys befallyn hym that he ys thus lad towarde hys dethe? Yet, pardeus,' seyde sir Launcelot, 'hit were shame to me to suffir this noble knyght thus to dye and I myght

---

[32] See Chapter 1, 12–13. See also Mahoney, ' "Ar ye a knyght" ', 322.

helpe hym. And therefore I woll helpe hym whatsomever com of hit, other ellys I shall dye for hys sake.' (777/1–6)

The speech, emphatically ascribed to Lancelot to indicate its authority, confidently identifies this shameful traitor's death as a 'misadventure', that is, something that should not rightly happen. It seems that the now penitent knight, no longer a threat to order, has recovered a right to kinder treatment from the text and its spokesman Lancelot. Once he is content to be a chivalric 'vassal', it becomes 'right' that he should receive help from a chivalric superior, and rejoin fellowship.[33] A joyful, but hieratic, tableau with Tristram, Isoude, Lancelot and Palamides results:

> For sir Launcelot, as sone as his helme was of, sir Trystram and sir Palomydes knew hym. Than sir Trystram toke sir Launcelot in his armys, and so ded La Beall Isode, and sir Palomydes kneled downe uppon his kneis and thanked sir Launcelot. And whan he sawe sir Palomydes knele he lyghtly toke hym up and seyde thus:
>   'Wyte thou well, sir Palomydes, that I, and ony knyght in this londe of worshyp, muste of verry ryght succoure and rescow so noble a knyght as ye ar preved and renowmed thorougheoute all this realme, enlonge and overtwarte.'
>   Than was there grete joy amonge them. (779/6–16)

It seems that no memory of recent incidents, for instance when Palamides beheaded Lancelot's horse (739/5–9), can withstand this impulse to 'joy' at the re-establishment of fellowship and hierarchy. In the fullness of his speech – 'I, and ony knyght', 'all this realme, enlonge and overtwarte' – Lancelot envisages all Britain as a field of honour.

Meetings and Partings

Malory loves these ineffable moments of 'joy', a foretaste of the joys of the company of heaven:

> Than cam the Haute Prynce, and he made of hym grete joy, and so ded sir Dynadan, for he wepte for joy. But the joy that sir Launcelot made of sir Lamerok there myght no tonge telle. Than they wente unto reste.
> (662/19–22)

Malory's moments of parting and dispersal are also sad beyond words: 'Than sir Lameroke departed from sir Launcelot and al the felyship, and aythir of them wepte at her departynge' (670/26–27).[34] Gawain's vision of

---

[33] Gawain is also described as 'noble' near his recantation to Lancelot, 1230/4.

[34] See also 868/3–5: 'Whan the quene, ladyes and jantillwomen knew of thys tydynges they

his sundering from Gareth (and Lancelot) is captured in one great line: ' "Alas," seyde sir Gawayne, "now ys my joy gone!" ' (1185/8). The sorrow of change as much as the joy of reunion asserts the values of fellowship and rank. Normally, 'adventure' – the disruption of stable order – merely provides a new field for its reassertion. The broad narrative rhythm of the *Tristram* is like this, not biographic progression, but alternate fellowship and departing – with only momentary 'stablysshynges' of the flux of narrative 'days'. Even after the reconciliation of Tristram and Palamides described above, the very next sentence renews the potential for incident: 'And the ofter that sir Palomydes saw La Beall Isode, the hevyar he waxed day be day' (779/16–18). Despite the romantic appearance of this textual surrender of stasis to new adventures, it must be seen as a fundamentally conservative strategy, employed to bring about more of the same. What most grieves Malory is not change but finality, the stasis of events whose terminal consequences cannot be undone. Only the deaths – of Uther, Lot, Balin, Pellinore, Lamerok, Tristram, Galahad, Gareth, Gawain, Mordred, Arthur, Guenevere and Lancelot – really change anything in the *Morte*, because they enforce an ending. Hence the emotionalism of this last meeting with Lamerok before his murder. In the *Tristram*, Malory declines to describe the treacherous or unfortunate ends of heroes – Lamerok, Tristram, Alexander – in much direct detail, as if unwilling to face them, but he frequently recalls their deaths with horror and lamentation. The horror is at their finality, with frustration that the dreadful moment cannot be renewed and redeemed: 'wolde God I had bene besyde sir Gawayne whan that moste noble knyght sir Lamorake was slayne!' (699/7–9). The death of the great is the incursion of intractable history into the malleable world of romance, the one closure that cannot be cancelled.

From Agent to Character

> Of an agent there is nothing to be said except that he performs a function: Betrayal, Judgement. When the agent becomes a kind of person, all is changed.[35]

In Malory, the opportunity for diverse agency is limited to major figures, who are made more complex by the sheer number of incidents and references involving them. The process is not haphazard. The weight and scope of narrative events are carefully adjusted both to continuing preoccupations (e.g., Lancelot's or Tristram's preeminence) and to the story's more local

---

had such sorow and hevynes that there myght no tunge telle', and Chapter 2, 34, n. 20 for other instances of this *topos*.

35 Frank Kermode, *The Genesis of Secrecy* (Cambridge, Mass.: Harvard UP, 1979) 98.

'needs of meaning'. When this is understood, worries about Malorian 'inconsistency' recede. The narrative practice is really quite consistent in foregrounding what it needs at the time, rather than respecting long-range biographical or thematic connections. For example, Gareth has a courtship and marriage story in the book devoted to him, but there is no reference to a wife in Book VIII, where he is called 'yonge' (1176/27). This is not to say he is unmarried or married there, simply that that aspect of his career does not concern the story at this time. Lancelot and Tristram are given the fullest range of incidents, including love interest, madness episodes, and (for Lancelot) miracles. They are frequently invoked also in comparisons with other knights and parallel situations, or through mention of their families. The most stable of all things in Malory is the 'name' of these great knights, and of Arthur. But with others there is less concern to safeguard reputation. So the effect of Palamides' agency is more uncertain, if less extended, than his betters', and several of his permanently distinguishing features, such as his Saracen race, his love for Isoude, and his quest for the Questing Beast, can be activated or left dormant, according to the episode in which he is involved. Malory cuts off narrative interest in Palamides' mother (590–92) and the nature of his involvement with Bors and Ector (528/29–32), limiting the ability of these episodes to elucidate him further. Significantly, the 'day' that Tristram and Palamides first appoint for combat (562/9–10) is commandeered for a greater encounter – Tristram and Lancelot – long since prophesied by Merlin (72/5–11, 568/10–20). Palamides learns of it from Dynadan only at second hand (595/34–596/7). His second-best status is maintained in this way.

In the symbiosis with Tristram, Palamides is certainly the more dependent partner, with far fewer connections outside his obsession wih Tristram and Isoude, whereas Tristram, apart from Isoude, has a vital link with Lancelot and others – Arthur, Dynadan, Gareth and especially Lamerok. Yet Tristram's long association with Palamides shows best how the Malorian method of repetition and recapitulation, through the alternation of episodes of good and ill will, gives to the extended narrative the dynamic of a continuing 'history' in which each person plays varying roles, and elicits varying roles from his counterpart. In any text as long as the *Tristram*, the extent of narrative incident will begin to form 'characters' of a kind, which even a careful attention to ideals of reputation cannot entirely standardise. As Frank Kermode has said,

> The more elaborate the story grows – the more remote from its schematic base – the more these agents will deviate from type and come to look like 'characters'.[36]

---

[36] Ibid., 77.

The opposing tendency in Malory, equally observable, is to reduce this potential for implicit 'character' to the explicit norms in which textual ideas of importance and goodness in agency are vested. Palamides' change from Saracen to Christian accompanies another battle – between schematised agent and character – in his long story of transition.

The emerging 'character' of Palamides is defined almost exclusively through the series of encounters with Tristram, Isoude and others that I have been reviewing. Given that these involve him in a perpetual love-sorrow, his isolated, self-questioning role has a particularly romantic appearance, rather lacking in Malory's Tristram himself, as Vinaver notices (1447). It can seem that Palamides shadows Tristram, rather as Gollum shadows Frodo Baggins, or Malory's Book VIII shadows his Book VII, as an 'unhappy' version of much the same situation.[37] In *Tristram*, this parallel is played out sometimes simultaneously, sometimes in alternation. An effect, I find, is that the boundaries between the buoyant Tristram and the despairing Palamides are sometimes eroded. Or rather, one understands (though it seems against the will of the text) that the history of each, winner and loser, is an outcome of the one discursive regime. I have so far treated Palamides both as a case study in ideologically determined agency and as a notional person. The instability he provides in the narrative is also understandable as a simple necessity for a tale which wishes to permit further narratives of combat for Tristram. (Still other pretexts are needed to bring about more fights between Tristram and Lamerok.)[38] But after Lonezep, Palamides' story becomes gradually easier to discuss in terms of character than of agency, and centres a growing effect of interiority and autonomy. Although, as I have argued, the highest prize in Malory is to keep all one's actions within the public sphere,[39] Palamides' relation with Tristram shows that a wisdom born of personal suffering can also receive its due. The private and interior realm, one might surmise, naturally belongs to the male loser, as to the woman,[40] denied an ideal self-declaration in the public eye.

I locate the moment of change for Palamides, or rather, for the critical discourse which his representation provokes, in a scene after Lonezep, just prior to a fight with Tristram, in which Palamides beholds himself in a fountain:

> and in the watir he sawe his owne vysayge, how he was discolowred and defaded, a nothynge lyke as he was.
>
> 'Lorde Jesu, what may this meane?' seyde sir Palomydes. And thus he seyde to hymselff: 'A, Palomydes, Palomydes! Why arte thou thus

---

[37] See Judson B. Allen, 'Malory's Diptych *Distinctio*: The Closing Books of his Work' in Spisak, *Studies in Malory*, 237–55, esp. 246–48.

[38] See above, 87–88.

[39] See Chapter 4, 95–96.

[40] See Chapter 6, 147–49.

defaded, and ever was wonte to be called one of the fayrest knyghtes of
the worlde? Forsothe, I woll no more lyve this lyff, for I love that I may
never gete nor recover.' (779/27–35)

A good knight's self-examination usually takes the form of beholding
himself as if from outside, to determine what his public 'worship' will be.[41]
Here, unusually, Palamides' self-analysis brings into consciousness a gap
between his existence as 'called' by others and as it is now in his own view.
He reconstitutes himself according to a personal assessment rather than
purely in terms of reputation, using the present moment to mediate between his past and future, as signalled by the energetic mixture of verb
tenses. Then, having broken the sense of a *necessary* connection between his
self and his situation, imagining a potential being which is neither the object
in the fountain nor that in the public eye, he rises above 'the self-absorption
of envy'[42] and decisively re-asserts himself as a subject-figure: ' "I woll no
more lyve this lyff" '. It is a unusual occasion, when a major personage
apostrophises himself without the appellation of 'sir', an absence in direct
address that elsewhere can accompany rebuke.[43] The moment of self-vision
that avoids shame is common enough (e.g., 719/10–11) but this is both more
intimate and more wide-ranging. A broader application is made, to a whole
way of life. It is now Palamides who rises, momentarily, above the alterna-
tives of victory or 'treason', and Tristram who seems blinkered, though he
restrains himself out of respect for 'name'. His terse anger intersperses
Palamides' clear-sighted and sublime melancholy. In a text noted for the
homogeneity of its speech acts,[44] where dialogue is rarely individualising,
this passage at least is dramatically contrastive:

 'Sir, well have ye uttyrd youre treson,' seyde sir Trystram.
 'Sir, I have done to you no treson,' seyde sir Palomydes, 'for love is fre
for all men, and thoughe I have loved your lady, she ys my lady as well
as youres. Howbehyt that I have wronge, if ony wronge be, for ye rejoyse
her and have youre desyre of her; and so had I nevir, nor never am lyke
to have, and yet shall I love her to the uttermuste dayes of my lyff as well
as ye.'
 Than seyde sir Trystram, 'I woll fyght with you to the utteryste!'
 'I graunte,' seyde sir Palomydes, 'for in a bettir quarell kepe I never to
fyght. For and I dye off youre hondis, of a bettir knyghtes hondys myght
I never be slayne. And sytthyn I undirstonde that I shall never rejoyse La
Beall Isode, I have as good wyll to dye as to lyve.' (781/20–34)

---

[41] See Chapter 1, 12.
[42] See Riddy, *Sir Thomas Malory*, 111. Merrill, *Sir Thomas Malory and the Cultural Crisis*, 10–14,
discusses this scene as the despair of a chivalric life cut off from God's grace.
[43] See 1184/8, ' "A, Aggravayne, Aggravayne!" seyde the kynge, "Jesu forgyff hit thy soule." '
[44] See Lambert's remarks on collective discourse in *Malory*, 16ff.

Something new has happened here. The accumulated weight of his history opens for Palamides a subject-position that outgrows the narrative function hitherto provided for him. Now that he, as character, breaks free, Tristram is left behind. They exist, for the moment, on different planes, and a mortal combat, could it ensue, would now prove different *kinds* of things about them. Palamides, exercising his new freedom as subject, is more concerned to state his case than to act his part. Tristram's accusation of 'treason' now appears inadequate and obsessive, especially when he becomes convinced that Palamides has contrived the hunting accident which postpones their agreed day of battle (783). Significantly, this view now makes Tristram singular, isolating him from others: 'in no wyse there was no knyght . . . that wolde belyeve that sir Palomydes wolde hurte hym, nother by his owne hondis nothir by none other consentynge' (783/12–15).

Tristram's hitherto praiseworthy determination in his role as punisher of treason can now be viewed as a potential failure of his knightly vision. Furthermore, his failure to keep his 'day' recalls, and implicitly rebukes, his reluctance to accept Palamides' explanation of a similar failure (782/12–26). Palamides, by contrast, comments with neither grief nor malice:

> 'Truly, I am glad of his hurte, and for this cause: for now I am sure I shall have no shame. For I wote well, and we had medled, I sholde have had harde handelynge of hym, and by lyklyhode I muste nedys have had the worse.' (784/19–22)

This speech represents another extraordinary emergence of Palamides, as notional 'person', from the narrative situation in which he has functioned as a necessary adjunct of Tristram's success, and which required his semblance of motivation only as a pretext. His role as inferior, and Tristram's prowess, continue to be endorsed, certainly, but by a narrative means that prizes Palamides' clear self-vision over the admitted fact that he would have 'the worse' in battle. And though it is ultimately impossible to preserve a veneration for combat while avoiding its effect of subordination, in the attempt to do so Malory for once valorises something more than sheer force of arms. The day of combat cannot be avoided, only postponed, but meanwhile the text embraces its opportunity to prove other things.

Redeeming Palamides: The Last Fights

The necessary intervention of chance makes it impossible for Tristram to find Palamides 'all that quarter of somer' (784/30). When they finally meet (it seems much later), Tristram has recovered from his wound, and Palamides has refound his old ill will. This apparent regression to the norm is to prepare for a final resolution of their conflict through the transformative medium of noble combat, occluding the placement of values in interior development entertained in the previous episode.

The final battle of Tristram and Palamides is one of those many achievements in the *Tristram*, which because they are not fully accessible in modern terms, have received too little praise, or the wrong kind. More than any telos of theme or plot, the manner of narration of this incident satisfies the material imagination of the text as an adequate resolution. The sheer length of the enriched incident, stretching over six sides of the Winchester manuscript, with its preamble and long aftermath, indicates its honorific power. And its appearance at the end of all the Tristram material Malory chose to relate places on it the whole weight of the Tristram/Palamides embroilment: 'Sir Trystram, now be we mette, for or we departe we shall redresse all oure olde sorys' (840/22–23). How it is that *both* knights can find redress rather than mere repetition of their grievances depends on the intercalation of fighting wih other important 'means', including speech. In Malory it often seems that speech and combat each enable the other, and that their discourses overlap, so that Palamides is 'stunned' by Tristram's words (696–97),[45] and a defeat in combat is a 'rebuke' (484/22).[46] The 'great strokes' of combat are felt as expressive concepts by their recipients. In this fight, Tristram, without armour, attacks Palamides so fiercely that his spear bursts into a hundred pieces, then gives him six great strokes on the helm. Palamides first 'beholds' Tristram, then transforms his epiphany into internal and outward expression:

And than sir Palomydes stode stylle and byhylde sir Trystram and mervayled gretely at hys woodnes and of hys foly.

And than sir Palomydes seyde unto hymselff, 'And thys sir Trystram were armed, hyt were harde to cese hym frome hys batayle, and yff I turne agayne and sle hym I am shamed wheresomevir I go.' (840/34–841/4)

Converted from aggression to appreciation, Palamides speaks to Tristram, and unites them in understanding:

'And well thou wotyste,' seyde sir Palomydes unto sir Trystram, 'I knowe thy strengthe and thy hardynes to endure ayenste a goode knyght.'

'That ys trouthe,' seyde sir Trystram, 'I undirstonde thy valyauntnesse.'

'Ye say well,' seyde sir Palomydes. (841/12–17)

Tristram's mad attack is the agent of an accord. But the matter cannot rest there, without further fighting. Each knight is reluctant to leave the place,

---

[45] Cf. 'And as ho stod ho stonyed hym wyth ful stor wordez', *Sir Gawain and the Green Knight*, 1290, in Andrew and Waldron, *The Poems of the Pearl Manuscript*.

[46] See also Chapter 6, 138.

which has become a 'field', because to do so would imply that he had had 'the worse'. A comic exchange of etiquette results:

> 'wyte thou well, sir Palomydes, as at thys tyme thou sholdyst departe from me, for I wolde nat have ado wyth the.'
> 'No more woll I,' seyde sir Palomydes. 'And therefore ryde furth on thy way!'
> 'As for that,' seyde sir Trystram, 'I may chose othir to ryde othir to go [walk].' (841/28–34)

The impasse is broken when Tristram seizes on the one more battle Palamides has vowed to perform before his christening as an opportunity to fight.

> 'Be my hede,' seyde sir Trystram, 'as for one batayle, thou shalt nat seke hyt longe. For God deffende,' seyde sir Trystram, 'that thorow my defaute thou sholdyste lengar lyve thus a Sarazyn ... So God me helpe, ... owthyr he [Palamides] shall sle me, othir I hym, but that he shall be crystynde or ever we departe in sundir.' (842–43)

Tristram may be grimly jesting at first – Malorian speech is a perfect medium for minimalist jokes – but the web of aggression and good will in his intention is impossible to unravel: Palamides may not 'live' a Saracen much longer either because he will die, or because he will complete his vow; the 'christening' may either be Palamides' fulfilment of the vow or a 'baptism of blood' through death at Tristram's hands. The fight that ensues, in the sight of Sir Galleron, 'the whyche was a noble knyght' (843/10–11), is pre-eminently noble in its length ('more than two owrys') (843/31), its equal maintenance ('as noble men that oftten had ben well preved in batayle') (843/28–29), the damage to armour (841/33), and the steady reciprocity by which mutual anger converts to faithfulness and trust: 'And ever sir Trystram fought stylle inlycke harde, and sir Palomides fayled hym nat but gaff hym many sad strokys agayne' (844/5–7). When Palamides loses his sword, Tristram makes this the occasion for repaying Palamides' forbearance of his own earlier 'avauntage'. The combatants each desire to win, but also want the battle itself to be as hard as possible. Advantage must be gained, not the fruit of chance. In response to Tristram's gesture, Palamides, as so often in the *Tristram*, proposes to end the fighting, able to do so because the conduct of the fight so far vouches that he does 'dare ryght well ende hyt'. Only *after* the fight has wrought its settlement can causes and consequences be taken into account. Palamides' breathless reasoning begins by treating Tristram's 'sad strokys' as quasi-judicial punishment for his 'offence', but then gives the *exchange* of strokes as a reason why he and Tristram should be 'freyndys'. He speaks as a chastised offender, but, typically, is also an appraising subject, with the authority of his experience of fellowship-in-combat:

'And sytthyn I offended never as to her owne persone, and as for the offence that I have done, hyt was ayenste youre owne persone, and for that offence ye have gyvyn me thys day many sad strokys (and some I have gyffyn you agayne, and now I dare say I felte never man of youre myght nothir so well-brethed but yf hit were sir Launcelot du Laake), wherefore I requyre you, my lorde, forgyff me all that I have offended unto you! And thys same day have me to the nexte churche, and fyrste let me be clene conffessed, and aftir that se youreselff that I be truly baptysed. And than woll we all ryde togydyrs unto the courte of kynge Arthure, that we may be there at the nexte hyghe feste folowynge.'

'Than take youre horse,' seyde sir Trystram, 'and as ye sey, so shall hyt be; and all my evyll wyll God forgyff hyt you, and I do.' (844–45)

In this forgiveness, Tristram fulfils the role of chivalric confessor and baptiser of Palamides, as well as one of his two godfathers, along with Galleron, the witness of their fighting. The full meaning of Palamides' vow to perform battles before his christening is realised at last in this sacramental equation between combat and christening.[47] Rejoining the fellowship of Tristram brings him into the Church, and to the Round Table, just in time for its brief completion on the day of Galahad's arrival. By means of this fight, God saves Tristram 'from senshyp [disgrace] and shame' (843/9) and Palamides from damnation. Tristram as God's agent (842/10, 843/3, 845/6–7) cleanses Palamides of his ill will ('my evyll will'). And yet, as we have seen, the same ill will – the 'olde sorys' – has been a vital part of the narrative's alternating mechanism, initiating the noble combat which alone can provide a resolution.

Changes in Malory's source material meant that the dilatory chivalric space of *Tristram* eventually reached this end. Though Malory was equal to the occasion, he hardly gives the impression of having looked for it. Thenceforth, as Riddy says, after the next tale – the *Sankgreal* – the instability of the 'world' would impress itself too strongly on the text to permit such leisurely and playful joys again.[48] They can be found only in brief moments, such as at the end of the Great Tournament,

So than there were made grete festis unto kyngis and deukes, and revell, game, and play, and all maner of nobeles was used. And he that was curteyse, trew, and faythefull to hys frynde was that tyme cherysshed,

(1114)

or after the healing of Urré: 'Thus they lyved in all that courte wyth grete nobeles and joy longe tymes' (1153). Time catches up with Malory, as with

---

[47] For a partial analogue, see *Sir Gawain and the Green Knight*, 2389–90: 'Thou . . . hatz the penaunce apert of the poynt of myn egge.'

[48] Riddy, *Malory*, 121–22.

Arthur and Lancelot, though all three postpone as long as possible the consequences of their situations.[49] But meanwhile, for as long as it lasts, the *Book of Sir Tristram de Lyones* is the very heart of *Le Morte Darthur* and its combat pageant.

---

[49] In fashioning earlier books, Malory had already avoided unhappy endings in his sources several times, such as Mordred's rebellion and Arthur's death in the alliterative *Morte Arthure*, and Lancelot's adultery in the French *Lancelot*. Similarly, he places Aggravain's breaking of the adultery to Arthur later than in the *Mort Artu*, to permit a happier atmosphere in *Launcelot and Guinevere*.

6

'Lamentacyon as they had be stungyn wyth sperys': Emotion, Gesture and Gender

And they departed; but there was never so harde an herted man but he wold have wepte to see the dolour that they made, for there was lamentacyon as they had be stungyn wyth sperys, and many tymes they swouned. And the ladyes bare the quene to hir chambre. (1253/29–33)

Like all the distinguishing marks of Malory's heroes, strong feeling is also a prominent feature of his writing. Emotion forms the prelude, the accompaniment and the response to the narrative's praiseworthy actions. Composed and even-tempered as its prose commonly sounds, *Le Morte Darthur* is still a record of the (sur)'passing' and the wonderful; as such it deals with the most deeply felt of things, providing their fitting written correlative.

For all that, the emotional cast of Malory's work can be hard to articulate, partly because the text seems sparing in interpretative commentary on the subject. The basic abstract vocabulary of feeling is relatively small,[1] and so are its common epithets – 'glad', 'heavy', 'wroth', 'ashamed', etc. The *Morte* seems much more given to intensifiers – 'full', 'well', 'right', 'passing', 'sore' – than to qualifications and distinctions of mental states.[2] As if to surmount this problem, the emotional life is frequently expressed through physical action, which has a much more developed discursive range. To Malory, the 'person' is founded on, virtually equivalent to, the body;[3] the odd-looking phrase 'with his body' is equivalent to our modern 'in person': 'and kynge Lotte had bene with hys body at the first batayle, kynge Arthure had be slayne' (76/14–16). Just as a knight consciously 'puts his person in adventure' in deeds of arms,[4] and through speech 'reports' himself to others, or 'dares say' his mind as an accountable act,[5] so his emotional life is bound

---

1   See Chapter 1, 13.
2   See Lambert, *Malory*, 28–33.
3   See, e.g., 54/17, 63/25.
4   See, e.g., 54/18–20; also 386/3–9, 1139/27–29.
5   For 'report me', see, e.g., 547/16–17, 754/3–6, 862/2–7 (Guenevere). For 'dare say', see, e.g., 276/31, 317/1 and many examples in Kato, *Concordance*.

up with bodily action, something he 'makes' or 'lets' (i.e., causes to) occur. Since, in this 'shame culture', the negotiation of identity is principally within the public sphere, then the 'personal' becomes more readily externalised, and attaches itself to sensible signs, speeches and tokens. In a time when politics was conducted face-to-face, the control of personal appearance, 'cheer' and 'countenance' was naturally of great importance. One sign of the power and extent of appearance in Malory is that 'seemly' and 'likely' are commonly words of praise, displaying the general assumption that what you see in another man's 'person' is what you get: Gareth is 'lykly' (303); Galahad is 'semely' (819). Malory can even use 'seem' to denote an unquestioned truth: Gareth has a shield 'wyth a maydyn whych semed in it' (1111/7–8).[6] The textual ideology does not usually invite much scrutiny of the distinction between public actions and interior qualities. 'Prevy' (private, secret) is frequently a worrying, often a pejorative word.[7] Unless we are dealing with a 'false' character like Mark or Meleagant, appearance is to be thought of as the conscious manifestation and proper place of inward promptings, rather than a surface above hidden depths. Feelings are important, but they are displayed and perceived in a surprisingly self-conscious form. Only if we understand Malory's preference for explicit over implicit communication in representing emotions, and withdraw the modern privilege granted to inferred or ironically obtained effects of 'character', is the emotional life in Malory rendered accessible in its own terms.

Emotion and Speech

A difficulty for modern readers of Malory in appreciating the emotional cast of his work, even leading to a false impression of deadpan emotional reticence, may stem from unfamiliarity with his non-dramatic representation of speech. It is noteworthy that in Malory virtually all personages speak in much the same way and with the same language conventions, so that our sense of the emotional character of an individual's speech depends on the nature and variety of speech occasions, and on the privileges of narrative access that some names are granted and others denied, rather than on the special quality of utterances recorded. Speech in Malory is not a dramatic impression, simulating what a by-stander might have heard, but rather a narration by direct means of the import of a spoken address, or, as it might be put, a continuation of the main narrative through the words of its personages, in keeping with the book's collective bent, and its sympa-

---

6 See also 54/18–20, 386/3–9, 1139/27–29. Another example is in *Guy of Warwick*, ed J. Zupitza (London, 1875; reissued as EETS ES 25–26, London: Oxford UP, 1966) line 7938.

7 See Kato, *Concordance*, under 'prevy'.

thetic closeness to oral utterance.[8] The public conventions of Malorian speech are exposed in the frequent occasions when two or more knights speak as if in chorus:

> But whan the ten knyghtes harde sir Mellyagaunteys wordys, than they spake all at onys and seyd,
> 'Sir Mellyagaunte, thou falsely belyest my lady, the quene, and that we woll make good uppon the, any of us. Now chose whych thou lyste of us, whan we ar hole of the woundes thou gavyst us.' (1132/25–30)[9]

The knights' speech here is energetically fitted to their general circumstances, yet perfectly appropriate for all who are subscribed to its utterance like joint signatories to a written statement; although each speaks individually ('my lady'), they are still consciously collective ('any of us'; 'whych thou lyste of us'). Such public speech is functionally aligned rather than self-expressive, and is even a 'performative utterance' in this case, since the words constitute a formal challenge of Meleagant. But the vigour of the first person carries with it also an effect of autonomy and sincerity; in its 'public' status, it is not contrasted with or alienated from 'private' consciousness. The speech is to be seen as spontaneous, yet part of what proves that, in Malory's method, is its very lack of singularity, much as the formulae of his battle descriptions are meant to vouch for the truth-value of what they recount. One good knight thinks, feels, gestures and speaks like another.[10] Like the gestures of some earlier medieval chivalric literature, and of Le Morte Darthur itself, these speeches suggest 'a spontaneous, convincing expression of emotion, though the acts themselves are conventional, as we know'.[11] To borrow terms originally applied to the gestures of later medieval theatre, the impression of 'labile' speech ('spontaneous but not fully crystallized in meaning') can still be given by 'stabile' words ('clear-cut in meaning but lacking immediacy').[12] We must first recognise the speech/gestural code, without simply imputing its formations to dramatic effects of personality.

The nature of Malorian speech is fitted to its matter, its addressee, its purpose and its occasion more than to the giving of an individual impression of the speaker, except in so far as he or she is presented as one who

---

[8] See Lambert, Malory, 2ff, 16ff; Chapter 2, above, 30–32.
[9] Other examples include 887/24ff, 888/5ff. See Lambert, Malory, 16–19, for more.
[10] See Field, Romance and Chronicle, Chapter 6; Lambert, Malory, 55: 'Fifteenth-century dialogue is a medium suited to presenting a reality in which there are central, normative truths.'
[11] Mosche Barasch, Gestures of Despair in Medieval and Early Renaissance Art (New York: New York UP, 1976) 90.
[12] Ibid., n. 12, citing M. Herrmann, Forschungen zur deutschen Theater gedichte des Mittelalters und der Renaissance (Berlin, 1914) 174ff.

knows the right sort of thing to say.[13] Most speeches are 'statements' rather than 'expressions',[14] and therefore closer to actions than opinions, although they may be denounced as mere 'langayge' ('words') by those who hold a contrary view.[15] In their speech, Malorian characters are as committed and as functionally selfless as the narrator himself. First person utterance loses much of its subjectivity, lacking the sense of an anterior personal being at a potential distance from the action in which he or she figures. The impression is that characters meld with the action itself. That speech can share the task of objective narration can be seen when a Malory sentence smoothly changes person, beginning in third person, then concluding, by the shortest way home, in *oratio recta*.[16] When necessary, the specific character of almost any knight can easily be held in abeyance, for the sake of the narrative input he can provide.

The Inner Life

Bearing this in mind, if the modern reader often needs to search for the *Morte*'s discourse of feeling, and its implication in dialogue, gesture and bodily sign, it is because the text assumes an audience consensus about these things which no longer obtains. The once explicit has become a more distant code. Even though the formality of Malorian speech and gesture sometimes appears to suggest the difference between seeming and being in individual personality, or the gap between chivalric ideology and its underlying historical reality, we still cannot read the 'real' feelings of Malory's characters, or the 'truth' of his narrative situations, 'between the lines'. As I have argued above, in relation to the healing of Urré episode, convention, not nature, is the sub-text.[17]

The lack of an 'inner' layer of self does not mean at all, however, that characters in Malory lack what we would call an 'inner life', that is, a life of feeling and thought. Indeed, as I show below,[18] the 'herte' holds a paramount importance in his discourse. But his characters (male characters, at any rate) are seen to display what comes from within in a peculiarly

---

13 See La Farge, 'Conversation', 236: 'What characterises a speech in Malory is not the individuality of the speaker, with its stress on background, past experience or gender, but the particularity of the state he or she is in.'

14 I.A. Richards, *Practical Criticism* (London: Routledge and Kegan Paul, 1929) 8, distinguishes between ' "statement" for those utterances whose "meaning" in the sense of what they *say*, or purport to say, is the prime object of interest' and ' "expression" for those utterances where . . . the mental operation of the writers . . . [is] to be considered'.

15 See, e.g., Gawain, insultingly, to Lancelot: 1200/13–14, 1202/1–3.

16 See Field, *Romance and Chronicle*, 55ff. A good example is 450/13–17, quoted above in Chapter 4, 105.

17 See Chapter 1, 6–8; Chapter 2, 44–46.

18 See this chapter, 145–47.

voluntary way, so that the interior/exterior division is, ideally, absent for them. We do not, normatively, have to 'catch them in the act' of confessing or betraying interiority, as we seem to do with the characters of traditional modern drama and novel. Whilst a Hamlet has 'that within which passeth show', a Lancelot or any Malorian knight allowed (as Balin is not) to succeed has the means of showing what is within him with far less anxiety or 'self-consciousness' (in the modern sense). Despite its public ethos, Malory's narrative practice only denies importance to the 'inner life'[19] in the sense that it does not really respect the distinction on which that term is grounded. We are used to the idea of penetrating a surface or narrative 'level' of actions and appearances in order to find the true feelings beneath. In Malory, by contrast, emotion is directly affiliated to physical action – deeds – and is displayed and perceived within them, to such an extent that 'feeling' is rarely a metaphor, whether we are speaking of someone's primary experience or their witnessing of another's. In Malory's discourse, the idea of spontaneous thought and emotion is not readily separable from that of deliberative action and reaction. His people 'make' sorrow, 'dole' and joy. They 'make cheer', as well as possess it, are 'abashed' both by swordblows and deep feelings, 'feel by' each other's words, and 'know' each other by fighting technique as well as by faces.[20] This is not to say that feeling in Malory is purely an action or only a physiological event. Rather, it comes from within, and its prime mover is the soul, but, as in Aristotle's view of pleasure, it is *realised* in action, in the full exercise of a person's faculties.[21]

In Malory, therefore, the emotional life is a deliberative matter, even if in representation its course may be so naturalised as to elide the impression of choice. (I am speaking of Aristotelian 'habits' of feeling, which a virtuous man will always display in a given situation, rather than more fleeting 'passions', or moments of weakness.[22]) Affectivity lies somewhere between the spontaneous and the willed action: when Perceval's sister, whom he has never seen before, meets him, she is still able to say 'ye ar the man that I

19 See Lambert, *Malory*, 179; Chapter 1, above, 14.
20 See Kato, *Concordance*, under 'sorow', 'dole', 'joy' and 'chere'. For 'abaysshed' used figuratively of the emotions see 38/24, 238/4, 389/32, 612/14 etc. For the same word used of an action or posture see 524/9, 534/20. For 'feeling' by intellection and utterance, see 146/5: ' "Well," seyde kyng Arthure, "I fele by you ye wolde have bene kynge of this londe" '; 146/16–17: ' "I fele by thy wordis that thou haste agreed to the deth of my persone' ", and 1249/14–17: ' "I fele by thys dolefull letter . . . that my lorde Arthur ys full harde bestad"'. For 'feeling' in combat, see 174/10, 299/9: ' "hit doth me good to fele your myght" '. For recognitions through combat prowess, see 512/2–3: ' "For there be som of us know the hondys of that good knyght overall well" ' and 1071/13–4: ' "I wolde sey hit were sir Launcelot by hys rydynge and hys buffettis that I se hym deale" '.
21 See H.M. Gardiner, R.C. Metcalf and J.G. Beebe-Center, *Feeling and Emotion: A History of Theories* (New York: American Book Company, 1937) 31; Aristotle, *Ethica Nichomachea*, X, 4, 7, 1174.
22 For the distinction, see Gardiner, ibid., 42–46.

moste love' (985/5–7).[23] Likewise, apparent instincts of the heart, such as anger, love or hatred, are part of courses of action for which credit or blame is appropriate. And to be a coward in Malory is never merely a physical weakness, but part of a wider and conscious programme of hostility towards good knights, as we see in Mark and Meleagant. Because the *Morte* much diminishes the distinction between physiological and psychological features of the emotions,[24] feelings of courage or love can be made thoroughly accountable in moral terms, through analysis of their associated actions. Because of this, a 'good knight' in Malory, i.e., a militarily effective one, is 'good' or 'noble' in a morally deeper, less technical, sense than most people would use today. As I have tried to show above,[25] the discourse of knightly combat provides Malory's chief imaginative resource for expressing ideas of 'goodness'. If this can be so, it is partly because he distinguishes much less between 'outward' actions and 'inner' motivations than has become customary for modern people.

In short, Malorian feeling, like other manifestations of the worshipful, is encountered as an aspect of behaviour rather than consciousness. It is difficult to separate it, as a topic for discussion, from the description of narrative 'deeds' of arms, love or courtesy. Quite unlike the private and unaccountable passions of Descartes' influential post-medieval view, Malorian feelings are basically volitional. To Descartes, the passions are not subject to the control of the will,[26] which at most can only refuse assent to their effects, so that a provoked anger, for example, is involuntary, though one may refrain from striking.[27] But in Malory, the will is much more deeply involved; an emotion usually belongs to a subsequent course of action sanctioned by the will; anger, for instance, is commonly the first stage of an ensuing (and pleasurable) act of requital, rather as Aristotle had seen it:[28] 'But whan the fyve knyghtes wyst that sir Kay had a falle they were wroth oute of mesure and therewithall ech of them fyve bare downe a knyght' (23/32–4). Tellingly, Malory so appreciates the nobility of this desire for quick battle revenge that he can use the phrase 'oute of mesure' in combat

---

[23] This may be a prompting of 'blood', like Gawain's towards Gareth (295). See also *Octovian*, ed. F. McSparran (EETS OS 289, London: Oxford UP, 1986) 184, lines 1141ff (Cambridge) and 1113ff (Lincoln). 'Love' is a matter of the blood here, when the boy loves the Emperor, his real father, more than the burgess Clement, his supposed one.

[24] For this distinction, attributed to William James, see J.-P. Sartre, *The Emotions: Outline of a Theory*, trans. B. Frechtman (New York: Philosophical Library, 1948) 23ff.

[25] Chapter 2, 43–44.

[26] For comments on Descartes' Sixth Meditation and differing medieval views, see Anthony Kenny, *Action, Emotion and Will* (London: Routledge and Kegan Paul; New York: Humanities Press, 1963) 6ff, 15ff.

[27] Ibid., 9.

[28] See also 29/19, 515/28ff, and many more examples under 'wrothe' in Kato, *Concordance*. For Aristotle, see Gardiner, *Feeling and Emotion*, 47ff, discussing *Rhetorica*, II, 2ff, 1378ff.

scenes with no sense of culpable *desmesure*, the exceeding of Aristotle's mean.[29]

Augustine's view of the emotions also helps to illustrate Malory's, and may have been indirectly influential upon it. For Augustine, the root of all affections and passions lies directly in the will:

> For what are desire and joy but a volition of consent to the things we wish? And what are fear and sadness but a volition of averseness to the things we do not wish? When consent takes the form of seeking to possess the things we wish, it is called desire; when it takes the form of enjoying the things we wish, it is called joy. In like manner when we turn with aversion from that which we do not wish to happen, this volition is termed fear; and when we turn away from that which has happened against our will, this sort of will is called sorrow. And generally, in respect of all that we seek or shun, as a man's will is attracted or repelled, so it is changed into these several affections.[30]

For Augustine, the course of emotions depends on what we 'love', and therefore what is loved is a strong indicator of the emotion experienced, following 'the Aristotelian commonplace that the emotions are specified by their objects'.[31] To take a simple example in Malory, the young Lancelot's desire for 'straunge adventures' (253) and his constant 'seeking upon his deeds' as a proved champion (1153), show the strongest possible contrast in courage with, say, Pedyvere's unwillingness to fight even in his own quarrel (285). The text endlessly repeats the recognition of supposedly inner qualities through the 'proof' of adventure, with degrees of honorific intensity, fashioning and revealing emotion as 'an organised and describable structure' of the relation between psychic being and the world.[32]

The realisation of suffering in Malory depends on a similar view. Aristotle had held that pleasure was the

> concomitant of the normal exercise of the faculties of a conscious living being. The exercise or actual realisation (ἐνεργεῖν, ἐνέργεια) of any faculty, or of the natural potentialities of life as a whole, is pleasant, and the pleasure is proportioned to the completeness of the realisation. On the other hand, any impediment experienced in the process of realising a faculty, or expressing a function, is felt as pain. Thus, in order to experience pleasure, the faculty must be in good condition and the object of its activity appropriate. When the faculty is in the best condition, and the

---

[29] For other discussions, see Field, *Romance and Chronicle*, 76; Lambert, *Malory*, 27, n. 19. Interestingly, 'oute of mesure' is used pejoratively of Lancelot's love for Guenevere, 897/15–16.

[30] Gardiner, *Feelings and Emotions*, 97–98, quoting *De civitate dei*, XIV, 5f.

[31] Kenny, *Action, Emotion and Will*, 16.

[32] Sartre, *The Emotions*, 24.

object affords the fullest scope to its exercise, the pleasure relative to that faculty is the greatest possible.[33]

It follows that those with the greatest potential faculties experience the deepest pain or pleasure when the exercise of their powers is either frustrated or satisfied.[34] To be great, like any Malorian knight capable of surpassing deeds, is therefore to feel greatly.

So, in Malory, the concentration of the will moved by feeling can be observed either in action or in frustrated action. The externalisation of feeling is most obvious in the mighty 'strokes' of knightly combat, which I have analysed at length in earlier chapters. Another venue is provided by heroic love-making, where the iconography of wounds and bleeding equally attests the depth of passion:

> And than they made their complayntes eyther to othir of many dyverce thyngis, and than sir Launcelot wysshed that he myght have comyn in to her.
> 'Wyte you well', seyde the quene, 'I wolde as fayne as ye that ye myght com in to me.'
> 'Wolde ye so, madame,' seyde sir Launcelot, 'wyth youre harte that I were with you?'
> 'Ye, truly,' seyde the quene.
> 'Than shall I prove my myght,' seyde sir Launcelot, 'for youre love.'
> And than he sette hys hondis uppon the barrys of iron and pulled at them with suche a myght that he braste hem clene oute of the stone wallys. And therewithall one of the barres of iron kutte the brawne of hys hondys thorowoute to the bone. And than he lepe into the chambir to the quene.
> 'Make ye no noyse,' seyde the quene, 'for my wounded knyghtes lye here faste by me.'
> So, to passe uppon thys tale, sir Launcelot wente to bedde with the quene and toke no force of hys hurte honde, but toke hys plesaunce and hys lykynge untyll hit was the dawnyng of the day; for wyte you well he slept nat, but wacched . . . and all the hede-sheete, pylow, and over-shyte was all bebled of the bloode of sir Launcelot and of hys hurte honde. (1131–32)

The knightly will is controlled in the service of passion here, its facilitator rather than slave. Lancelot's careful assurance of Guenevere's 'herte' is, of course, in extreme contrast to Meleagant's heedless ravishment of her. Lancelot's 'myght' in action translates the prompting of the 'herte' into an actuality – the assault on the window and the embrace. Lancelot's words ' "Than shall I prove my myght . . . *for youre love*" ' are delicately ambivalent in this context, meaning both 'because I love you' and 'as an act of love towards you'. Love of the queen is Lancelot's motive force, but his will to

---

[33] See Gardiner, *Feeling and Emotion*, 31, citing *Ethica Nichomachea*, X, 4, 7, 1174.
[34] See Kenny, *Action, Emotion and Will*, 148, on Aristotle and the senses.

action (sexual and quasi-military) still depends on her, and this deed must be seen to be done in her interests also. Only then is the heroic potential for 'plesaunce and lykyng' fulfilled. Its visible tokens are the broken window bars, the wounded hand and the 'bloode of sir Launcelot' on the sheets. In other circumstances, when the lovers' will is most overcome by emotion, and can neither resist nor act, a bodily outcome of sorts still results – the swoon – indicating the greatness of the passions frustrated, as in the parting of Lancelot and Guenevere (1253). The swoon is testimony to a disordered emotional situation, yet it may also be seen as an heroic deed in itself, 'proving' the great power of an individual's feeling. Like several others of Malory's emotional gestures, it is also an honorific feature of knightly combat, produced by the expense of noble blood.[35]

I have spoken so far of the emotions of surpassing individuals, but if emotion in Malory is properly an act subject to the will, and an external realisation and utterance of the self, it is necessarily strongly normative, a shared thing, made intelligible to a wider peer group, on whose sanction its value relies. One good person's emotional life differs from another's in degree rather than in kind, and the genuineness of emotional acts, even their spontaneity, is attested, not discredited, by their adherence to proper norms. One good knight or lady will feel as another does; they will also feel *for* another, with a naturalised sympathy. Especially, it is always acknowledged that the best will feel most, and especially feel most for each other, whether 'joy' or 'sorrow'. This view also had philosophical and religious connections.

Thomas Aquinas held that Christ, perfect in his human nature, suffered more than any other person, because the sufferings were magnified by the sufferer's sensitivity.[36] Similarly, Malory's noblest knights naturally have a deeper affective life, seen in the ineffable joy of chivalric and lovers' fellowship in *Tristram*, Arthur's joy in his knights' safe return from quests, and Lancelot's spectacular sorrows for Guenevere and Arthur. That the emotional hierarchy forms part of a natural class system is a commonplace in romance literature from Chrétien onwards. The process does not only reflect on the emotional subject. Through their greater capacity for

---

35 For swooning in combat, see, e.g., 89/16, 90/4 (Balin and Balan). Gawain's swoon at the news of Gareth's death (1185) is particularly expressive.

36 *Summa Theologiae* (London: Blackfriars, 1974) vol. 49, 3a, q. 15, art. 5, p. 205: 'And he [Christ] was not without feeling, since his soul was perfectly endowed with all the natural faculties. Hence there is no doubt that Christ suffered real pain.' See also 3a, q. 46, art. 6, vol. 54 (1965), p. 27: 'Christ's body, formed miraculously by the workings of the Holy Spirit, was excellently put together . . . Consequently in Christ the sense of touch, by which pain is perceived, was extremely sensitive. Moreover, it was with the greatest clarity that his soul by its inner powers perceived all the causes of sadness.' See also ibid., art. 7, pp. 31–35. I am grateful to Paul Duncan, Yarra Theological Institute, Melbourne, for these references.

perception, the truly noble ennoble their whole world, bringing out a potential for joy or suffering within it that others can not.

Besides its practical or declarative value, the capacity for strong feeling, like other knightly features in Malory, comes to be seen as a good in itself. In their Christian but earthly world, Lancelot and Arthur are heroes of strenuous affectivity, like secular saints. Lancelot's transformation from 'sinful earthly knight' to ascetic contemplative is made easier and more credible through the essential continuity of his emotional life. In emulating Guenevere's conversion, *faute de mieux*, his 'herte' does not change; he simply transfers the theatre of its activities from knightly action to religious contemplation. As before, Guenevere remains the chief object: 'and ever for you I caste me specially to pray' (1253).[37] Implying a similar continuity in her affective life, Elayne of Ascolat assumes that her love pains for Lancelot may be counted towards her sufferings in Purgatory (1093). In these instances from the later books, emotion achieves a pure, almost mystic, status, and seems to transcend its earlier appearance as the problematical disturber of psychic and physiological balance, as we saw it in the madness episodes of Lancelot and Tristram.

So it is through the nature of their objects, and their alignment towards praiseworthy actions, that the emotions in Malory are to be understood. Yet just how this understanding takes place is to be carefully controlled. We have already seen that to be 'takyn with the deed', as Mordred and Aggravain attempt to take Lancelot and Guenevere in the chamber (1163), can be of less probative account than a previous good reputation, and that all occasions of judgement must respect a wider context of 'name'.[38] The implied reader of Malory (that is, the reader who co-operates with the dominant mode of interpretation offered within the text) is not invited, in the manner of a modern audience, independently to elicit the emotional life of characters from dramatic hints and suggestions, as if privately present without their knowledge or consent. Such clue-hunting is unworthy: Aggravain's spying on Lancelot and Guenevere (1046, 1153, 1162); Meleagant shamefully opening Guenevere's bed-curtains (1132–33); or, in another context, the unrepentant Gawain and his fellows seeking the Grail which is only for the knight 'clene of hys synnes' (869). When we know how a Malorian character feels, especially a good one, it is because we have been properly admitted to that knowledge, through approved means. We 'behold' their 'chere' and 'countenaunce', like the spectators of one of Edward IV's tournaments.[39] Only in combat, by those who 'feel their might' or 'know their hands' directly, can the great personages be understood any better. A typically 'suspicious' modern reader of Malory will strongly sense

---

37 See Riddy, *Malory*, 162–63.
38 Chapter 1, 14–15.
39 See Introduction, xi–xiii.

his or her excluded and 'privy' status, because it is made clear that along with admission to knowledge goes the expectation of shared judgement. So an emotion ideally spreads from the great figures at its epicentre to include a wider audience, amongst them the book's preferred readers. The great scenes of shared emotion, such as the parting of Lancelot and Guenevere, offer analogies to the 'affective' religious meditation, in which the reader/speaker/hearer of the formal textual utterance is bound closer in feeling to the icon of grieving Mary or suffering Christ, so that even the 'hard-hearted' (1253/29–30) may shed tears of compunction. Malory's representation of emotion is predicated on the existence of heroically great personages as both foci and exemplars of feeling. Their 'faculties', whether in sorrow or joy, are credited as an inexhaustible reservoir of potential happenings both within and beyond the narrative.

I have been sketching in a general view of the prime importance of feelings in Malory. One should note that their function still does not amount to 'motivation' of the action in the modern sense, because the malleable concept of 'adventure' is interposed to save knights from the appearance of willing all the outcomes of their emotional promptings. The basic drive towards 'arms' or 'love' might well seem solipsistic and culpably reckless, in that each man's ambition prompts his 'taking the adventure' in an apparent disregard of the consequences to others. But because the particular form events will take remains hidden until it occurs, the link between initial feelings and their deeds seems more indirect. The assent of the will, and of 'love', can be given to 'adventure', rather than to the specific outcome itself. Problems may arise: Balin, as I have argued,[40] has a good motivation but is denied a happy outcome. In the *Sankgreal*, for the most part, the feeling which initiates an adventure is made accountable for its upshot, especially when some condemnation of a bad action is required: a striking allegorical instance of this occurs when Galahad's fight with seven knights is understood as salvific triumph over sin, whilst Gawain's fight with the same figures is a culpable earthly violence (890–92).[41] We have also seen, especially in the *Tristram*, false and cowardly motives, and how envy as motivation may be necessary to distinguish right from wrong in military ambition.[42] But mainly, in simply 'seeking on his deeds', a knight is permitted to fashion his environment for the better, through the effective expression in action of what he loves and wills.

[40] Chapter 1, 21–27.
[41] See also Chapter 3, 72.
[42] See Chapter 5, 112–13.

The 'Herte'

Physiology is not the *cause* of emotion in Malory, as I have said. But just as emotion is inseparable from action, so the expression of the emotional life is inseparably bound up with the body, especially the 'herte'. As Malory uses the term, it denotes the central and the principal bodily organ, and is metonymic for courage or 'spirits', depth of feeling, and an inner core of true selfhood: ' "though sir Trystrames hath beatyn his body, he hath nat beatyn his harte" ' (410); 'Than wepte kynge Arthure for routhe at his herte' (222); ' "love muste only aryse of the harte selff, and nat by none con-straynte" ' (1097).

The 'herte' also has an important role in perception and understanding, one that goes beyond assessment by other likelihoods. Balin, about to draw the sword, says

> 'Thoughe that I be pourely arayed yet in my herte mesemyth I am fully assured as som of thes other, and mesemyth in myne herte to spede ryght welle.' (63/12–15)

Lancelot's heart has a similar capacity: ' "Now lat se and helpe me up that I were there, for ever my harte gyvith me that I shall never dye of my cousyne jermaynes hondys" ' (1074/26–28). Bors, the cousin in question, who has given the wound without knowing that his opponent was Lance-lot, marvels ' "that my herte or my bloode wolde serve me" ' (1083/28–30). The heart has privileged knowledge, it seems, at least the heart of a special person does, and acts according to a natural sense of fitness, rather than ordinary cognition. Its almost mystical functions are highly personal and self-declarative – '*my* herte'. Its powers 'sustain' the body, as Lancelot puts it, but even the excess of feeling that impairs this service can be counted to the heart's strength:

> 'so whan I sawe his corps and hir corps so lye togyders, truly myn herte wold not serve to susteyne my careful body . . . wyt you wel,' sayd syr Launcelot, 'this remembred, of their kyndenes and myn unkyndenes, sanke so to myn herte that I myght not susteyne myself.' (1256/30–8)

The taking of feelings 'to heart', a sign of their intense and intimate power, is here associated with the belief of medieval physiology that in grief and fear blood and 'animal spirits' sank towards the heart from the extremities, whilst in joy and anger they swelled outwards.[43] In his great sorrow for

---

43 See Gardiner, *Feeling and Emotion*, 114ff. Cf. *The Riverside Chaucer*, *The Book of the Duchess*, 487ff: 'Hys sorwful hert gan faste faynte/ And his spirites wexen dede;/ The blood was fled for pure drede/ Doun to his herte, to make hym warm –/ For wel hyt feled the herte had harm –', etc.

Arthur and Guenevere, Lancelot's heart exercises its potential for 'feeling' so strongly that his other life functions are attacked; he literally pines and dwindles away beyond recognition:

> Thenne syr Launcelot never after ete but lytel mete, nor dranke, tyl he was dede, for than he seekened more and more and dryed and dwyned awaye . . . that he was waxen by a kybbet shorter than he was, that the peple coude not knowe hym. For evermore, day and nyght, he prayed, but somtyme he slombred a broken slepe. Ever he was lyeng grovelyng on the tombe of kyng Arthur and quene Guenever. (1257/1–9)

And so, what no opponent could ever achieve in combat Lancelot's own courageous heart accomplishes – victory over his 'grovelyng' body (1257/8).[44] If the result is a spiritual defeat for the 'orgule and pryde' (1256/33–34) of terrestrial chivalry, it still shows the affective heroism of a surpassing *knight*, and fulfils the hermit's prophecy, made on another occasion when Lancelot's heart has wounded him: ' "A, sir Launcelot, . . . youre harte and youre currayge woll never be done untyll youre laste day!" ' (1087/1–2).

As this complex example shows, the heart is both the author of great deeds and the receptive organ which best registers their force, either to 'encourage' or make 'down-hearted'. As Trevisa puts it, quoting Aristotle, 'it is the welle of lif, and al meuynge and al felinge is therinne'.[45] As the principal organ within the 'person', the heart corresponds in status to the rank of Malory's premier heroes. Tristram's reaction to Lamerok's murder: 'hit sleyth myne harte to hyre this tale', displays his own nobility, and Lamerok's, in the strongest possible terms (699/28–29). Courage, necessary aggression to the point of becoming 'wood wroth', immediacy of reactions ('lightly and deliverly'), even being 'well-breathed', take their origins from the (obviously male) heart:

> Herto in *Tegni* Galien seith that vertue and complexioun of the herte is iknowe be these tokenes: be grete breth and blowynge; by swift puls and thicke; and hasty strengthe therof to worchinge; by wratththe, hardynes, and woodnes; by largenes of brest and herines therof. Alle these tokeneth that hete hath maistrie in the herte, and the contrary tokenes bitokeneth the contrarye hereof.[46]

It follows that the heart, active or passive, is another major element of Malorian discourse which asserts a continuity between its 'virtue' (inherent

---

[44] See below, 155, and n. 61.
[45] *On the Properties of Things*, 241.
[46] Ibid.

power)[47] and the virtuous deeds of combat; fighting provides the chief means by which a Malory hero can 'florysh hys herte in thys worlde' (1119/24).

Gender and Gesture

Trevisa's statement reminds us incidentally that emotions and their expression are also a highly gendered area of discourse in Malory. As I have said, the story delights in external 'proof' of the 'manhode and worship . . . hyd within a mannes person' (63/25), and which ideally exists in a continuous relation with the outer self. But there is a gender distinction in all this. In the case of men, the story provides a multitude of combats which serve as a public 'pageant' and a display of noble blood.[48] Malorian gestures associated with fighting celebrate at the same time the military effectiveness of great 'strokes' and the icon of the knightly body and its actions. And although the men's fights are strongly 'gestural' in the sense that they lay stress on description of strokes, damage to shields and armour, and wounds and bleeding, at least as much as on practical questions of cause and effect, Malory's women, denied the field except as spectators, must reveal their moral and emotional alignment almost solely through the expressive opportunities of speech, body language and affective reactions. While for men these other means of expression are validated by the proof of combat – ' "ye spake a grete worde and fulfylled hit worshipfully" ' (129/21–22) – women cannot normally 'fulfil' their words directly, or perform self-validating gestures. Because of this, women's public self is rendered always more mysterious than men's, and their gestures can more easily be read as either deceptive outward 'appearance' (the sword bearer in 'Balin', whom only Merlin can tell is ' "the falsist damesell that lyveth" ' (67/24–25)), or an indulgence of pure emotionalism (Hallewes the Sorceress (280–81), Guenevere), rather than as the proper external realisation of inner qualities. If the internal in Malory is gendered feminine, and the public masculine, as Catherine La Farge has shown,[49] it is because in his representation of women there is much less interpretative access to the interior from their limited range of external actions, and far less apparent continuity between inner feeling and public efficacy. Whatever is hidden within the woman's person tends to stay there. Because Malory's women are far less often named than his knights, and, even if named, appear less frequently, they

---

[47] See Chapter 2, 34, and n. 43.
[48] See 748/9, 759/31 and Chapter 2, 49, for 'pageaunte(s)' used of a knight's tournament prowess. For the major importance of 'blood' in Malory's discourse, see Chapter 3, 53, and the many examples under its variant spellings in Kato, *Concordance*.
[49] La Farge, 'The Hand of the Huntress', 264.

tend to accrue less subjective history from one episode to the next. The Malorian woman typically has an ancillary function, existing like a Proppian 'actant' in the service of a male-centred tale. Knightly heroes, in contrast, through repetition of their names in varied narrative circumstances, can attract a stronger semblance of complex and autonomous subjectivity, even when the ideological function of their agency is also clear.

Whilst the *Morte* often shows women in danger from men, physically and politically, it never suggests that women's interests can be legitimately different from those who have sworn 'allwayes to do ladyes, damesels, and jantilwomen and wydowes socour: strengthe hem in hir ryghtes, and never to enforce them' (120/20–22). As the careful social reference of this list indicates, women in Malory are seen as holding a common interest with 'gentle' men either by birth or marriage. Women's status depends on this ideal commonalty with men, and to infringe it is to be 'false' (67/22–68/15). Whilst behaviour towards women is only one standard of knightly conduct, a woman is more completely judged, like Guenevere, as either a 'maynteyner' or a 'destroyer' of 'good knyghtes' (1054/1–21), and she draws her value from her relations with men. Guenevere, says Bors, is ' "oure moste noble kynges wyff whom we serve" ' (1054/12–13); his genitive construction literally comprehends duty to her within his knightly duty to Arthur. Similarly, Lamerok loves Morgawse for her rank, marital status and male progeny in a way the text is happy to literalise:

> 'O, thou fayre quene of Orkeney, kynge Lottys wyff and modir unto sir Gawayne and to sir Gaherys, and modir to many other, for thy love I am in grete paynys!' (579/23–25)[50]

The most obvious limitation of women's agency within Malory is their inability to participate directly in the main narrative mode of significance or 'proof' – martial combat. A woman cannot perform 'dedys full actuall' (34/17–18, cf. 165/28), or be noble 'of her hands'. Women's heavy involvement with the allurements of magic and sex can be seen mainly as a consequence of their debarment from the 'fair field' of knightly action and from knightly 'means', necessitating ways of influencing events which are represented as much inferior. Women who must act for themselves against enemies often resort to treachery, bad magic and poison. Examples are provided by the behaviour of Tristram's stepmother (373–74); the mother of Isoude (389–90); Brangayne's female enemies (419–20); and the mother of Plenorius, the victim of Urré (1145). Denied the 'field', these women's grievances, and others', issue in behaviour which replicates that of male traitors and cowards.[51] Morgan is involved in ambush and secret impris-

---

[50] See also 486/14–16.
[51] For an extended association between the behaviour of the bad, active woman and the cowardly, emasculated male, see *Le Roman de la Rose*, ed. F. Lecoy (Classiques Français du

onment (137ff, 256ff, 504–05, 510–12, 792–98), like Tarquin (254–56) and
Meleagant (1120ff), and, significantly, in league with the coward Mark
(638ff). Both Tristram's step-mother (373–74) and Morgan (157–58) attempt
poisonings, like the treacherous Pyonell (1048–49); Morgan, again, makes
shameful disclosures to cause mischief (429–30, 554–55) in a way Malory
again links with King Mark (616–17), and very much in the manner of
Mordred and Aggravain (1161–64). The sense of grievance that breeds
praiseworthy anger in battle, where knights routinely become 'wood
wrothe out of mesure' seems to breed only culpable ill will for the women
kept outside the fighting.

These self-reliant women's 'means' are shown to be inefficient as well as
dishonourable. Though Malorian knights may be sorely troubled by female
practices, they are rarely overcome by them. The 'incurable' wounds of
Melyot, Tristram and Urré are finally healed (278–82, 383–85, 1145–52),
prisons amoureuses are broken (256–59, 553–56, 639–44), while Lancelot,
Tristram, Alexander, Perceval (910–15) and Bors (962–68) manage to resist
the sexual temptations of ordinary women, sorceresses and devils in female
guise. The narrative ambience suggests a widespread fear of women's
power to harm, but does not ultimately substantiate it in the 'on-stage'
adventures.

Even when apparently manipulating events, like Morgan with Accolon,
or the sword-damsel with Balin, the woman cannot herself alone provide
their resolution. The sword destines Balin to kill his brother, but his fate has
several other causes, including the beheading of the 'Lady of the Lake', the
death of Colombe and the Dolorous Stroke. Arthur is repeatedly saved from
Morgan's treachery. He dies 'a worshipfull dethe' (44) from a battle-wound
ordained by God, not her.[52] Women feature most frequently in Malory as
co-operative figures who inform, liberate, cure and 'maintain' the knights,
often countering other female figures who try to 'destroy' them. Like
everyone else, they are more empowered within the male-centred textual
world of 'worship' than outside it. Besides the nunnery, there seems virtually no other place for the woman to inhabit.

Malory does not have a separate discourse for the actions of women, but
the effect of his common one is made both different and more noticeable by
the factors I have been outlining. If bodily action becomes 'gesture' when

Moyen Age, Paris: Champion, 1973–75) vol. 3, 20028ff: 'car escoilliez, certain an somes,/
sunt couart, pervers et chenins,/ por ce qu'il ont meurs femenins/ . . . car a fere granz
deablies/ sunt toutes fames trop hardies:/ escoilliez en ce les resamblent,/ por ce que
leur meurs s'entresemblent'.

[52] Geraldine Heng, 'Enchanted Ground: The Feminine Subtext in Malory' in *Courtly Literature, Culture and Context: Selected Papers from the 5th Triennial Congress of the International
Courtly Literature Society* (Amsterdam and Philadelphia: John Benjamins Publishing Company, 1990) 283–300, overvalues (see 284, 288) the status accorded to women's independent
agency in Malory by ignoring the failure of their schemes and the frequent association of
active women with male cowards and traitors.

it has meaning but does not serve any practical purpose,[53] then women's lack of power makes many of their actions 'gestures' in a weak sense, and such weakness itself is feminised in comparison with victorious male 'deeds' of arms. There is no mistaking the threat in feminisation. One need only think of the incident at the Tournament of Surluse (669/24ff), where Lancelot disguises himself as a damsel and overthrows Dynadan.[54] The whole jest is based on an acknowledgment that to be treated like a woman is to be shamed as a social inferior.

Unless they occasion an affirmative male response, the status of female affective gestures falls sharply in Malory. Arthur treats the lady of the white brachet's 'dole' only as 'noyse' until Merlin insists that her sorrows consti- tute 'adventures' for his court (103/9–17), and Bors rebukes Guenevere by noting the practical uselessness of her emotive gesture:' "Now, fye on youre wepynge!"'seyde sir Bors de Ganys.'"For ye wepe never but whan there ys no boote"' (808/5–6); Elayne, who weeps with Bors, is not rebuked. The indulgence of feeling in gestures without any 'boote', i.e., male redress, indicates one's incapacity as a fighter, and is easily suspected of weakness or private malice.

I am not arguing at all that Malory feminises gestures per se, or denies them to his worshipful male characters. It is rather that where Le Morte Darthur suggests an impatience with gesture, or a criticism of it, that it becomes more readily seen as both private and feminised. Conversely, where women's gestures are viewed favourably, they partake in some way of the public male world. A more detailed analysis of some places in the narrative will show, I think, the interest of gender readings in this area of representation. I choose episodes involving Guenevere and La Beale Alys, demonstrating in turn how gestures may be either feminised and devalued as weakness, or shared between men and women with some appearance of equality.[55]

It is not surprising, perhaps, that a gender bias in gesture emerges when the narrative relation of external action to inner feeling is under unusual pressure. The 'Poisoned Apple' story beginning immediately after the conclusion of the Sankgreal is built around a worrying disjunction between outer appearance and inner thoughts which has become more evident in the moral light of the Holy Grail narrative, with its unusual emphasis on interiority and motivation. Primarily, this split condition is Lancelot's. We are alerted to the gap between his 'semynge outewarde' of devotion to God

---

53 See Barry Windeatt, 'Gesture in Chaucer' in Medievalia et Humanistica: Studies in Renaissance Culture, New Series no. 9 (Cambridge: Cambridge UP, 1979) 143–61, citing W. Habicht, Die Gebärde in englischen Dichtungen des Mittelalters (Bayerische Akademie der Wissen- schaften) Neue Folge XLVI, 1959, 8.
54 See Chapter 3, 68.
55 Another striking example of a woman's exploit mediated through male discourse is the episode of Perceval's sister's death. See Chapter 3, 71–72.

and his 'prevy thoughtes and . . . hys myndis' of Guenevere (1045/10–20). From this hidden love comes the wish and the necessity to disguise his relations with her by acting as the legal champion of many other women. But the new episode, having established this, then operates to associate with Guenevere the culpable privacy and inwardness of Lancelot's behaviour, and to transfer the stigma of a split self from Lancelot to her. A speech of Lancelot's foreshadows the outline of the entire episode, in which his male power to *act* (militarily) will save the woman from the consequences of unbridled but helpless *feeling*:

'if that ye falle in ony distresse thorowoute wyllfull foly, than ys there none other remedy other helpe but by me and my bloode.' (1046/22–24)

As the story progresses, Guenevere's jealous misreading of Lancelot's behaviour becomes the new focus of interest, diverting attention from his impossibly divided longing for both the 'dyligente laboure' (1046/14) of the Grail quest and the 'prevy draughtis' (1045/19) of love with her. The issue changes from Lancelot's lack of integrity to his vindication from Guenevere's charges. The logic of this transition is underscored by gestures that represent Guenevere's inner self as wild emotionalism and, as Bors says, a typically female 'hastynesse' (1047/18–20):

and whan he had all seyde she braste oute on wepynge, and so she sobbed and awepte a grete whyle. And whan she myght speke she seyde,
   'Sir Launcelot, now I well understonde that thou arte a false, recrayed knyght and a comon lechourere, and lovyste and holdiste othir ladyes.'
                                (1046/33–1047/3)

With Lancelot banished, Guenevere now takes on as surrogate his inner/outer split:

So whan sir Launcelot was departed the quene outewarde made no maner of sorow in shewyng to none of his bloode nor to none other, but wyte ye well, inwardely, as the booke seythe, she toke grete thought; but she bare hit oute with a proude countenaunce, as thoughe she felte no thought nother daungere. (1048/5–11)[56]

Again like Lancelot, Guenevere attempts to disguise her inner feelings by public activity, giving a dinner 'for to shew outwarde that she had as grete joy in all other knyghtes of the Rounde Table as she had in sir Launcelot' (1048/12–15). The outcome is disaster, when Sir Patryse is secretly poisoned by Pyonell. In keeping with the masculine, public mode, it is assumed that

---

[56] It is interesting that with Guenevere 'countenaunce' is used solely in its sense of a deceptive outer appearance (see also 803/31), whereas Arthur (151/34, 185/8–186/6, 241/23) is celebrated for his kingly or knightly 'countenaunce' as an active way of 'looking' which is a true sign of the heart.

Guenevere as giver of the dinner is responsible, ignoring her claims of 'good entente' and lack of personal motive (1050/28–29). For over-indulgence in the private realm ('prevy draughtis') she is made to suffer in the public one. Left without a male champion, she is inarticulate and incapacitated, only capable of gestures represented as quite useless:

> Than the quene stood stylle *and was so sore abaysshed that she wyst nat what to sey* . . . for they all had grete suspeccion unto the quene bycause she lete make that dyner. And the quene was so abaysshed that *she cowde none otherwayes do but wepte so hartely that she felle on a swowghe.*
>
> (1049/22–34)

Guenevere's abashment of spirits is quickly registered as a massive fall in her personal status, particularly in relation to the 'blood of Sir Lancelot': Arthur finds her on both knees before Bors, pleading for his 'mercy' (1052). Even then, she is so little regarded by Bors that he refuses to act as her champion until formally 'required' by Arthur (1052/25–29). He accepts only 'for my lorde sir Launcelottis sake, and for youre (Arthur's) sake' (1053/2–3). It is now only through his fealty to Arthur and his blood loyalty to Lancelot that Guenevere exists for him.

There is no need to dwell on the outcome of the trial by combat. Lancelot, banished from court by the jealous Guenevere, returns to solve a problem now seen solely as hers, to which his response is ' "A, Jesu! . . . thys ys com happely as I wolde have hit." ' (1053/16–17). After a brief exile and return in disguise, his identity is triumphantly re-integrated through new recognition as the victorious champion:

> And evermore the quene behylde sir Launcelot, and wepte so tendirly that she sanke allmoste to the grownde for sorow that he had *done* to her so grete kyndenes where she *shewed* hym grete unkyndenesse.
>
> (1058/36–1059/2)

The re-naturalisation of Lancelot's behaviour as 'kyndenes', after his worrying moral position at the start of the story, is achieved through an access to knightly action – what he has 'done' – which is easily able to establish and declare Guenevere's innocence, while her own 'entente' is silenced and inadequate. Conversely, the 'grete unkyndenes' Guenevere 'shewed' Lancelot can be fittingly redressed only by new gestures of affective *re*-action. Her silent weeping is now a mark of correct sensibility, as she rightly 'beholds' Lancelot again. 'Beholding' the worshipful is an important action in Malory for both sexes, and many weep at such moments of epiphany (1083/12–16, 1097/1–3).[57] But in this context, I think, Guenevere's

---

[57] For a survey of the significance and gendering of weeping and affective reactions, see Andrew Lynch, ' "Now, fye on youre wepynge!": Tears in Medieval English Romance' in

additional sinking gesture also acknowledges the subordinate place of the woman when behaving according to her 'kynde', and the fact that she holds status only on sufferance from men, especially of Lancelot's family. In a sense, she, as well as Mador, is defeated in this combat.

No gesture in *Le Morte Darthur* is inherently feminised or unworthy, but for a woman's gestures to retain value in Malory's narrative context, they must be shared with men, sanctioned by male pity, or even, as sometimes happens, be borrowed from the male realm. My contrasting example for analysis is a passage in the *Tristram* book, where an episode of sexual attraction and courtship shares its motifs of gesture between men and women. The union of Alexander and La Beale Alys depends for its resolution and in key aspects of its representation on a gestural discourse derived from armed combat:

Whan La Beale Alys sawe hym juste so well, she thought hym a passyng goodly knyght on horsebacke. And than she lepe oute of hir pavylyon and toke sir Alysaundir by the brydyll, and thus she seyde:

'Fayre knyght! Of thy knyghthode, shew me thy vysayge.'

'That dare I well,' seyde sir Alysaundir, 'shew my vysayge.'

And than he put of his helme, and whan she sawe his vysage she seyde, 'A, swete Fadir Jesu! The I muste love, and never othir.'

'Than shewe me youre vysage,' seyde he.

And anone she unwympeled her, and whan he sawe her he seyde, 'A, Lorde Jesu! Here have I founde my love and my lady! And therefore, fayre lady, I promyse you to be youre knyght, and none other that beryth the lyff.'

'Now, jantyll knyghte,' seyde she, 'telle me youre name.'

'Madame, my name is sir Alysaundir le Orphelyne. Now, dameselle, telle me your name,' seyde he.

'A, sir,' seyde she, 'syth ye lyst to know my name, wyte you well my name is Alys la Beale Pellaron. And whan we be more at oure hartys ease, bothe ye and I shall telle of what bloode we be com.'

So there was grete love betwyxt them . . .

And there Alys tolde of what bloode she was com, and seyde,

'Sir, wyte you well that I am of the bloode of kynge Ban, that was fadir unto sir Launcelot.'

'Iwys, fayre lady,' seyde sir Alysaundir, 'my modir tolde me my fadir was brothir unto a kynge, and I am nye cousyn unto sir Trystram.'

(645/16–646/30)

For Alys, Alexander's erotic appeal stems from his prowess, viewed in the standard terms of professional evaluation – 'a passyng goodly knyght on horsebacke'[58] – and her response is quasi-military. Her forward action

Parergon: Bulletin of the Australian and New Zealand Association for Medieval and Renaissance Studies, New Series vol. 9, no. 1, June 1991, 43–62.

[58] See Malory 105/8, 159/15, 167/17, 699/16, 741/4, 1189/8 etc. That women love knights

in seizing his bridle is conventionally a sign that a tournament opponent has been captured, suggesting that he can be led at will. It is a deed that shames Alexander later when employed against him by Mordred in a tournament (647/4–11), but here it seems to hint at the power of sexual desire. Her compelling Alexander to remove his helmet may also suggest the 'racing' (pulling) off of an opponent's helm, a standard formula of victory (e.g., 51/4, 658/27, 734/14).[59] Their whole encounter, charged with the eroticism of parallel speech and disvestment, exhibits the perfect symmetry and mutuality of a good fight,[60] and, like Malory's descriptions of fighting, employs a discourse of increasing intimacy, moving from the externals of 'vysayge' to the power of 'name', and then to the bodily mysteries of 'bloode'.

The motif of erotic combat is resumed in the next incident when a damsel, who has previously been Alexander's lover and helped him to escape from Morgan's prison (643–44), rescues his fortunes in combat by awakening him from the traditional lover's trance as he beholds Alys:

> So whan the damesell . . . sawe how shamefully he was lad, anone she lete arme her and sette a shylde uppon her shuldir. And therewith she amownted uppon his horse and gate a naked swerde in hir honde, and she threste unto Alysaundir with all hir myght, and she gaff hym suche a buffet that hym thought the fyre flowe oute of his yghen. (647/12–18)

Though the intervention of a fighting woman is unusual, the discursive link between sexuality and combat is not. In other episodes Malory uses the two phrases 'have ado with' and 'medyll (togydirs)' indifferently of fighting and sexual contact (53/26, 316/9, 38/32; 213/23, 238/21, 991/2), while Guenevere, suspecting Lancelot of sexual infidelity, repeatedly calls him 'recrayed', as if he had cravenly yielded in a combat (1047/1, 1087/23, 1189/11). Alexander eventually returns to his country with *both* women, and they live there 'in grete joy' (648/1–3). Gestures of combat provide a fitting ideological mediation of this solemn lovers' betrothal in the name of Jesus, all the more so when their love is revealed as a union of the blood of Lancelot and Tristram, the two greatest fighters and lovers of the age.

It is impossible to generalise convincingly from selected examples, much less to establish a fully consistent reading of Malorian gesture, which will always depend on the immediate narrative context for its shifting determinants. Moreover, it is not helpful to characterise the discursive reflexes of action and feeling as invariably 'masculine' or 'feminine', as if the gendering

more after seeing their prowess in combat is a commonplace of Arthurian literature from Geoffrey of Monmouth onwards.

[59] See Chapter 2, 51, and n. 80.

[60] See Lambert, *Malory*, 45ff; Mann, 'Knightly Combat', 338; Chapter 3, 59 and n. 18. For other instances in Malory, see Mahoney, ' "Ar ye a knyght?" ', 318–24, esp. 319: 'The reward of love becomes . . . a way of defining true knighthood.'

of textual detail could be perfectly policed. Gesture is an interesting area of narrative representation partly because it reveals some traffic across arbitrary gender boundaries, and can extend the emotional and agentive range of both male and female characters. Nevertheless, I think that in Malory a broad shift in the treatment of affective gesture can be traced, in line with the developments of the story after the end of the Holy Grail quest, especially in the *Morte* proper.

In the concluding stages of the 'whole book', I think, a change occurs in the valuation of affective reactions and gestures generally, which could be said to 'feminise' the consciousness of the text in Malorian terms, or, to put it more carefully, to re-evaluate the 'feminine' status of certain affective gestures outside the realm of male combat. As Vinaver's 'Books Seven and Eight' progress, men's principal gestures become increasingly associated with the newly predominant sense of impasse and incapacity, arising from the tangled situation at Camelot. Although there is no 'boote', no hope of a purely military redress, since this is a battle of friend against friend, Lancelot, Arthur, Pedyvere, Ector and others all swoon, lament and weep in an unprecedentedly intense manner, and often without the normal resolution of emotional tension provided by ensuing combat episodes. As has often been noticed, the description of fighting becomes both less frequent and less detailed than before. Since it also bears less narrative responsibility for 'proving' the greatness of Malory's heroes, other kinds of action are raised in status, often with the effect of parallelling male and female affective reactions, most famously in the parting of Lancelot and Guenevere (1251–54). With actual combat at an end, its related discursive field becomes more gender-free: Guenevere, as well as Lancelot, can be 'stungyn wyth sperys' (1253).

Extreme affective gestures have occurred before in Malory, but usually with worrying associations of madness, shame and temporary femininisation. One thinks of the distraught Palamides, without his sword, making 'many straunge sygnes and tokyns', including wailing and hand-wringing (528/33ff). By contrast, even when affective reactions in the later instances to which I refer specifically resemble madness (e.g., 1200/10–12), there is no stigma, and the greatest heroes of the story are blamelessly involved. Lancelot lies two nights on Gawain's tomb 'in dolefull wepynge' (1251/6–7), and continually lies 'grovelyng' on the tomb of Arthur and Guenevere (1257/7–11), in a posture that Malory normally uses to indicate the loser in a foot combat. Now it becomes a posture for repentance and prayer, though in this instance, as in others, Lancelot's religion and repentance seem inseparable from his earthly attachments.[61] Like Guenevere

---

61 For 'grovelynge' as a defeated posture in combat, see Malory 306/9, 1057/23 and 1167/25. For prostration and kneeling as a preferred posture for prayer, see Richard C. Trexler, 'Legitimating Prayer Gestures in the Twelfth Century: The *De Penitentia* of Peter the

before (1058–59), Lancelot sinks to the earth to show his sense of 'unkyn-denes' (1256/37). Like Elayne of Ascolat (1092–94), he defends himself against clerical rebuke of his emotional display by asserting the power of rightful feeling over his helpless actions, displayed in involuntary but still appropriate gestures – 'truly myn herte wold not serve to susteyne my careful body' (1256/31–32). The male body has become, like the female, the register of emotion rather than its practical arbiter. In a formula borrowed from the stanzaic *Morte Arthure*, tears in this 'most piteous tale' often become the heroised subject of the sentence, bursting out from within to prove the power of feeling even though no 'actual' deeds can retrieve the situation.[62] Fighting prowess, which has led to the deaths of Gareth and Gaheris, is in this context displaced as the leading 'proof' of manhood and worship. To 'save' and 'suffir' Arthur (1192), avoiding a military closure for reasons of emotional attachment, shows Lancelot in a better light. He forbids Bors to kill the king and thus ' "make an ende of thys warre" ' (1192/14):

> So whan kynge Arthur was on horsebak he loked on sir Launcelot; than the teerys braste oute of hys yen, thynkyng of the grete curtesy that was in sir Launcelot more than in ony other man. And therewith the kynge rod hys way and myght no lenger beholde hym, saiyng to hymselff, 'Alas, alas, that ever yet thys warre began!' (1192/28–33)

Accompanying this narrative impasse, in which Lancelot, not for the first time, shows his greatness by preventing any resolution, the discursive emphasis has inevitably shifted from efficacious action towards the domin-ion of gesture and feeling. The knightly impulse towards action, though still great, is made more 'intransitively' gestural, without causality. One might see it as a further extreme of Malory's tendency to celebrate arms independently of their political goals: now the narrative scarcely needs either actual physical combats or effective rule to display its heroes' worth. Together with other developments in the plot, such as the virtuous changing of Guenevere, the return of Arthur's sword to the lake, and the final coming of Morgan as Arthur's ally, the end of the hierarchical distinction of mascu-line knightly action over a feminine gestural realm of impractical feeling serves to bind Malory's Arthurian society together in sensibility even as it disintegrates politically. Right to the end, 'many bataylles' (1260/14) are mentioned, but if, as Jean-Claude Schmitt has said, 'discourse on gesture is,

Chanter', 147–62, especially 113, and J.-C. Schmitt, 'The Prayer Gestures of Saint Dominic' in J.-C. Schmitt, ed., *History and Anthropology, Vol. 1, Part 1: Gestures* (Paris: Harwood Academic Publishers, November 1984).

62 See Lynch, 'Now, fye on youre wepynge!', 59–62. Cf. 1200/10–12: 'Than all the knyghtes and ladyes that were there wepte as they were madde, and the tearys felle on kynge Arthur hys chekis.'

in each period, a discourse on social order and its exclusions',[63] then the 'disparbeling' of the masculinist culture of the Round Table is represented partly through the transvaluation of combat gesture in Malory's last book, and the dispersal of its engendering powers.

---

[63] Schmitt, *Gesture*, Introduction, 2.

Select Bibliography of Works Cited

Editions of Malory

Brewer, D.S., ed., *Malory: The Morte Darthur: Parts Seven and Eight* (York Medieval Texts, London: Arnold 1968).
Vinaver, Eugène, ed., *King Arthur and his Knights: Selected Tales of Sir Thomas Malory* (London: Oxford UP, 1956).
Vinaver, Eugène, ed., *The Works of Sir Thomas Malory*, 3 vols, 3rd edn, rev. PJ.C. Field (Oxford: Clarendon Press, 1990). Quotations are from this edition.
The Winchester Malory, A Facsimile, ed. N.R. Ker (EETS SS 4, London: Oxford UP, 1976).

Concordance

Kato, Tomomi, *A Concordance to the Works of Sir Thomas Malory* (Tokyo: University of Tokyo Press, 1974).

Other Medieval Texts

The Book of the Ordre of Chyvalry, ed. A.T.P. Byles (EETS OS 168, London: Oxford UP, 1926).
Chaucer, Geoffrey, *The Riverside Chaucer*, ed. L.D. Benson (Oxford: Oxford UP, 1988).
Excerpta Historica, or, Illustrations of English History (London: Samuel Bentley, 1831).
Guy of Warwick, ed. J. Zupitza (London: 1875; reissued, EETS ES 25–26, London: Oxford UP, 1966).
Knyghthode and Bataile, ed. R. Dyboski and Z. Arend (EETS OS 201, London: Oxford UP, 1935).
Kyng Alysaundir, ed. G.V. Smithers (EETS OS 227, London: Oxford UP, 1952).
Langland, William, *Piers Plowman: The B Version*, ed. G. Kane and E.T. Donaldson (London: Athlone Press, 1975).
Layamon's Brut, ed. G.L. Brook and R.F. Leslie, 2 vols (EETS OS 250 and 277, London: Oxford UP, 1963 and 1978).
The Legend of Fulk Fitz-Warin in Ralph of Coggeshall, *Chronicon Anglicanum; [etc.]*, ed. J. Stevenson (London: HMSO, 1875; Lichtenstein: Kraus Reprint Co., 1965) 277–415.
Octovian, ed. F. McSparran (EETS OS 289, London: Oxford UP, 1986).
On the Properties of Things: John Trevisa's Translation of Bartholomaeus Anglicus De Proprietatibus Rerum, ed. M.C. Seymour, 3 vols (Oxford : Clarendon Press, 1975).

Pageant of the Birth Life and Death of Richard Beauchamp Earl of Warwick KG, 1389–1439, ed. Viscount Dillon and W.H. St John Hope (London: Longman, 1914).

The Paston Letters, ed. N. Davis, 2 vols (Oxford: Clarendon Press, 1976).

The Poems of the Pearl Manuscript, rev. ed. M. Andrew and R. Waldron (Exeter: University of Exeter Press, 1987).

The Receyt of the Ladie Kateryne, ed. G. Kipling (EETS OS 296, London: Oxford UP, 1990).

Le Roman de la Rose, ed. F. Lecoy (Classiques Français du Moyen Age, Paris: Champion, 1973–75).

Malory Reception

Ascham, Roger, *The Schoolmaster*, ed. L.V. Ryan (Folger Documents of Tudor and Stuart Civilization, Ithaca, NY: Cornell UP, 1967).

Brewer, Elisabeth, and Taylor, Beverly, *The Return of King Arthur* (Cambridge: D.S. Brewer; Totowa, NJ: Barnes and Noble, 1983).

Johnson, Samuel, *The Yale Edition of the Works of Samuel Johnson*, ed. W.J. Bate and A.B. Strauss (New Haven: Yale UP, 1969).

Knowles, J.T., *The Story of King Arthur and His Knights of the Round Table* (London: Griffith and Farrar, 1862).

Lang, Andrew, *Tales of King Arthur and the Round Table* (London: Longman, Green and Co., 1905).

Mead, W.E., *Selections from Sir Thomas Malory's Le Morte Darthur* (Boston: Ginn and Co., 1897).

Milton, John, *Poetical Works*, ed. Douglas Bush (London: Oxford UP, 1966).

Parins, Marilyn Jackson, ed., *Malory: The Critical Heritage* (London and New York: Routledge, 1988).

Rhys, Ernest, *Malory's History of King Arthur and the Quest of the Holy Grail* (London: Walter Scott, 1886).

Sidney, Philip, *A Defence of Poetry*, ed. J.A. Van Dorsten (London: Oxford UP, 1966).

Southey, Robert, ed., *The Byrth, Lyf and Actes of Kyng Arthur*, 2 vols (London: Longman, 1817).

White, T.H., *The Once And Future King* (London: Fontana, 1958).

Background, Historical and Critical Studies

Aers, David, *Chaucer, Langland and the Creative Imagination* (London: Routledge and Kegan Paul, 1980).

Allan, Alison, 'Yorkist Propaganda: Pedigree, Prophecy and the "British History" in the Reign of Edward IV' in Ross, ed., *Patronage*.

Allen, Judson, B., 'Malory's Diptych *Distinctio*: The Closing Books of his Work' in Spisak, *Studies in Malory*.

Anglo, Sidney, 'Archives of the English Tournament – Score Cheques and Lists', *Journal of the Society of Arhivists*, vol. 11 no. 4, 1961.

Archibald, Elizabeth, 'Malory's Idea of Fellowship', *Review of English Studies* XLIII, August 1992.

Auerbach, Eric, *Mimesis: The Representation of Reality in Western Literature*, trans. Willard R. Trask (Princeton: Princeton UP, 1954).

Barasch, Mosche, *Gestures of Despair in Medieval and Early Renaissance Art* (New York: New York UP, 1976).

Barber, Richard, and Barker, Juliet, *Tournaments* (Woodbridge: Boydell Press, 1989).

Barber, Richard, 'Malory's *Le Morte Darthur* and Court Culture under Edward IV', *Arthurian Literature* XII, 1993.

Barthes, Roland, *S/Z: Essai* (Paris: Seuil, 1973).

Barthes, Roland, *Michelet* (Paris: Seuil, 1974).

Beckerling, Philippa, 'Perceval's Sister: Aspects of the Virgin in the *Quest of the Holy Grail* and Malory's *Sankgreal*' in Hilary Fraser and R.S. White, ed., *Constructing Gender: Feminism and Literary Studies* (Nedlands, WA: University of Western Australia Press, 1994).

Begent, Peter J., *Justes Royale: The Tournament in England* (Begent: Maidenhead, 1984).

Bennett, Michael, *The Battle of Bosworth* (Gloucester: Alan Sutton, 1985).

Benson, L.D., *Malory's Morte Darthur* (Cambridge, Mass. and London: Harvard UP, 1976).

Bloch, R. Howard, *Medieval French Literature and Law* (Berkeley: University of California Press, 1977).

Boardman, A.W., *The Battle of Towton* (Gloucester: Alan Sutton, 1994).

Brewer, D.S., and Takamiya, T., eds, *Aspects of Malory* (Cambridge: D.S. Brewer, 1981).

Brooks, Peter, *Reading for the Plot* (Oxford: Clarendon Press, 1984).

Cadden, Joan, *Meanings of Sex Difference in the Middle Ages: Medicine, Science and Culture* (Cambridge: Cambridge UP, 1993).

Cherewatuk, Karen, 'Sir Thomas Malory's "Grete Booke" ' in D. Thomas Hanks, ed., *Malory and the New Historicism*, forthcoming.

Cherewatuk, Karen, ' "Gentyl Audiences" and "Grete Bookes": Chivalric Manuals and the *Morte Darthur*', *Arthurian Literature*, forthcoming.

Culler, Jonathan, *The Pursuit of Signs* (London: Routledge, 1981).

Culler, Jonathan, *Roland Barthes* (London: Fontana, 1983).

Davis, Nick, 'Narrative Composition and the Spatial Memory' in *Narrative: From Malory to Motion Pictures*, ed. J. Hawthorn (Stratford-upon-Avon Studies, 2nd Series, London: Arnold, 1985).

Denholm-Young, N., 'The Tournament in the Thirteenth Century' in *Studies in Medieval History Presented to F.M. Powicke* (Oxford: Clarendon Press, 1948).

Docherty, Thomas P., *Reading (Absent) Character* (Oxford: Clarendon Press, 1983).

Drewes, Jeanne, 'The Sense of Hidden Identity in Malory's *Mort Darthur*' in Hanks, *Sir Thomas Malory*.

Duby, Georges, *The Chivalrous Society*, trans. C. Postan (London: Arnold, 1977).

Du Boulay, F.R.H., *An Age of Ambition* (London: Nelson, 1970).

Ferguson, Arthur B., *The Indian Summer of English Chivalry* (Durham, North Carolina: Duke UP, 1960).

Field, P.J.C., *Romance and Chronicle* (London: Barrie and Nelson, 1971).

Field, P.J.C., *The Life and Times of Sir Thomas Malory* (Cambridge: D.S. Brewer, 1993).

Firmin, Sally, 'Deep and Wide: Malory's Marvelous Forest' in Hanks, *Sir Thomas Malory*.

Foucault, Michel, *The History of Sexuality: An Introduction*, trans. Robert Hurley (Harmondsworth: Penguin, 1981).

Fries, Maureen, 'Malory's Tristram as Counter-Hero to the *Morte Darthur*', *Neuphilologische Mitteilungen* 76, 1975.

Fries, Maureen, 'Indiscreet Objects of Desire: Malory's "Tristram" and the Necessity of Deceit' in Spisak, *Studies in Malory*.

Gardiner, H.M., Metcalf, R.C., and Beebe-Center, J.G., *Feeling and Emotion: A History of Theories* (New York: American Book Company, 1937)

Gravatt, Christopher, *Knights at Tournament* (London: Osprey, 1988).

Gray, Douglas, *Themes and Images in the Medieval English Religious Lyric* (London: Routledge and Kegan Paul, 1972).

Green, Richard Firth, *Poets and Princepleasers: Literature and the English Court in the Later Middle Ages* (Toronto: University of Toronto Press, 1980).

Griffith, R.R., 'Arthur's Author', *Ventures in Research*, Series 1 (Greenvale, NY, 1973).

Griffith, R.R., 'The Authorship Question Reconsidered: A Case for Thomas Malory of Papworth St Agnes, Cambridgeshire' in Brewer, *Aspects of Malory*.

Guerin, Wilfred, L., 'The Tale of the Death of Arthur: Catastrophe and Resolution' in *Malory's Originality*, ed. R.M. Lumiansky (Baltimore: Johns Hopkins Press, 1964).

Hallam E., ed., *The Chronicles of the Wars of the Roses* (London: Weidenfeld and Nicolson, 1988).

Hanks, D. Thomas Jr, ed., *Sir Thomas Malory: Views and Reviews* (New York: AMS Press, 1992).

Heng, Geraldine, 'Enchanted Ground: The Feminine Subtext in Malory' in *Courtly Literature, Culture and Context: Selected Papers from the 5th Triennial Congress of the International Courtly Literature Society* (Amsterdam and Philadelphia: John Benjamins Publishing Company, 1990).

Hicks, M.A., 'The Changing Role of the Wydevilles in Yorkist Politics to 1483' in Ross, *Patronage*.

Jacob, E.F., *The Oxford History of England VI: The Fifteenth Century: 1399–1485* (Oxford: Clarendon Press, 1961).

Jacquart, D., and Thomasset, C., *Sexuality and Medicine in the Middle Ages*, trans. M. Adamson (Cambridge: Polity Press, 1988).

Keen, Maurice, *Chivalry* (New Haven and London: Yale UP, 1984).

Kelly, Robert L., 'Wounds, Healing and Knighthood in Malory's *Tale of Launcelot and Guenevere*' in Spisak, *Studies in Malory*.

Kennedy, Beverly, *Knighthood in Le Morte Darthur* (Cambridge: D.S. Brewer, 1985, 2nd edn, 1992).

Kennedy, Beverly, 'Notions of Adventure in Malory's *Morte Darthur*', *Arthurian Interpretations* 3 (2), 1989.

Kenny, Anthony, *Action, Emotion and Will* (London: Routledge and Kegan Paul; New York: Humanities Press, 1963).

Kermode, Frank, *The Genesis of Secrecy* (Cambridge, Mass.: Harvard UP, 1979).

Knight, Stephen, *Arthurian Literature and Society* (London: Macmillan, 1983).

Koch, H.W., *Medieval Warfare* (London: Bison Books, 1978).

La Farge, Catherine, 'Conversation in Malory's *Morte Darthur*', *Medium Aevum* LVI 2, 1987.

La Farge, Catherine, 'The Hand of the Huntress: Repetition and Malory's *Morte*

Darthur' in Isobel Armstrong, ed., *New Feminist Discourses* (London: Routledge, 1992).

Lambert, Mark, *Malory: Style and Vision in Le Morte Darthur* (New Haven and London: Yale UP, 1976).

Lewis, C.S., 'The English Prose *Morte*' in J.A.W. Bennett, ed., *Essays on Malory* (Oxford: Clarendon Press, 1963).

Lindley, David, *Lyric* (London: Methuen, 1985).

Lynch, Andrew, ' "Now, fye on youre wepynge!": Tears in Medieval English Romance' in *Parergon: Bulletin of the Australian and New Zealand Association for Medieval and Renaissance Studies*, New Series vol. 9, no. 1, June 1991.

Macherey, Pierre, *A Theory of Literary Production*, trans. Geoffrey Wall (London: Routledge and Kegan Paul, 1978).

Maddern, Philippa, 'Honour among the Pastons: Gender and Integrity in Fifteenth-century English Provincial Society', *Journal of Medieval History* 14, 1988.

Mahoney, Dhira B., 'Narrative Treatment of Name in Malory's *Morte D'Arthur*', *ELH* 47, 1980.

Mahoney, Dhira B., ' "Ar ye a knyght and ar no lovear?": The Chivalry Topos in Malory's *Book of Sir Tristram*' in K. Busby and N.J. Lacy, eds, *Conjunctures: Medieval Studies in Honour of Douglas Kelly* (Amsterdam: Rodopi, 1994).

Mann, Jill, 'Knightly Combat in *Le Morte Darthur*' in *The New Pelican Guide to English Literature, Vol. 1, Part 1*, ed. B. Ford (Harmondsworth: Penguin, 1982).

Mann, Jill, ' "Taking the Adventure": Malory and the *Suite du Merlin*' in Brewer, *Aspects of Malory*.

Mann, Jill, *The Narrative of Distance, The Distance of Narrative in Malory's Morte Darthur* (The William Matthews Lectures, London: Birkbeck College, 1991).

Matarasso, Pauline, *The Redemption of Chivalry: A Study of the Queste del Saint Graal* (Geneva: Droz, 1979).

Matthews, William, *The Tragedy of Arthur: A Study of the Alliterative Morte Arthure* (Berkeley and Los Angeles: University of California Press, 1960).

Merrill, Robert, *Sir Thomas Malory and the Cultural Crisis of the Late Middle Ages*, American University Studies, Series 4 vol. 39 (New York: Peter Lang, 1986).

Moorman, Charles, *A Knyght There Was: The Evolution of the Knight in Literature* (Lexington: University of Kentucky Press, 1967).

Morgan, D.A.L., 'The House of Policy: The Political Role of the Late Plantagenet Household, 1422–1485' in David Starkey, ed., *The English Court: From the Wars of the Roses to the Civil War* (London and New York: Longman, 1987).

Ong, Walter J., *Orality and Literacy* (London and New York: Methuen, 1982).

Parker, Patricia, *Inescapable Romance: Studies in the Poetics of a Mode* (Princeton: Princeton UP, 1979).

Pochoda, Elizabeth, *Arthurian Propaganda: Le Morte Darthur as an Historical Ideal of Life* (Chapel Hill: University of North Carolina Press, 1971).

Richards, I.A., *Practical Criticism* (London: Routledge and Kegan Paul, 1929).

Riddy, Felicity, *Sir Thomas Malory* (Leiden: E.J. Brill, 1987).

Ross, Charles, *Edward IV* (London: Eyre Methuen, 1974).

Ross, Charles, ed., *Patronage, Pedigree and Power in Later Medieval England* (Gloucester: Alan Sutton; Totowa, NJ: Rowman and Littlefield, 1979).

Sartre, J.-P., *The Emotions: Outline of a Theory*, trans. B. Frechtman (New York: Philosophical Library, 1948).

Saunders, Corinne, 'Malory's Book of Huntynge: The Tristram Section of The *Morte Darthur*', *Medium Aevum* LXII 2, 1993.

Schmitt, J.-C., 'The Prayer Gestures of Saint Dominic' in J.-C. Schmitt. ed., *History and Anthropology, Vol. 1, Part 1: Gestures* (Paris: Harwood Academic Publishers, November 1984).

Schueler, Donald G., 'The Tristram Section of Malory's *Morte Darthur*', *Studies in Philology* 65, 1968.

Spisak, J.W., ed., *Studies in Malory* (Kalamazoo: Medieval Institute Publications, 1985).

Starkey, David, 'The Age of the Household' in *The Later Middle Ages*, ed. Stephen Medcalf (London: Methuen, 1981).

Thornton, Ginger, 'The Weakening of the King: Arthur's Disintegration in *The Book of Sir Tristram de Lyones*' in Hanks, *Sir Thomas Malory*.

Todorov, Tzvetan, *The Poetics of Prose*, trans. R. Howard (Oxford: Blackwell, 1977).

Trexler, Richard C., 'Legitimating Prayer Gestures in the Twelfth Century: The *De Penitentia* of Peter the Chanter' in J.-C. Schmitt, *Gestures*.

Ullmann, Walter, *A History of Political Thought: The Middle Ages* (Harmondsworth: Penguin, 1965).

Vinaver, Eugène, *Le Roman de Tristan et Iseut dans l'oeuvre de Thomas Malory* (Paris: Champion, 1925).

Wheeler, Bonnie, 'Romance and Parataxis and Malory: The Case of Sir Gawain's Reputation', *Arthurian Literature* XII, 1993.

Wilson, Robert, H., 'Malory's Naming of Minor Characters', *Journal of English and Germanic Philology* XLII, 1943.

Windeatt, Barry, 'Gesture in Chaucer' in *Medievalia et Humanistica: Studies in Renaissance Culture*, New Series no. 9 (Cambridge: Cambridge UP, 1979).

Thematic Index

Index of Names

ARTHURIAN STUDIES